66017699

x

WALLACE STEVENS

The Making of
Harmonium

Wallace Stevens

THE MAKING OF

Harmonium

BY ROBERT BUTTEL

PRINCETON UNIVERSITY PRESS
PRINCETON, NEW JERSEY
1967

Permission to quote from previously unpublished writings of
Wallace Stevens, which appear for the first time in this book, must
be obtained from Holly Stevens, c/o Alfred A. Knopf, Inc., 501
Madison Avenue, New York, N.Y.

"Tea," "The Wind Shifts," "Anecdote of the Prince of Peacocks"
from COLLECTED POEMS and "The Silver Plough Boy"
and "Blanche McCarthy" from OPUS POSTHUMOUS as
well as scattered lines from both volumes, are protected by
copyright and have been reprinted here by special permission
of the publisher, Alfred A. Knopf, Inc.

"Tea," "The Wind Shifts," and "Anecdote of the Prince of
Peacocks" from COLLECTED POEMS OF WALLACE
STEVENS have been reprinted here by permission of the British
publisher, Faber and Faber Ltd.

Publication of this book has been aided by
the Whitney Darrow Publication Reserve Fund
of Princeton University Press.

Printed in the United States of America
by Princeton University Press, Princeton, New Jersey

For Helen and Ed Thwaits
and Helen, Jeff, and Steve

Preface

ON A STYLE that ranges from the exquisiteness of a miniaturist to the rhetoric of a bold comedian or the sober eloquence of a deeply thoughtful poet, Wallace Stevens took great risks. And though we are well beyond the time when a good many critics assigned his poems to the periphery of serious literature as merely the impeccable, opulent, and clever creations of a dandy, his style does present a challenge to the critic: even the most sympathetic readers must cringe occasionally when Stevens' effects seem finical or capricious or when rhetorical virtuosity seems to become an end in itself. But more often than not, the style is not divorced from substance, and the sensuous, urbane, dazzling, and initially perplexing surfaces of the poems—surfaces enjoyable in themselves—draw the reader into surprising depths of thought, emotion, and aesthetic pleasure. It is this that makes Stevens' voice a major one in twentieth-century poetry and his style worthy of study.

As Frank Doggett has said, "In Stevens' case, the beginnings of style are hidden between the undergraduate pieces and the maturity of *Harmonium*. There his style suddenly is, and its seems enough for some critics that it remain that way."[1] An examination of the undergraduate writings, plus ten poems that were published in *The Trend* in 1914 and the considerable amount of manuscript material generously made available by Stevens' daughter Holly, does help though to uncover those beginnings and make possible an analysis of Stevens' development as he achieved his first certain and mature style in the poems of *Harmonium*. There were, of course, variations and developments in the

[1] "Wallace Stevens' Later Poetry," *ELH* (June 1958).

poetry beyond that volume, but they grew out of the early achievement.

To consider briefly the literary situation inherited by Stevens' generation is to understand why he demanded a new freedom within which he could experiment and discover techniques equal to his emerging view of poetry's high function; he would come to claim, in fact, that "After one has abandoned a belief in god, poetry is that essence which takes its place as life's redemption."[2] Not that he was the first to hold this attitude toward poetry; indeed, he was no doubt familiar very early with Pater's desire for a religion of art and Santayana's insistence on a greatly enlarged role for poetry and the imagination—in place of formal religion—as the means by which man could establish a harmony between himself and nature. Arnold and Ruskin, furthermore, had realized that the old cultural order was dying and that a new order was imminent. And yet the poets generally had not discovered satisfactory means for coping with the cultural and epistemological changes that were taking place.

Stevens began writing poetry at a time when realism and naturalism were profoundly altering the course of fiction but when American poetry for the most part lay becalmed in the doldrums of the genteel tradition, when the shadow of the Victorians and Romantics hung over American and British poetry. Swinburne, who anticipated Stevens in some important ways, was only partially successful in the results he derived from his inordinate emphasis on a music of poetry insulated from mundane discourse, as though this alone would compensate for the desolation he felt over life's brevity and the absence of an afterlife—a daring atti-

[2] "Adagia," *Opus Posthumous.*

tude for him to assume at the time. The influence of the Pre-Raphaelites, who sought, in reaction to the ugliness of a materialistic age, a rarefied beauty combining art and a neo-medieval religiosity, was still strong. The English Parnassians and Decadents were responding to the example of French poetry, but the results were largely ephemeral. Stevens' early poems are marked by many of the poetic sentiments and practices of the era; indeed, even his later poems incorporate with subtle modulations some of the qualities drawn from these sources. But, aside from foreshadowings in his undergraduate work and manuscript poems, Stevens' authentic style did not really emerge until he felt the impact of the new movements in art and literature which attained full force in the period just before World War I. In his autobiography, Yeats, in referring to the effect on him of his sojourn in Paris, quotes Synge as saying to him, "Is not style born out of the shock of new material?" Stevens must have experienced such a shock when he saw before him the wealth of new material and techniques which he could seize upon and make his own. While Pound, in a letter to William Carlos Williams, said that he "sweated like a nigger to break up the clutch of the old . . . Harper's etc.," Stevens worked in his own way toward the same end, encouraged by his association with friends among the avant-garde and by the general explosion of the new poetry. He assimilated the innovations and influences that inspired many other experimental poets of the period, but this surely does not account for his distinctiveness. The chief concern is not the influences themselves so much as what Stevens did with them in shaping his own style and technique as he rose far beyond the level of mere experimentalism.

Stevens' style arises out of his deeply felt need to discover valid ideas of order in an age of cultural change and confusion. Furthermore, he is a direct descendant of the Romantic poets in his unceasing exploration of the relationships between the inner, subjective, human point of view and outer, objective nature—or, as he so often stated it himself, between imagination and reality. The Romantic problem was intensified for Stevens, however, since science and the new philosophies had made it vastly more difficult to accept a transcendental solution; he recognized a naturalistic and changing reality, or what he called in "July Mountain" (*Opus Posthumous*) "an always incipient cosmos." For Stevens, then, the problem lay in reconciling the stasis of poetic art with this constant change. In his poem "Anecdote of the Jar," for example, the jar and the wilderness in Tennessee are interdependent. By placing an aesthetic object, the jar, in the midst of the tangled wilderness, he gives a focus to nature: "The wilderness rose up to it, / And sprawled around, no longer wild." At the same time, he creates an order that accords with human value, "a momentary stay against confusion," as Frost put it. But the jar alone is a dead thing, "gray and bare": "It did not give of bird or bush." The poem, however, includes both the life and beauty of nature and the order and beauty of art, plus the wit and feeling of the human consciousness reflecting on their conjunction; here is the "blissful liaison, / Between himself and his environment" ("The Comedian as the Letter C"). This is what Stevens learned to demand of his poems, that as imaginative creations they contain and elicit the essence of reality itself. Of course, most art has this intention, but for Stevens it became a consuming imperative in an age which generally considered poetry irrelevant. For him "life and poetry are one" ("The Rela-

tions Between Poetry and Painting," *Necessary Angel*).
Consequently his development reflects the search for a
style that demonstrates and dramatizes by its daring and
refinement the power of the imagination to apprehend and
order reality, making it a felt presence.

Tentatively at first and then with growing assurance,
Stevens mastered the means of incorporating his feelings
and perceptions in indelible forms. Characterized by bold,
bizarre, and immaculate phrasing, imagistic concreteness,
incisive prosody, and the pictorial and tonal effects of color,
his poems achieve a remarkable vividness, a palpability; and
with techniques derived from the Symbolists, he extended
this mastery to the intangible, imbuing those areas of reality accessible only to the imagination with the same
vividness. At the same time, by disarming ridicule with
such forms of irony as an objective, amused view of self,
and by a recognition of the banal as he sought those supreme points of identification with reality, he could suc-
ceed as a Romantic poet in the twentieth century. And,
finally, although he freed himself from the "clutch of the
old," he never really dispensed with the nobility of poetic
tradition. With these stylistic elements at his command,
he ranged from serious playfulness to the sublime in his
desire to create poems which could withstand the hostile
pressures of, and have meaning in, a materialistic age and
naturalistic universe. Stevens' style, then, developed as an
integral and organic manifestation or correlative of his
central themes. The poem itself "is a nature created by the
poet," said Stevens in "Adagia."

In reaching the point of poetic maturity, he evaded many
tempting dead ends: a rarified aestheticism, the decorative
arabesques and mordant ironies of the Decadents (akin to
the followers of Art Nouveau in the other arts), the Sym-

bolists' obsessive desire to penetrate the veil of the absolute through the magic of art, the limitations of Impressionism and Imagism, and the eccentricities of innovation for the sake of innovation. He flirted with all these dangers and others as well; but acquiring what he needed from the new, he maintained a balance that necessitates our reading him as a significant poet in the perspective of the whole English and American tradition. Contemporaries of Stevens faced many of the same problems and drew on many of the same sources of inspiration that he did, though few cast their nets so wide or brought their sources together for such concentrated thematic purpose. Although he was to reach his thirty-sixth year before achieving his mastery and uniqueness, it is in the Harvard writings that we see the first slight indications of his later style.

ACKNOWLEDGMENTS

My gratitude to Holly Stevens—to put first things first—is profound, for by letting me use a large number of her father's early manuscript poems and other material she has made possible the kind of study I have undertaken. I am all the more grateful to her since she has allowed the manuscript poems to appear in print for the first time in this book even though they will become part of a projected edition of Stevens' juvenilia. Nor do her contributions to my book end here: she has patiently answered numerous questions and provided much crucial information and many clues and suggestions without my having to ask; furthermore, she has read portions of my manuscript and as a result saved me the embarrassment of many omissions and errors.

Samuel French Morse was most obliging in helping me get the study underway, directing me to sources, sending me material, and sharing with me, in letters and conversations, his knowledge of Stevens; also, his publications on the poet have been a continuing fund of insights for me. The late Richard Chase, with what was his customary clear-minded, succinct criticism, guided the study through its dissertation stage. Also, Professors Lewis Leary, Joseph Ridgely, Robert Gorham Davis, Bert M. P. Leefmans, Walter Sokel, and John Unterecker contributed their thoughtful readings and helpful advice. I am especially pleased that A. Walton Litz read a later version, for his critical discernment led me to rewrite several sections. And I am lastingly indebted to Hallett Smith and William York Tindall, who devoted serious attention to the poet's work in courses I had with them many years ago, at a time when Stevens' importance had not yet dawned on most academicians. Furthermore, it was because of a later conversation I had with Professor Tindall that I began this study.

I would require long and detailed comments to express in full my appreciation to those of my friends who have read parts of the manuscript, reacted candidly to some of my points in discussion, steered me to sources, and helped and encouraged me in a host of other ways. I regret that I must resort to listing their names here: Louis Cellucci, Denis Donoghue, Thomas Goethals, George Johnson, George McFadden, Glen A. Omans, Morse Peckham, Judith Puchner, James Redwine, James K. Robinson, William Rossky, and James Zito.

At the Princeton University Press, Miriam Brokaw, in some early discussions I had with her, helped me to resolve a number of difficulties, and Eve Hanle has with her editorial tact and patience eased me through the many details of getting a manuscript into book form. I am thankful, also, to the trustees and administration of Temple University for a Summer Research Grant and for an additional grant for secretarial assistance, both of which sped the preparation of the final manuscript. Beverly Breese, Susan Shapiro, and Lynne Weldon have aided me in numerous ways related to this book, exceeding their duties in the Temple English Department, as is typical of them. As for Helen Buttel's contributions—her lucid, no-nonsense criticisms, her game, persistent efforts at the typewriter, her time, resiliency, and encouragement—I cannot begin to repay her for them, unless finally getting the manuscript out of the house was a start in that direction.

I wish also to thank the following:

Mrs. William Carlos Williams for permission to quote from unpublished letters of her husband's to Stevens.

Matthew Josephson for permission to quote from an unpublished letter of his to Stevens.

The editors of *ELH* and The Johns Hopkins Press for permission to print the first chapter of my book, a version of which appeared in *ELH* and later in *The Act of the Mind: Essays on the Poetry of Wallace Stevens* (1965).

The University of Chicago Library and Robert Rosenthal, Curator of the Harriet Monroe Collection, for permission to quote from the Stevens manuscripts in that collection and from Harriet Monroe's correspondence with Stevens.

The editors of the *Harvard Advocate* for permission to quote Stevens' undergraduate writings.

Wyncote, Pa., June 1966

Contents

WALLACE STEVENS
The Making of
HARMONIUM

I. Part of His Education

*W*HEN Wallace Stevens entered Harvard in 1897, he was not an untutored provincial. True, Reading, Pennsylvania, was a provincial city, surrounded by fertile Pennsylvania Dutch farm country and by woods and mountains where Stevens was fond of hiking, but it was not without culture. It was a vigorous industrial city with a tradition extending back to William Penn, a city of burghers who nevertheless loved music and had a sense of pageantry, apparent, for example, in their annual evening festival on the Schuylkill River, with canoes and other boats floating downstream in a line, lighted by Chinese lanterns. More directly, Stevens' own home provided a favorable cultural environment. He was one of a family who "were all great readers," and his father, a lawyer who contributed poems to the *Reading Times*, was a man seriously concerned with his son's intellectual and aesthetic development, writing Stevens letters of sensible advice on his studies and the arts while he was at Harvard. Before he left for college, Stevens had demonstrated a flair for language by winning the *Reading Eagle* Prize for Essay and the Reading Boys' High Alumni Medal for Oration; he had also written some poetry.[1] He was, then, a young man ready by background, inclination, and ability to make his way in the

---

[1] The festivals on the Schuylkill are briefly described in editorial comment concerning some pictures of the Reading era in the *Historical Review of Berks County*, xxiv, iv (Fall 1959), 108. The rest of the information is from Michael Lafferty's article, "Wallace Stevens, A Man of Two Worlds" in the same issue, pp. 109-113, 130-132. Also, Stevens reflected Reading's interest in music: according to his daughter, Holly Stevens, he sang in a choir and a quartet.

undergraduate literary circles at Harvard. In his sophomore year some of his poems and prose began to appear in the *Harvard Advocate,* the college literary magazine of which he would become president before he left Harvard in 1900.

With a literary interest already nurtured at home, Stevens was to find a further stimulus at Harvard, where under the elective system he took a high proportion of his courses in composition and literature, French and German as well as English.[2] The faculty itself was distinguished and independent-minded, encouraging and cultivating the able student. It could boast such men as Santayana, for example, whom Stevens got to know and whose thought, even though he did not have a course with him, would play an influential part in Stevens' own thinking.[3] The *Harvard Monthly* and the *Advocate* were centers of lively student interest in writing, and Stevens formed friendships that would last beyond college with such students as Witter Bynner, Arthur Davidson Ficke, Walter Conrad Arensberg, and Pitts Sanborn. All were strongly interested in the arts; Arensberg, for example, according to a contemporary, "knew all that was to be known about Walter Pater."[4]

Stevens' undergraduate writing reveals the seriousness of his own interest in aesthetic matters at this early stage of his career. And yet, although this work manifests a growth in

[2] See Appendix 1 for the complete transcript of courses Stevens took at Harvard.

[3] Any study of Stevens' intellectual development would have to take Santayana's work into account. As Frank Kermode says, "Santayana's *Interpretations of Poetry and Religion* (1900) is a key book for the thought of Stevens." *Wallace Stevens* (Edinburgh and London, 1960), p. 81. See also p. 18 and note 12.

[4] See Lafferty, p. 113. Also, William Ivins is the contemporary who referred to Arensberg's knowledge of Pater: see Fiske Kimball, "Cubism and the Arensbergs," *Art News Annual*, xxiv (1955), 117.

experiment and discovery, he was to remark on a later visit to Harvard that when he was a student there, "it was commonplace to say that all the poetry had been written and all the paintings painted."[5] Surely there was a general sterility in English and American poetry at that time. The early poems of Yeats were still permeated with the style and mood of Pre-Raphaelite verse; the poetry of Hardy and Housman was not significantly changing the direction of poetry at large. Such Decadents as Wilde, Symons, and Dowson were reduced to mocking and shocking middle-class moral attitudes while they celebrated art for art's sake in the ivory tower Tennyson had warned against in "The Palace of Art"—thus marking the end of an era and at the same time contributing to the poetry of the era to come by helping to introduce French Symbolism into English poetry. In America, the sweeping innovations of Whitman and the incisive wit and haunting suggestiveness of Emily Dickinson were largely ignored. Edmund Clarence Stedman, the well-known poet, critic, and editor of his day, spoke of the time when his *An American Anthology* appeared (1900) as a "twilight interval."[6] Poetry seemed less and less significant in a world of science, industrialism, and middle-class culture. The Decadents and aesthetes responded by establishing a cult of artifice and beauty, while at the opposite extreme the realistic and naturalistic writers were making a determined effort to explore the actual world, sordid though it might be. The ever-recurrent problem of reconciling art and life, a problem recognized and

[5] Stevens, "The Irrational Element in Poetry," *ca.* 1937, *Opus Posthumous*, ed. Samuel French Morse (New York, 1957), p. 218. This book will be referred to hereafter as *Opus*.

[6] See Horace Gregory and Maria Zaturenska, *A History of American Poetry, 1900-1940* (New York, 1942), p. 10.

5

worried over by the Romantics and Victorians, had by the end of the century become especially acute.

The French poet, Henri Regnier, in a series of lectures given in the spring semester of 1900 at Harvard and other American colleges and universities, noted that the Symbolists had faced this conflict between the two extremes, which he put in terms of idealism and realism (or naturalism):

> . . . In the early eighties followed the reaction of idealism against realism. The new movement was headed by Paul Verlaine, Mallarmé, and others. With them slowly arose the new school of poets called "decadents" or symbolists.

> . . . Villiers d'Isle Adam was held in great respect by the young school, who considered him as a living protest against the naturalistic tendencies of the time, and as a living incarnation of idealism.

> . . . Poetry in France had been in great peril from the ever-rising wave of naturalism and realism, to which all poets were making concessions.[7]

Whether or not Stevens attended these lectures, he had already become sensitive to the nature of the conflict; in several prose pieces antedating Regnier's visit, he had developed his plots in terms of the contrasts between ideal beauty, art, and the imagination on the one hand and coarseness, disorder, and reality on the other. In these stories and sketches Stevens emphasized both the lifelessness of beauty and art detached from the actual world and the futility of the actual world ungraced by the imagination.

[7] From summaries printed in the *Harvard Crimson*, xxxvii, 15 (Friday, March 2, 1900), 1; 17 (Monday, March 5, 1900), 1; and 23 (Monday, March 12, 1900), 1.

More and more his Harvard work juxtaposed the world of imagination and the world of reality, and thus began his lifelong meditation on their interrelationship. Out of his constant awareness of this interrelationship evolved all the later, more specific variations of that theme and the experiments with style and technique which were refined and developed into the mature poetry of *Harmonium*.

BETWEEN THE fall of 1898 and the spring of 1900, many of Stevens' poems appeared in the *Harvard Advocate*, several in the *Harvard Monthly*, and one in *East and West*, a short-lived New York periodical. Also, ten short stories and sketches were published in the *Advocate*, not to mention many editorials after Stevens became its president.[8] As one might expect, many of the Harvard poems are typical of the undergraduate and magazine verse of the era, verse in the ebbing Romantic and Victorian traditions. But following the appearance of most of his prose exercises, in which Stevens not only concentrated on the theme mentioned above but also anticipated some elements of his mature style, three of his later undergraduate poems show among other qualities a new wit, irony, sophistication, and forcefulness.

In the very early Harvard poems Stevens was fond of the sonnet and quatrain forms, but whatever skill he displayed in versification, the poems suffer not only from their dated stylistic qualities but also from their tendency toward sentimental effects. Indeed, most of the undergraduate poems, not just the earliest ones, are little more than competent exercises in the prevailing poetic fashions of the time. A

[8] See Appendix II for a full chronological index of the Harvard poems and stories.

good example is the sonnet "Vita Mea," the second Stevens poem to appear in the *Advocate* (December 12, 1898):

> With fear I trembled in the House of Life,
> Hast'ning from door to door, from room to room,
> Seeking a way from that impenetrable gloom
> Against whose walls my strength lay weak from strife,
> All dark! All dark! And what sweet wind was rife
> With earth, or sea, or star, or new sun's bloom,
> Lay sick and dead within that place of doom,
> Where I went raving like the winter's wife.
>
> "In vain, in vain," with bitter lips I cried;
> "In vain, in vain," along the hallways died
> And sank in silences away. Oppressed
> I wept. Lo! through those tears the window-bars
> Shone bright, where Faith and Hope like long-sought
> stars
> First gleamed upon that prison of unrest.

It is a melodramatic utterance to be sure, but at the same time, it displays proficiency in the development of the house-prison imagery, the fulfillment of the rhyme-scheme, and the not ungraceful use of the basically iambic pattern—with such effects as "and sank in silences away." Also, a faint glimmer of Stevens' later boldness of metaphor is apparent in "raving like the winter's wife" (though the effect seems unintentionally humorous here).

The movement, imagery, and diction of the poem are distinctly Victorian and a reminder, for example, of Tennyson's *Maud*, Part Three, which proceeds from Stanza 1: "My life has crept so long on a broken wing / Through cells of madness, haunts of horror and fear, . . ." to Stanza 5: "It is better to fight for the good than to rail at the ill; / . . . , / I embrace the purpose of God, and the doom assigned."

The central metaphor in "Vita Mea" echoes the title of Rossetti's sonnet sequence, *The House of Life*. One notes also a similarity to lines in James Thompson's "The City of Dreadful Night": "I paced from room to room, from hall to hall, / Nor any life throughout the maze discerned." Such imagery, diction, and tonal quality were simply part of the poetic atmosphere of the time. Santayana, for example, while teaching at Harvard in the Nineties, was writing more controlled sonnets, but in a mood and style like that of "Vita Mea," as the following passage from his "Though utter death should swallow up my hope" suggests:

> Yet have I light of love, nor need to grope
> Lost, wholly lost, without an inward fire;
> The flame that quickeneth the world entire
> Leaps in my breast, with cruel death to cope.

And E. A. Robinson had included in his *The Torrent and the Night Before* (1896) not only many distinctive departures from conventional verse but also such poems as "Credo," which with its mixture of despair and idealism is close in effect to "Vita Mea."

> I cannot find my way: there is no star
> In all the shrouded heavens anywhere;
>
> .   .   .   .
>
> No, there is not a glimmer, nor a call,
> For one that welcomes, welcomes when he fears,
> The black and awful chaos of the night;
> For through it all,—above beyond it all,—
> I know the far-sent message of the years,
> I feel the coming glory of the Light!

"Vita Mea," with its own unaccountable shift to hope at the end, was anthologized in *Harvard Lyrics* (1899) by

9

alumnus C. L. Stebbins; it is in company with a number of other student poems whose overwrought speakers insist on a vague idealistic answer to their despair over the darkness of Life. No wonder Stevens was to say many years later, "Some of one's early things give one the creeps" (*Opus*, p. xvii).

Another "Sonnet" in the *Advocate* (April 10, 1899) echoes Keats' "Bright Star." It is formally competent and as effective as its conventional and imitative manner allows.

> There shines the morning star! Through the forlorn
>> And silent spaces of cold heaven's height
>> Pours the bright radiance of his kingly light,
> Swinging in revery before the morn.
> The flush and fall of many tides have worn
>> Upon coasts beneath him, in their flight
>> From sea to sea; yet ever on the night
> His clear and splendid visage is upborn.
>
> Like this he pondered on the world's first day,
>> Sweet Eden's flowers heavy with the dew;
> And so he led bold Jason on his way
>> Sparkling forever in the galley's foam;
> And still he shone most perfect in the blue,
>> All bright and lovely on the hosts of Rome.

It, too, is similar in style to several poems in *Harvard Lyrics*. Compare its imagery, for example, with that in a student poem called "Worth" in that volume:

> I saw the old white moon above the trees
>> That shone on Adam in his paradise,
>> That shines on the everlasting rise
> And fall of realms and races, land and seas.

Such poetic idiom illustrates the extent to which the language of poetry in general had by the end of the century fallen into a conventionalized literary style which could not evoke the intensity of effect intended.

That Stevens during this period had no particularly original point of view which demanded original means of expression, and that most of these poems are essentially exercises in the current modes, can be seen by looking at another "Sonnet" which appeared in the *Harvard Monthly* (March 1899):

> If we are leaves that fall upon the ground
> To lose our greenness in the quiet dust
> Of forest-depths; if we are flowers that must
> Lie torn and creased upon a bitter mound,
> No touch of sweetness in our ruins found;
> If we are weeds whom no one wise can trust
> To live our hour before we feel the gust
> Of death, and by our side its last, keen sound;
>
> Then let a tremor through our briefness run,
> Wrapping it with mad, sweet sorcery
> Of love; for in the fern I saw the sun
> Take fire against the dew; the lily white
> Was soft and deep at morn; the rosary
> Streamed forth a wild perfume into the light.

In its concern with mortality and the spiritual beauty of earth, the poem in a very remote way anticipates the theme of "Sunday Morning." More evidently, however, it expresses the *carpe diem* theme rather than that of Faith and Hope—despite the religious connotations of "lily white" and "rosary" in the sestet—in a tone and manner reminiscent of Ernest Dowson, for one. The style of the sestet, in

11

fact, definitely places the poem in the Pre-Raphaelite-aesthetic tradition. A tender, if sentimental, delicacy of feeling is conveyed, and yet at the same time, as in "Vita Mea," the voice is melodramatic and the figures too sentimentally handled: "if we are flowers that must / Lie torn and creased upon a bitter mound. . . ." But the poem is partly redeemed by "For in the fern I saw the sun / Take fire against the dew," an image that is specific and vital, with the visual particularity that would be conspicuous in his later poetry. Also, the management of cadence and enjambment shows both skill and control.[9]

[9] Although all Stevens' Harvard sonnets need not be discussed, the reader might wish to note in the young poet's other poems in this form his adherence to the period's prevailing stylistic qualities, which include, for example, echoes of the *Rubaiyat* in "Sonnet" ("Lo, even as I passed"). The pseudonyms are characteristic of Stevens' reticence. (I do quote and discuss one further and exceptional "Sonnet," pp. 17-18.)

Sonnet

I strode along my beaches like a sea,
The sand before me stretching firm and fair
No inland darkness cast its shadow there
And my long step was gloriously free.
The careless wind was happy company
That hurried past and did not question where;
Yet as I moved I felt a deep despair
And wonder of the thoughts that came to me.

For to my face the deep wind brought the scent
Of flowers I could not see upon the strand;
And in the sky a silent cloud was blent
With dreams of my soul's stillness; and the sand
That had been naught to me, now trembled far
In mystery beneath the evening star.

John Morris, 2nd
(*Harvard Monthly*, July 1899)

(n. 9, cont.)

To the Morn

If this be night, break softly, blessed day.
Oh, let the silent throat of every bird
Swell tenderly in song, as though he heard
Some brother singing deep within the ray!
Send but an unseen breeze aloft, away
From darkness and dull earth, to be a word,
A half-discovered sound, to make me gird
Myself, and persevere this cheerless way.

But softly, softly, thou most blessed morn.
Mine eyes too long accustomed to the dark
May fail when thou in glorious heav'n art born,
May fail against that far-entreated light,
Catch but the glimmer of a distant lark,
And drop, all blasted, at the sovereign sight.

> Hillary Harness
> (*Harvard Monthly*, December 1899)

Sonnet

Lo, even as I passed beside the booth
Of roses, and beheld them brightly twine
To damask heights, taking them as a sign
Of my own self still unconcerned with truth;
Even as I held up in hands uncouth
And drained with joy the golden-bodied wine,
Deeming it half-unworthy, half divine,
From out the sweet-rimmed goblet of my youth,

Even in that pure hour I heard the tone
Of grievous music stir in memory,
Telling me of the time already flown
From my first youth. It sounded like the rise
Of distant echo from dead melody,
Soft as a song heard far in Paradise.

> R. Jerries
> (*Harvard Advocate*, May 23, 1900)

13

In the quatrain form, Stevens also achieved a conventional facility, as in "Quatrain" (*Advocate*, November 13, 1899) with its tenderly coy personification:

> Go not, young cloud, too boldly through the sky,
>   To meet the morning light:
> Go not too boldly through that dome on high—
>   For eastward lies the night.

In its apostrophe to the cloud and its prettiness and grace, it is not unlike the quatrain (Part I, XVII) in Tennyson's *Maud*:

>   Go not, happy day,
>   From the shining fields,
>   Go not, happy day,
>   Till the maiden yields.

Similarly graceful is Stevens' "Song" (*Advocate*, March 13, 1899):

(n. 9, cont.)

Sonnet

> Come, said the world, thy youth is not all play,
> Upon these hills vast palaces must rise,
> And over this green plain that calmly lies
> In peace, a mighty city must have sway.
> These weak and murmuring reeds cannot gainsay
> The building of my wharves; this flood that flies
> Unfathomed clear must bear my merchandise,
> And sweep my burdens on their seaward way.
>
> No, cried my heart, this thing I cannot do,
> This is my home, this plain and water clear
> Are my companions faultless as the sky—
> I cannot, will not give them up to you.
> And if you come upon them I shall fear,
> And if you steal them from me I shall die.
>
>   (*East and West*, May 1900)

> She loves me or loves me not,
>> What care I?—
> The depth of the fields is just as sweet,
>> And sweet the sky.
>
> She loves me or loves me not,
>> Is that to die?—
> The green of the woods is just as fair,
>> And fair the sky.

This is an attractive version of a traditional theme, echoing Sir Walter Raleigh's "Shall I Like An Hermit Dwell" and George Wither's "The Author's Resolution in a Sonnet." It has lightness and restraint, qualities decidedly lacking in some of Stevens' poems, such as the following mawkish "Song," which appeared in the *Advocate* a year after the one above (March 10, 1900), and well after Stevens had begun to explore new directions in his stories:

> Ah yes! beyond these barren walls
>> Two hearts shall in a garden meet,
> And while the latest robin calls,
>> Her lips to his shall be made sweet.
>
> And out above these gloomy tow'rs
>> The full moon tenderly shall rise
> To cast its light upon the flow'rs
>> And find him looking in her eyes.

This and several other equally embarrassing efforts published during Stevens' final semester are the weakest of the Harvard poems, very possibly written earlier and then used as fillers when Stevens became president of the *Advocate*.[10]

[10] One other poem in quatrain form, aside from those quoted in the text, published while Stevens was an undergraduate is the following:

But it is just as possible that his performance was as uneven as the late appearance of these poems would suggest, for some of the later manuscript poems are almost as trite.

Indeed, "Who Lies Dead?" the first of his poems to appear in the *Advocate* (November 28, 1898), shows as much promise as any of the poems discussed so far.

> Who lies dead in the sea,
>   All water 'tween him and the stars,
> The keels of a myriad ships above,
>   The sheets on a myriad spars?
>
> Who lies dead in the world,
>   All heavy of heart and hand,
> The blaze of a myriad arms in sight,
>   The sweep of a myriad band?

The image in the first quatrain, dependent as it is on the unusual point of view—looking upward from the ocean floor—has a particularity and freshness that make it far

---

Night Song

I stand upon the hills tonight
  And see the cold March moon
Rise upward with his silver light
  And make a gentle noon.

The fields are blowing with the breeze,
  The stars are in the sky,
There is a humming through the trees,
  And one cloud passes by.

I wonder if that is the sea,
  Rid of the sun's annoy,
That sings a song all bold and free,
  Of glory and of joy.

Kenneth Malone
(*Harvard Advocate*, May 10, 1900)

more effective than the lugubrious "impenetrable gloom / Against whose walls my strength lay weak from strife" in "Vita Mea." The device of the unanswered questions is an attempt to leave the import of the martial images oblique rather than heavily explicit. What seems to be suggested is the paralysis of those unresponsive or dead to the beauty, wonder and purpose in life. Such a concern reflects Stevens' lifelong insistence on the need for the self to discover significant relationships with the objective world. Here, of course, the chief impression is of vague lament and a poetic impulse toward beauty and spectacle, matched by the young poet's attempt to achieve a lofty impressiveness. Still, "Who Lies Dead?" is a respectable effort within the limitations of its conventional style, which here includes the grand martial imagery and the phrase "heavy of heart."[11]

The imagery in this poem is surpassed, however, by that in the concluding four lines of "Sonnet," which appeared some six months later in the *Harvard Monthly* (May 1899), at a time when Stevens was beginning to acquire greater thematic assurance in his prose sketches. The whole sonnet is noteworthy:

Cathedrals are not built along the sea;
  The tender bells would jangle on the hoar

[11] The imagery in "Who Lies Dead?" may be an echo of some of the details in Arnold's "Stanzas from the Grande Chartreuse," a poem which laments the spiritual paralysis in the world and includes martial spectacle to suggest the glory that lies beyond the safety of the "abbey wall": "we are like children reared in shade / . . . . [who] catch a glance / Of passing troops in the sun's beam— / Pennon, and plume, and flashing lance!"; " 'Fenced early in this cloistral round / Of reverie, of shade, of prayer, / How could we grow in other ground? / . . . . / —Pass banners, pass, and bugles, cease; / And leave our desert to its peace!' "

And iron winds; the graceful turrets roar
With bitter storms the long night angrily;
And through the precious organ pipes would be
A low and constant murmur of the shore
That down those golden shafts would rudely pour
A mighty and a lasting melody.

And those who knelt within the gilded stalls
Would have vast outlook for their weary eyes.
There they would see high shadows on the walls
From passing vessels in their fall and rise;
Through gaudy windows there would come too soon
The low and splendid rising of the moon.

Stevens took a copy of this poem to Santayana one evening, and the mentor was so impressed that he was moved to compose that very night a poem in response: "Cathedrals by the Sea (Reply to a sonnet beginning 'Cathedrals Are Not Built Along the Sea')."[12] Obviously, the contrast between the precious, ornate church art—which is out of tune with nature and sustained only by being divorced and protected from nature's eternal variety and energy—and the beauty of nature and life is a theme that Santayana must have found congenial. More than this, here was a precocious student indeed, one who could adroitly develop the contrasts in the poem with a cogent and convincing pattern of word and image, as he does in setting the "iron winds" in conflict with the "tender bells" and "golden shafts." It is a remarkable poem, on a theme he treated more extensively about a year later in his series called "Street Songs,"

[12] Holly Stevens has informed me, in a conversation, about Stevens' visit to Santayana and the exchange of poems. See S. F. Morse, J. R. Bryer, and J. W. Riddel, *Wallace Stevens Checklist* (Denver, 1963), p. 50, for further details about this poem.

and, indeed, during the rest of his life. The novel conception of the poem and Stevens' acute response to sensory data, as well as his ability to convey it—apparent in the aural details in the octet and the visual details in the sestet—are early instances of the originality, sensitivity, and technical skill that he would bring to fulfillment in his later work.

This poem was an exception at this point. Generally, lacking such thematic certainty, Stevens was writing verse which in thought and style was quite in keeping with that written by the more established poets of the era as well as by other students. His poems seem to reflect the spiritual malaise of the Nineties, with the desire for an idealized beauty and meaning overcast by a tone of sadness and despair. Although technically competent, for the most part, the poems contain at best very dim indications of the course Stevens' development would follow.

It is in the stories and sketches, all published in the *Advocate* between January 1899 and June 1900, that Stevens, free of the restrictions of popular poetic practice, could begin to work out what more and more became his central concern: the relationships between the actual world and that world as observed or transformed by the imagination. In place of the moody, self-conscious speakers in the poems, he could present a variety of characters in a variety of situations. The tonal range of the stories is greater too, including irony and humor, qualities so obviously missing in the poems discussed thus far. But assuredly the stories are not accomplished works of art. They are too wooden and contrived for that and are full of such immaturities as, "The warm afternoon beat against the windows courageously." Samuel French Morse, in his introduction to *Opus Post-*

humous, refers to the stories as *"fin de siècle* sketches," an apt characterization on the whole. Nevertheless, they contain in embryo many of Stevens' later attributes of style.

One important way that the stories differ from the early poems is in their specific use of the unpleasant details that the naturalistic novelists included in their works. A good example occurs in the third sketch of "Four Characters," Stevens' last piece to appear in the *Advocate* (June 16, 1900). In this sketch—one of a series of four contrasting beauty and sordidness—the narrator and a reporter (appropriately enough for the naturalistic situation), upon investigating a death, find an old woman in a tenement lamenting over the corpse of her husband whom she has laid out on an ironing board between two chairs and covered with her only sheet; the bare mattress is also described. Here the negation in the world is not presented in the vague manner of "Vita Mea," as a prison with walls of "impenetrable gloom"—the squalor is unsparingly real. This sketch is preceded by one which describes a beautiful summer day and followed by one concerning a woman reminiscing about the past splendor of her home ("painted in imitation of the ducal palace in Venice") before it became a boarding house, with a seamstress, an artist, a student, and an electrician among its boarders, the "dreadful sundry of this world," as Stevens would say in "O Florida, Venereal Soil" (1922). The dead body, the sheet, and the milieu of the sketch look ahead to "The Emperor of Ice-Cream" (1922) with its lines, "Take from the dresser of deal / . . . that sheet / . . . and spread it so as to cover her face."[13]

[13] *Collected Poems of Wallace Stevens* (New York, 1954): "O Florida," p. 47; "The Emperor," p. 64. While most of Stevens' poems referred to hereafter are to be found in *Harmonium,* all of them will be found in *Collected Poems* unless other sources are

It is "Part of His Education," the third story in the *Advocate* (April 24, 1899), which most dramatically illustrates Stevens' interest in the interrelationship of aesthetic values and crude reality.[14] Here he reinforces his meaning by using the antithetical motifs of crème de menthe and beer. Geoffrey, a prissy aesthete, visits a barroom with Billy, "a regular fellow," in order to "see the side of life that gave the other fellows so much sport; the side of life he had never seen." In an atmosphere of coarse faces,

---

specifically cited. The dates following the titles are of first publication.

[14] Even the first two stories in the *Advocate* are rudimentary attempts at working out the conflict between the beautiful or imaginative and the negations in reality. In a melodramatic piece called "Her First Escapade" (January 16, 1899), beauty and romance are obliterated by a heartless if materially successful man. Rothwald, a wealthy farmer, momentarily jealous when his young housekeeper tries to escape with a poor young farmer (Rothwald has been too obtuse to realize the girl's potential as a wife for himself), shoots in their direction, intending merely to frighten them, and unknowingly kills the girl. "A Day in February," the next story to appear (March 6, 1899), has as its basis the dualism between winter, associated with barren college studies in philosophy, mathematics and economics, and summer, which stimulates romance: a hint of warm air in February causes the narrator to feel like a knight, though he is in street clothes, and evokes pleasant memories of summer fields in Pennsylvania. After a walk, he resolves to be less Faust than Pan and pitches a stack of his writings into the wastebasket. The story ends enigmatically with his bowing to an imaginary person (the spirit of summer, perhaps, or Pan) and saying, "Ah, old man, old fellow, you don't know, you haven't any idea how glad I am to meet you again." Only hindsight would lead the reader to see the possible origin here of the later symbolic role of winter and summer in Stevens' poetry; the sketch is hardly distinguishable from one any student might have written on the subject of nature versus books.

21

smoke, and pictures of fighting cocks—very naturalistic details—Geoffrey asserts his preciosity by ordering crème de menthe. One wonders, incidentally, if Stevens took a hint from Frank Norris' *McTeague*, published only two months before (February 1899), which includes a saloon scene in which McTeague orders a glass of beer while Marcus Schouler "calls for a 'Creme Yvette' in order to astonish the others." In any case, upon being ridiculed for ordering the crème de menthe, Geoffrey makes a fool of himself by calling the men pigs for desecrating a ballade; but finally he realizes his absurdity and atones by ordering beer all around. Divorced from reality, his precious elegance cannot sustain itself. He accepts reality, crude but vital, much as the men, after laughing at him and being entertained at his expense, come to accept Geoffrey. As Billy had said earlier of the men, "They're like thirsty flowers longing for dew," the dew presumably suggesting the beauty and meaning absent from their lives. The final reconciliation is contrived, but the story stresses the need for such a reconciliation. Geoffrey must drink the "beer of reality," but the crème de menthe forms a beautiful rainbow and becomes a point of poetic illumination in the story when Geoffrey, making a defiant gesture, inadvertently causes the liqueur to fly out of his glass. Up to a point, "Part of His Education" is an awkward *fin de siècle* piece. It does not, however, endorse an escape from reality; the aesthete is humorously thrust into the roughness of life. Stevens still had much to learn, but this story, in its attempt at thematic complication and in its skeletal symbolic construction, is a real turning point in his early writing.

Although the theme of conflict and interdependence of the mundane and imaginative worlds runs through all of them, two other stories clearly illustrate this theme and

Stevens' search for ways of dramatizing it. One is "Pursuit" (October 18, 1899) in which a group of boys who "had eyes only for what was bright and rare" chase an extraordinary butterfly with "argent wings," an obvious symbol of aesthetic perfection. The boys are laughed at by the boorish wife of a farmer, but when the butterfly "sailed down in its luxury" at the feet of the farmer and his wife, clearly philistines, "There was a piercing scream and in a wild panic the farmer and wife were gone." The wife, overwhelmed by a sense of the power of pure beauty, is left "a breathless heap in the dust. . . . The vanquished clod [her husband] cut across the country through a thicket of tall, pink-blooming milkweeds." After capturing the perfect butterfly, the boys, for a while forgetful of ordinary things, remember the events the butterfly had brought about and they return, as to reality and necessity, to look for the farm woman in the dust, but she is gone.

The other story which illustrates Stevens' theme particularly well is "The Nymph" (December 6, 1899). Here, the narrator is in the woods in Massachusetts in search of wildness. Instead, he finds a tall, slim girl of seventeen in a faded blue skirt and white sweater, with a spray of eglantine in her hair and a sketching pad in her hand, who responds to his curiosity by declaring herself to be a nymph. "And in the winter—" wonders the practical youth. "That's my secret," she replies. She makes fun of his hard tack, dry beef, and canned beans, offering in their stead—while playfully stepping on one of his crackers—blackberries, mushrooms, wild cherries, and grapes. Naming the woodland dainties in French, thus civilizing them and intensifying the sense of their delicacy, she lists them on her sketching pad. The distinction between this fare and the gross food of the young man reminds us of that between crème de

menthe and beer in "Part of His Education." This encounter of boy and girl is considerably more striking than
"Two hearts shall in a garden meet" (from "Song"); the
scene is sophisticated and idyllic—nature heightened and
ordered by the power of the girl's imagination. But alas, the
idyll is interrupted by an insistent voice calling to Dora
(the nymph's actual name): "The potatoes are cold, the
flies are in the jelly—oh, such a lunch as you'll have." The
comic deflation becomes complete when, arriving at a clearing, the narrator finds that the nymph works for a group
of men who are playing cards outside their tents; a banner
proclaims them the "Eureka Camping Club of Billville,
Mass." Such is the fate of Parnassian nymphs in the modern
world, although this one has in the face of banality created
her imaginary mythological character and a few moments
of rare beauty; these remain despite the comic deflation, or
rather because of it.

The nymph's playful indoctrination of the youth into the
world of sophisticated experience foreshadows the plot of
the girls in the *Harmonium* poem, "The Plot against the
Giant," to check, abash, and undo the giant by providing
the most delicate and beautiful stimulants to his senses.
But "The Plot" is not unique, for "Last Looks at the Lilacs"
and "Two Figures in Dense Violet Night" both concern
the humorous disparity between gauche male and suave
female. Imagine the nymph in a less humorous context, and
she becomes an early version of Stevens' queen in "To the
One of Fictive Music," who "Gives motion to perfection
. . . / . . . out of our imperfections wrought," just as the
comically presented narrator in "The Nymph," in search
of wilderness, is a precursor of the more experience-hungry
Crispin—that "marvelous sophomore" in "The Comedian
as the Letter C."

24

Stevens' delight in the bizarre and the comic-grotesque, as well as the humor seen in the previous examples, is best illustrated by "In the Dead of Night" (May 23, 1900),[15] a farcical piece which can be characterized as something between a college humor sketch and some of Washington Irving's burlesques of the ghostly in *Tales of a Traveller*. Here Stevens' imagination was thoroughly liberated from the "impenetrable gloom" of "Vita Mea." Cavanaugh, a servant disgruntled over being let go because of his mysterious behavior in the house, takes revenge by drugging the apple dumplings. The result is a wild midnight scene of mass hallucination in which the father of the house soberly discusses the Philippine question with Cavanaugh, who is trying to escape with the silverware. Outdoor, daytime activity is transposed indoors in the middle of the night when the group begins tobogganing on the main stairway to the accompaniment of shrieks and the singing of "Jingle Bells." Meanwhile, a Mrs. Fann, losing her inhibitions, keeps asking to be folded. The story is an early caper by the poet who was to lament in "Disillusionment of Ten O'Clock" that

> The houses are haunted
> By white night-gowns.
> None are green,
> Or purple with green rings,

.   .   .   .

[15] In the story "Hawkins of Cold Cape" (March 10, 1900), Stevens again combines humor and weirdness. On the basis of a falling meteor, a rumor develops that the end of the world is at hand. In this eerie atmosphere, full of the threat of imminent cataclysm, Hawkins, the unsuccessful editor of the local newspaper, uses the rumor and his imagination to create panic among the gullible townsfolk, and thus manages to acquire most of the town's livestock as well as a thriving butter and egg business.

> People are not going
> To dream of baboons and periwinkles . . .

. . . .

Although less impressive than the basic conceptions of these stories and Stevens' management of the comic point of view in them, the imagery and diction are occasionally worth mentioning. Compare, for example, the trite and heavy treatment of the wind in "Vita Mea"—"And what sweet wind was rife / With earth, or sea, or star, or new sun's bloom, / Lay sick and dead within that place of doom"—with the more playful and striking use of it in "The Nymph," where the wind is likened to a giant. When the girl is summoned back to camp, she runs with the narrator in pursuit and cries over her shoulder, " '*Mûres de ronce*' . . . with a tantalizing laugh. '*De ronce, de ronce*,' repeated the giant. '*De ronce*,' I added instinctively." Here the obligato of the personified wind adds to the scene a quality that is at once slightly haunting and whimsical. It is also somewhat ludicrous, but nevertheless it is an effort that foreshadows Stevens' large comic manner and his joy in the sounds of French words, which he seems to play on here in terms of the story's theme (the literal meaning of *mûres de ronce* being berries from briars). Conspicuously better than many descriptions in these stories is that of the butterfly in "Pursuit," in which Stevens, with an appropriate Parnassian grace, evoked its exalted and aesthetic quality: its "argent wings" moved with "such an opening of light, such a closing of radiance." Finally, the instance in the stories most indicative of the later exuberance of word and sound occurs in "Part of His Education" at a point where Stevens wanted to convey the excitement and vitality of the music in the barroom: "the banjo . . . thrilled and rattled with a volume of clattering notes and chords." This is a far cry from the later extravagant virtuosity seen, for instance, in "Bantams in Pine Woods," but "thrilled," "rattled," and "clattering" have some of the later almost tactile vibrato of diction and sound, played "not on the psaltery, / But on the banjo's categorical gut" ("The Comedian as the Letter C").

The stories also reflect Stevens' growing interest in color, both as a visual effect and as a symbolic device. The third sketch in "Four Characters" contains this specific but merely decorative color description: "The horizon was blue, rimmed in the east with a pink mistiness; in the west, with a warm yellowish red that gradually died into thin whiteness." But in "The Revelation" (November 13, 1899), Williams, a picture-frame maker, in helping a college youth decide on an appropriate color for the frame of the photograph of his beautiful girl friend, provides half-seriously a brief glossary of color symbolism. Black is considered ominous, brown is thought poetical, and white symbolic of clear weather. Finally Williams suggests and uses gold, the color he reserves for framing pictures of Madonnas, because the girl, in her visits to the shop to get her photograph of the youth framed, has become Williams' ideal. Thus Williams finds his Madonna in the actual world, a point which Stevens achieved obliquely, partly through the symbolic use of color which would play such a major role in his later poetry.

In the first of three editorials in the *Advocate* regarding a proposed plan for fencing Harvard Yard (March 24, April 13, June 16, 1900), Stevens said: "Putting a fence around the Yard strikes us as being the easiest way of achieving order out of chaos . . . ; we have no point of concentration . . . ; a fence would unquestionably bring back to the Yard

27

some of the prestige which it has lost . . . ; the Yard would regain the hold on our imagination which it is gradually losing." For Stevens, the imagination, order, and art were not simply literary matters; they were relevant to experience, to the actual world. It was such concentration of interest that enabled him in the stories to work out some of the elements of his theme and to move, however inexpertly at this stage, in the direction of his later style. And the same interest had a corresponding effect on some of his later undergraduate poetry.

By March 1900, all but two of the stories ("In the Dead of Night" and "Four Characters") had appeared in the *Advocate*, and at that point (March 24, 1900) Stevens published "Outside the Hospital," a poem very different from the earlier ones:

> See the blind and the lame at play,
>   There on the summer lawn—
> She with her graceless eyes of clay,
>   Quick as a frightened fawn,
> Running and tripping into his way
>   Whose legs are gone.
>
> How shall she 'scape him, where shall she fly,
>   She who never sees?
> Now he is near her, now she is by—
>   Into his arms she flees.
> Hear her gay laughter, hear her light cry
>   Among the trees.
>
> "Princess, my captive." "Master my king,"
>   "Here is a garland bright."
> "Red roses, I wonder, red with the Spring,
>   Red with a reddish light?"

"Red roses, my princess, I ran to bring,
  And be your knight."

Here is a pastoral scene with flowers, but it takes place on a hospital lawn, not "beyond these barren walls," as in "Song." With its ironic juxtaposition of the grotesquely real and the gracefully imaginative which transcends the real, this is the second poem in which Stevens' central theme is unmistakably present (the first being the Sonnet "Cathedrals are not built"). Also, the couple's lack of self-pity and their dialogue are in telling contrast with the feverish and sentimental qualities in several of Stevens' Harvard poems. In fact, although the subject provides a greater risk of sentimentality than do the subjects of the other poems, it reveals instead a higher degree of control. The very conception of the poem is more forceful; in the chiasmic reversal, the girl sees excellently in her mind's eye, and the legless boy runs in his imagination like a knight. The pair are like the nymph, Dora; although they do not speak French, they act and speak with regal elegance. The use of the word "garland" would be trite in the context of the earlier poems, but here it adds appropriately to the effect of light fantasy which is set off by the blunt statement of facts: a girl with "eyes of clay" plays with a boy "whose legs are gone." One thinks how frequently in his later poetry Stevens gave new life to archaic, poetic words, like "tinct" in "Cy Est Pourtraicte, Madame Ste Ursule, et Les Unze Mille Vierges."

Here, also, Stevens uses color more as he would in his later poetry. The girl in her imagination sees color very particularly—"red with a reddish light"—almost as though she had in mind the painter's method of highlighting a color with a stroke of a brighter shade. By *Harmonium*, of course, Stevens, struck by the bold use of color in modern painting, would much more distinctly simulate the technique of painting in order to create visual emphasis and a sense of texture, as he does so flamboyantly in "Nomad Exquisite"—"Beholding all these green sides / And gold sides of green sides." It might be that in "Outside the Hospital" Stevens was inspired by the Pre-Raphaelites' interest in an alliance of poetry, tapestry, and painting, and especially by their use of color in poetry. One thinks particularly, in this connection, of such poems as William Morris' "Golden Wings" and "Two Red Roses across the Moon" with their orchestrations of colors.

The suggestion of medieval courtly love in "Outside the Hospital" may also be a mark of Pre-Raphaelite influence, though this is not to forget the medievalism in Tennyson; indeed, this element, like many in Stevens' Harvard work, is quite typical of Victorian poetry in general. The most important point about this poem, however, is that in it he combined a medieval love motif with a hospital setting and the cruel fact of physical disability. One wonders, in regard to the hospital scene, if Stevens had read William Ernest Henley's *In Hospital*, a series of poems which uncompromisingly depict the painful and unattractive details of hospital life. Whatever the sources, to create a unity out of such diverse materials was a stroke of originality that prefigures much in Stevens' later poetry.

Although the actual dates of composition cannot be proved, the general trend of publication in the *Advocate* shows Stevens becoming increasingly absorbed, in his poems as well as his prose sketches, by the ideas that would hold an inexhaustible interest for him throughout his career. Following "Outside the Hospital" there appeared a sequence of four poems collectively called "Street Songs"

(April 3, 1900). These are uneven in quality, but they are more ambitious than "Outside the Hospital" and make an interesting companion piece to "Cathedrals are not built," extending the implications of that poem.

I

The Pigeons

Over the houses and into the sky
    And into the dazzling light,
Long hosts of fluttering pigeons fly
    Out of the blackened night,
Over the houses and into the sky
    On glistening wings of white.

Over the city and into the blue
    From ledge and tower and dome,
They rise and turn and turn anew,
    And like fresh clouds they roam,
Over the city and into the blue
    And into their airy home.

II

The Beggar

Yet in this morn there is a darkest night,
Where no feet dance or sweet birds ever rise,
Where fancy is a thing that soothes—and lies,
And leads on with mirages of light.
I speak of her who sits within plain sight
Upon the steps of yon cathedral. Skies
Are naught to her; and life a lord that buys
And sells life, whether sad, or dark, or bright.

The carvings and beauty of the throne
Where she is sitting, she doth meanly use

31

To win you and appeal. All rag and bone
She asks with her dry, withered hand a dreg
Of the world's riches. If she doth abuse
The place, pass on. It is a place to beg.

III

Statuary

The windy morn has set their feet to dancing—
    Young Dian and Apollo on the curb,
The pavement with their slender forms is glancing,
    No clatter doth their gaiety disturb.

No eyes are ever blind enough to shun them,
    Men wonder what their jubilance can be,
No passer-by but turns to look upon them—
    Then goes his way with all his fancy free.

IV

The Minstrel

The streets lead out into a mist
    Of daisies and of daffodils—
A world of green and amethyst,
    Of seas and of uplifted hills.

These bird-songs are not lost in eaves,
    Nor beaten down by cart and car,
But drifting sweetly through the leaves,
    They die upon the fields afar.

Nor is the wind a broken thing
    That faints within hot prison cells,
But rises on a silver wing
    From out among the heather bells.

The title, "Street Songs," seems to have been chosen to give an air of casualness and detachment, though at our remove from the turn of the century it may seem closer to a pseudo-Neapolitanism. To read the poems, however, as a random collection of songs, as though they were merely descriptive vignettes, would be quite misleading, for beneath the casual air runs a serious theme. This was Stevens' first attempt to write a suite of poems amounting, really, to one long poem in which the connections between the parts are oblique and the meaning is presented symbolically. ("Four Characters," written two months later, was such an attempt in prose.) The more one studies "Street Songs," the more one realizes that it is a very primitive version of what Stevens later did so magnificently in "Sunday Morning": in spite of great stylistic differences and some differences in emphasis, the two poems have similar things to say about nature, religion, and the imagination. The trouble is that in the early poem the style and technique were not adequate for the elaborate aim.

That Stevens was trying to work by indirection and to bring his imagery into a definite pattern becomes apparent when we examine the movement and theme of the poem. To begin with, the pigeons, coming out of the darkness into the light, are vaguely mystical—they are "hosts / . . . / On glistening wings of white." Their ascent out of the blackness "Over the city and into the blue" suggests a transcendent renewal and, in the context of the whole poem, a stimulus to the imagination. In "The Beggar" a reversal occurs: in the midst of light there is darkness. The imagination here cheats one ("fancy is a thing that . . . lies"), and art ("The carvings and beauty of the throne") is perverted. The beggar woman, with an obliviousness to actual nature ("Skies / Are naught to her"), seems to suggest that the

church and formal religion have turned lifeless and materialistic ("life a lord that buys / And sells life"). In place of
the excitement of the pigeon's ascent, futility and ugliness
prevail. "Statuary" is an antidote to all this. The combination of nature ("The windy morn") and art (the statuary)
inspires dancing, gaiety, and a free imagination. Significantly, Dian and Apollo are pagan, pre-Christian gods with
attributes of nature—the woods, moon, and sun—but also
they are associated with music, poetry, and prophecy.
Whether one imagines in "Statuary" actual youths trans-
figured by the imagination and described by the metaphor
of statuary, or the actual statuary described by the meta-
phorical "movement" of dancing, a motion within stillness
("No clatter doth their gaiety disturb"), a vitally imaginative scene is suggested. It is one that leads to the figure of
Stevens' green "fluent mundo" in "Notes toward a Supreme
Fiction," who "will have stopped revolving except in crystal." Finally, since the imagination has been set free by the
atmosphere of pagan innocence and joy, "The Minstrel"—
a minstrel rather than any other type of evangelist—is able
to take one with a now pristine vision to nature itself. But
it is a nature from which we derive both aesthetic and spiritual elevation: it is a world of green and amethyst, the latter
word suggesting the poetic or artistic. And not only is it a
world "Of daisies and of daffodils" but also one "Of seas
and of uplifted hills," a phrase with Biblical and spiritual
connotations. Suggestions of art are found in the title
itself and in the "bird-songs." Further suggestions of the
spiritual quality in nature are found in the "heatherbells,"
rather than church bells, and in "rises on a silver wing"—
reminding us of the flight of pigeons in the first poem, which
in retrospect can be seen as a kind of symbolic annuncia-
tion. Thus in the four-part poem a rejection of formal re-

ligion is followed by an avowal of a mixture of art and a kind of pantheistic religion.

On an elementary level, then, "Street Songs" is concerned with essentially the same theme as the later "Sunday Morning," including the motif of death and renewal in nature: in "The Minstrel," in a mist "Of daisies and of daffodils," the wind "rises on silver wings" following the death of the bird-songs "upon the fields afar"; in "Sunday Morning," Part VIII, "Sweet berries ripen in the wilderness," and

> At evening, casual flocks of pigeons make
> Ambiguous undulations as they sink,
> Downward to darkness, on extended wings.

But other parallels, not merely thematic, also indicate that "Street Songs" was an embryonic version of the mature poem. The symbolic, transcendent pigeons appear in both poems; the pagan Dian and Apollo in "Statuary" become the more "savage source" in "Sunday Morning," Part VII. The "sweet birds" in "The Beggar" as well as "bird-songs," the "world of green," and the mist and fields in "The Minstrel" become in "Sunday Morning," Part IV, the birds with "their sweet questionings," "April's green," and "misty fields." Also, the question, "Why should she give her bounty to the dead?" in Part II of "Sunday Morning" is a vivid reminder of "The Beggar" in "Street Songs":

> . . . she doth meanly use
> To win you and appeal. All rag and bone
> She asks with her dry, withered hand a dreg
> Of the world's riches.

Finally, the movement from city to country in "Street Songs" is roughly parallel to the more subtle movement from the Matisse-like urban luxury to the fields and the deer on the mountains in "Sunday Morning."

But to compare the two poems at all is to measure the growth in Stevens' poetry in the fifteen-year period between them, for "Street Songs," while a very respectable undergraduate poem and competent by any standards, was merely a probationary effort for Stevens. In "The Beggar," for example, an ill-disguised spite breaks through the carefully assumed air of detachment apparent in the group as a whole. In contrast to this lack of control is the more playful urbane satire of the later "A High-Toned Old Christian Woman," as well as the controlled ambivalence with which Christian myth is treated in "Sunday Morning" itself. Also, part of the purpose of the whole group is obscured by the rather trite treatment of nature versus the city. "The Minstrel" becomes almost entirely a conventional poem on this theme. Further, the diction and imagery "Of daisies and of daffodils," "beaten down by cart and car," and "faints within hot prison cells" are in the manner of Stevens' weakest undergraduate poems. The subtlety of "heather bells" as a substitute in nature for church bells is ruined by the insipid prettiness of the diction.

Yet there are in "Street Songs" hints of the later poet—despite "yon cathedral" and the "doth's." "The Pigeons" certainly has a tighter relationship between form, meaning, and rhythm than do the earlier poems. The repetitions, especially in the line "They rise and turn and turn anew" (which heralds the similar technique for a different effect in the *Harmonium* poem, "Domination of Black," with its ominous turning of leaves), help to give a sense of the sweeping, circling upward movement of the pigeons, and of the excitement and awe inspired by their radiant flight. "The Beggar" ends with the sudden simplicity of style in the sentence, "It is a place to beg." In its abrupt statement of what is, it faintly anticipates "The Emperor of Ice-Cream":

> If her horny feet protrude, they come
> To show how cold she is, and dumb.

In "Statuary" the word "jubilance" and the light play on "fancy free" have a touch of the later flair. And in the title "The Minstrel" (not identified within the poem), there is an oblique relevance, an added implication, that we find in many of the later, usually more humorous and ironic, titles. As a whole, "Street Songs" is a mélange of new purpose and old style, but the new purpose was beginning to have its effect on the style.

This point is apparent in the *Advocate* poem "Ballade of the Pink Parasol" (May 23, 1900), the undergraduate poem which in style seems most indicative of what was to appear in *Harmonium*.

> I pray thee where is the old-time wig,
>> And where is the lofty hat?
> Where is the maid on the road in her gig,
>> And where is the fire-side cat?
>> Never was sight more fair than that,
> Outshining, outreaching them all,
>> There in the night where the lovers sat—
> But where is the pink parasol?
>
> Where in the pack is the dark spadille
>> With scent of lavender sweet,
> That never was held in the mad quadrille.
>> And where are the slippered feet?
> Ah! we'd have given a pound to meet
>> The card that wrought our fall,

37

The card none other of all could beat—
    But where is the pink parasol?

Where is the roll of the old calash,
    And the jog of the light sedan?
Whence Chloe's diamond brooch would flash
    And conquer poor peeping man.
Answer me, where is the painted fan
    And the candles bright on the wall;
Where is the coat of yellow and tan—
    But where is the pink parasol?

Prince, these baubles are far away,
    In the ruin of palace and hall,
Made dark by the shadow of yesterday—
    But where is the pink parasol?

"Ballade," like the two poems before it, is obviously a variation on Stevens' central theme. It is a seemingly frivolous lament for the ordered elegance a past age had created in the midst of, or out of, reality. Time, a central element of reality, obliterates such creations. And what, it is implied, has the present that will serve the function previously served by the pink parasol? In "Ballade" Stevens found a subject and form which, at that point in his career, enabled him to convey a serious attitude and at the same time follow his penchant for the exuberant and elegant. Taking its inspiration from the ballade vogue of the late nineteenth century, the poem is an important step toward Stevens' later style.

This is especially evident in the obsolete diction deliberately chosen for its evocation of a recherché and sophisticated elegance. Also, such words as "wig," "spadille," "quadrille," "calash," and "sedan chair" carry with them, in their outdatedness, an effect of the absurd, which enabled Stevens to include a conception of refinement and beauty without being sentimental. He could afford to indulge in the thing he simultaneously ridiculed in a gentle way. Notice particularly the gusto of "Where is the roll of the old calash," wherein the wit and humor are reinforced by the repetitions of sound. The joy in language and sound here brought Stevens much closer to the verbal virtuosity of *Harmonium*. Stevens also avoided sentimentality by finding in the ballade form the means to objectify and dramatize his theme; as he did in "Outside the Hospital," he avoided self-conscious, humorless speakers. One can simply compare "Lo, even as I passed beside the booth / Of roses . . . ," from the beginning of "Sonnet" (see note 9) which appeared in the same issue of the *Advocate* as did "Ballade," with "I pray thee where is the old-time wig" in order to see how Stevens was working toward wit and a lightness of touch.

The pink parasol is decidedly functional in this poem, unlike the trite and ineffectual booth of roses just mentioned. The parasol, dainty and feminine, is treated with a gaiety which is heightened by the color and alliteration. More important, however, the parasol seems to have been chosen with some precision as the central symbol of the poem. What, after all, was the function of the parasol but to enable the user to go out in the "sun of reality" without losing her aristocratic pallor, so artfully maintained? Without the protection of the parasol, itself a thing of elegant beauty, the accessories of civilized artifice—the painted fan, the scent of lavender, the coat of yellow and tan—would be reduced to quaint relics by exposure to the sun. Only the shadow of the parasol can offset the dark "shadow of yesterday." And so, under the mask of lightness and wit, a genuine, if at the same time amusing, sense of lament emerges in the concluding quatrain.

For Stevens' use of the ballade form there were many precedents, ranging from Villon's ballades to several by E. A. Robinson, which appeared in the two volumes of poems he published in 1896 and 1897, to an anonymous and insipid one called "The Life of Gold," published in the Advocate a year and a half before Stevens'.[16] But William Ernest Henley, Andrew Lang, and Austin Dobson made extensive use of the form, and in ways which would be more likely to inspire Stevens. The titles, for example, of Henley's "Ballad of a Toyokuni Colorprint" and Lang's "Ballade of Blue China," point to their exotic and rococo details.

Austin Dobson, however, is the most interesting of the possible influences, for in his other work, as well as in the ballades, we find a thoroughgoing affection for the eighteenth-century world of graceful and quaint artifice, both English and French. In "A Gentleman of the Old School," he writes of a "canary vest / With buds brocaded," which

[16] For a pertinent discussion of the ballade form and its influence, see James K. Robinson, "Austin Dobson and the Rondeliers," MLQ, 14 (March 1953), 33, and also his "A Neglected Phase of the Aesthetic Movement: English Parnassianism," PMLA, LXVIII (September 1953), 733-754. E. A. Robinson was drawn not only to the ballade form but also to villanelles and rondeaux "in the spirit of Austin Dobson," according to C. T. Davis in E. A. Robinson: Selected Early Poems and Letters, p. xi. Robinson's ballades—with the exception of the "Ballade of the White Ship" which was first published in the Advocate, LII (October 16, 1891), 22—originally appeared in The Torrent and the Night Before in 1896 and Children of the Night in 1897. For ballades, see Selected Early Poems, pp. 4, 9, 19, 30. For "The Life of Gold" see Advocate, LXVI (December 20, 1898).

is very like a vest "embroidered with a multitude of little pink roses" worn by a former variety-stage juggler in Stevens' prose sketch, "The Higher Life" (*Advocate,* June 12, 1899).[17] Dobson's "The Old Sedan Chair" recalls past elegance:

> And yet,—Can't you fancy a face in the frame
> Of the window,—some high-headed damsel or dame
> Be-patched and be-powdered, just set by the stair,
> While they raise up the lid of that old sedan chair?
>
> Can't you fancy Sir Plume, as beside her he stands,
> With his ruffles a-droop on his delicate hands,
> With his cinnamon coat with his laced solitaire,
> As he lifts her out light from that old sedan chair?

These examples would certainly have appealed to Stevens, but this would seem even more true of Dobson's ballade "On a Fan That Belonged to the Marquise de Pompadour," which seems in many ways a possible model for "The Ballade of the Pink Parasol":

> Chicken-skin, delicate, white,
> Painted by Carlo Vanloo,

---

[17] In this sketch the juggler has become a college student, deciding that if he wants to elevate himself "from the variety stage to grand opera or fine tragedy . . . education is necessary. Poor me!" "In another year," he says, "I shall be able to gabble your French and bluster your German." He continues to wear his clothes from the past, including the vest, but he now feels himself superior to Rose, Lily, and May, women from his variety-stage days who are coming to visit him: "They are low, they are vulgar." When they arrive at his room, he has enigmatically disappeared, possibly suggesting that in seeking the higher life he has cut himself off from the essential force and beauty of life itself, reducing himself to a cipher in an embroidered vest.

Loves in a riot of light,
    Roses and vaporous blue;
    Hark to the dainty *frou-frou!*
Picture above, if you can,
    Eyes that could melt as the dew—
This was the Pompadour's fan!

See how they rise at the sight,
    Thronging the Œil de Boeuf through,
Courtiers as butterflies bright,
    Beauties that Fragonard drew,
    Talon-rouge, falbala, queue,
Cardinal, Duke—to a man,
    Eager to sigh or to sue—
This was the Pompadour's fan!

Ah, but things more than polite
    Hung on this toy, *voyez-vous!*
Matters of state and of might,
    Things that great ministers do;
    Things that, maybe, overthrew
Those in whose brains they began;
    Here was the sign and the cue—
This was the Pompadour's fan!

Envoy

Where are the secrets it knew?
    Weaving of plot and of plan?
—But where is the Pompadour, too?
    This was the Pompadour's *fan!*

However accurate and repellent "Chicken-skin" is for describing the fan, that feminine accessory evokes nostalgia and sophisticated wit. The speaker savors recherché words, emphasizes elegance and beauty, and even refers to intrigue, with death implied, as does Stevens' speaker:

42

Ah, we'd have given a pound to meet
The card that wrought our fall,
The card none other of all could beat—

And of course what stands out in Stevens' poem, when one
compares the two, is the line "Answer me, where is the
painted fan / . . . ?" It seems certain that Stevens learned
much from Dobson, and from "On a Fan" in particular.

What Stevens seems to have found in Dobson's poem,
with all its rococo details and the reference to Fragonard—
and possibly in other Dobson poems such as one called
"After Watteau"—he would also find in the *fêtes galantes*
elements in Verlaine's poems and in the paintings by Fragonard and Watteau. But whether Stevens had already in
college discovered Verlaine and the paintings is difficult to
say. Nonetheless, Stevens' fondness for the *fêtes galantes*
atmosphere at this time can be seen in the fourth sketch of
"Four Characters" (see above, p. 20) in which the lady
who owns the boarding house describes her former garden
parties:

> . . . the garden! How we used to dance there in summer
> evenings!—with the trees bright with little lanterns,
> and the rose bushes tied up with little ribbons, and
> the sweetest orchestra of guitars and mandolins hidden
> somewhere in the foliage. . . .

"Ballade of a Pink Parasol" is derived from a vogue that
was part of a general attempt to bring new effects into
English poetry. Stevens' ballade, like Dobson's, does not
avoid a precious aestheticism and quaintness, but resur-
rected along with the language and trappings of eighteenth-
century culture are the detachment and wit which prevent
the staleness of some of the more prevalent nineteenth-

century modes. The very literature overthrown by Romanticism had by the end of the nineteenth century become remote enough to be itself "romantic." Here was one way of instilling new life into a stagnant tradition. Modern poets would try other ways generally overlooked by nineteenth-century English and American poets. Stevens, for one, had by "Ballade" come abreast of the movement that increasingly brought French influences to bear on English poetry. In his undergraduate interest in things French—the French-speaking nymph, the ballade vogue, the *fêtes galantes* atmosphere—he found a means of introducing details into his work that were exotic, elegant, and at that time relatively fresh. This was an interest that would lead more distinctly to Verlaine and then to the French Symbolists and ironists—though this is not to say at all that he was to be exclusively swayed by French influences.

It is clear, at any rate, that at this stage of his career Stevens had discovered what was then in the vanguard of English poetry: *fin de siècle* aestheticism or Parnassianism. He revered the ideal beauty represented by the silver butterfly in "Pursuit" and the pink parasol in "Ballade" (though, to be sure, he maintained at the same time an equal reverence for the beauty in nature: the butterfly, symbol of aesthetic perfection, is captured in a natural outdoor setting). He exalted the precious and took an anti-philistine attitude, and yet he refused to escape from or deny the actual world or the mortal condition. He was discovering, as Stephen Dedalus would discover, that the imagination must forge beauty "out of the sluggish matter of the earth." We see this realization in the theme of "Quatrain," his last poem to appear in the *Advocate* (June 2, 1900):

He sought the music of the distant spheres
 By night, upon an empty plain, apart;
Nor knew they hid their singing all the years
 Within the keeping of his human heart.

Certainly Victorian poets—and, indeed, Romantic poets —had been concerned with the fate of subjective, imaginative, and artistic ideals in a world of science and materialistic values. But the pressures of this world were increasing, and art to survive at all in a meaningful way had to change, to become somehow more potent and not retreat into the quiet, genteel territory reserved for it. Stevens seems to have surmised this as he became absorbed with his theme and took steps to make his writing more vital. In the undergraduate work, he began to liberate his matter and style from the confines of the poetic practices of the time. His characteristic irony, wit, and humor began to emerge, along with more color, more boldness, more control. Here was a promising beginning, with tendencies that would be fulfilled later. His first real triumphs, in fact his first published poems after he left college, were still fourteen or fifteen years away, but the Harvard work established the direction he was to follow in his later poetry.

II. Abodes of the Imagination

WHEN Stevens left Harvard in 1900, the American literary world, with the exception of a few novelists, was spent and sterile. The chief poets of the era were duplicating out of custom the models that to them were manifestly poetic. No periodicals existed which were ready to publish work more adventurous than Stevens' undergraduate accomplishments: the *Atlantic Monthly, Harper's Magazine, Current Opinion, The International,* among others, were printing poems by such poets as Henry Van Dyke, Charles Hanson Towne, George Edward Woodberry, Arthur Davidson Ficke, Madison Cawein—competent and professional poems in the current styles. Reading through them, one realizes the aptness of Edmund Clarence Stedman's epithet, "twilight interval," and agrees with Louise Bogan's analysis:

> The weight of British Victorian tradition lay heavily upon American poets in general; and the strong native moralizing bent of the American poets of the school readers—Bryant, Whittier, and Longfellow—still operated. A feeble reflection from the English aesthetic movement of the eighties and nineties was also apparent, but recently this influence had been stigmatized morally and more or less forced underground, both in England and America, by the scandal attendant upon the trial and conviction in 1896, of Oscar Wilde.[1]

And William Stanley Braithwaite, though not exactly an apostle for the avant-garde, declared in 1914, "From 1900 to 1905, poetry had declined; and I think there has never

[1] Bogan, *Achievement in American Poetry, 1900-1950* (Chicago, 1951), pp. 3-4.

been another period in our history when so unintelligent and indifferent an attitude existed toward the art."[2] Frost, Pound, Eliot, and others decided they had to cross the Atlantic to find a more promising climate for poetry, and E. A. Robinson, who stayed in this country, struggled against great odds to get a hearing. Even after Harriet Monroe's *Poetry*, with its eclectic policy, opened its pages to new poets in 1912, Pound had difficulty getting Eliot's "Love Song of J. Alfred Prufrock" published there. Indeed, Arthur Davidson Ficke's "Poetry" was honored by being placed first in the initial issue of that periodical. It epitomizes much of the poetry of the preceding decade and earlier, as may be seen in the first of its two parts:

> It is a little isle amid bleak seas—
> An isolate realm of garden, circled round
> By importunity of stress and sound,
> Devoid of empery to master these.
> At most, the memory of its streams and bees,
> Borne to the toiling mariner outward-bound,
> Recalls his soul to that delightful ground;
> But serves no beacon toward his destinies.
>
> It is a refuge from the stormy days,
> Breathing the peace of a remoter world
> Where beauty, like the musking dusk of even,
> Enfolds the spirit in its silver haze;
> While far away, with glittering banners furled,
> The west lights fade and stars come out in heaven.

Under such conditions it is no wonder that Stevens' development in these years was uncertain and transitional, some

---

[2] Braithwaite, *Anthology of Magazine Verse for 1914 and Yearbook of American Poetry* (New York, 1914), p. xii.

of his work fully characteristic of the era and some of it experimental.

Upon leaving Harvard, he appears at first to have attempted to combine his literary interest with the necessity of earning a living, for he tried his hand briefly at newspaper reporting and at magazine editing.[3] Even as he studied law, though, and was establishing himself in the business world, he did not drop his literary and poetic ambitions or his interest in art in general. In the evenings he read intensively and widely—nineteenth-century and current fiction, philosophy, a great diversity of literature from the Greeks to French poets; he attended concerts, pored over Japanese prints, and played a little music now and then for his own amusement. At the same time he was writing verse; in a journal he kept, he mentions in 1906, for example, writing a poem but concealing the fact from his business colleagues.[4]

A good number of the poems he composed between 1900 and 1914 have survived in manuscript; many of these belong particularly to 1908 and 1909, when he wrote out in neat longhand a "June Book" for each of these years, slender sheaves of his poems which he presented to the

[3] Michael Lafferty, "Wallace Stevens, A Man of Two Worlds," *Historical Review of Berks County*, XXIV (Fall 1959), 113. For further discussion of this part of Stevens' career, see William Van O'Connor, *The Shaping Spirit* (Chicago, 1950), pp. 3-15.

[4] I gathered the rest of the information in this paragraph from conversations with Holly Stevens. Also, Carl Van Vechten in "Rogue Elephant in Porcelain," *Yale University Library Gazette*, XXXVIII (1963), 45, reports that Stevens at the office "stealthily composed his tiny verses on tiny bits of paper cunningly disposed in big books . . . against the curious inspection of . . . his associates and underlings."

girl he would marry in 1909, Elsie Viola Moll.[5] Six of these poems appeared in print several years later in *Trend*—five of them in his "Carnet de Voyage" group of eight in September 1914, and one as one of "Two Poems" in November of the same year. Many of the poems are no more than conventional lyrics, but some seek out new areas of inspiration, new subject matter, new styles—new "abodes of the imagination," to use a phrase from his later essay "Two or Three Ideas" (*Opus*). In attempting to convey the grandeur and exquisite beauty perceived by the imagination, as well as the feelings arising from speculations about man's relationship with nature and his desire for order, Stevens experimented variously with the possibilities of standard twilight-interval settings and imagery, the *fêtes galantes* and rococo worlds, the vogue for orientalism, and native American details. Signs of his later individuality and command are barely discernible in these experiments, and

[5] In a letter, Holly Stevens has listed for me the manuscript poems that were originally in each of the June Books. Exact copies or in some cases variations of the best of these June Book poems are included among the manuscript pieces she has let me use, which suggests that Stevens kept copies of his June Book poems in a file of his own, and occasionally revised them and sent them out in hopes of publication. This, of course, was just the case with those that appeared in *Trend* in 1914. This also leads me to believe that, except for those written by 1908 or 1909 for the June Books, most of the manuscript poems I have used were written or revised between 1909 and 1914. The *parenthetical* dates and titles for various manuscript poems in my text refer to original June Book titles and dates. The titles *not* in parentheses are the ones given to the manuscript poems in the file I used. Undated manuscript poems, as suggested above, probably belong to the 1909-1914 period. See Appendix III for index and varying titles of manuscript and *Trend* poems.

yet, even the finger exercises of Wallace Stevens hold interest, particularly since qualities that are characteristically
his emerge from them.

TYPICAL of much of the 1908-1909 work is "April" (1909,
"In April"). Below the manuscript copy of the poem appears the isolated phrase "The Imagination Revived," evidently considered as an alternate title and rejected, perhaps
as too pointed a statement of theme.

> Once more the long twilight
>   Full of new leaves,
> The blossoming pear-tree
>   Where the thrush grieves;
>
> Once more the young starlight,
>   And a known mind,
> Renewed, that feels its coil
>   Slowly unbind,
>
> Sweeping green Mars, beyond
>   Antique Orion,
> Beyond the pleiades
>   To vivid Zion.

With its tone of solemn exaltation and the poetic grandeur
of the classical and Biblical references, "April" is very close
in quality to the early Harvard sonnet, "There shines the
morning star!" Both poems aim at a poetic intensity but
achieve little more than facility in an outworn mode. The
twilight setting is fitting for a poem which conforms so well
to the prevailing style of the period.

Like "April," "Noon, and a wind on the hill" (1908,
"New Life"), also concerns the inspiration of nature which
leads, in this case, to the speaker's assertion of imaginative
divination in the second stanza.

Noon, and a wind on the hill.
Come, I shall lead you away
To the good things, out of these ill,
At the bright of the world today.

I shall show you mountains of sun
And continents drowned in the sea.
I shall show you the world that is done
And the face of the world to be.

"Mountains of sun," although a little vague, antedates his later more forceful use of the sun as a symbol—in its effect the image is not far from the majestic transcendence desired; and the final two lines of the poem have a firmness and conviction that put them beyond any in Ficke's "Poetry." But any degree of successful romantic evocation in Stevens' poem is rendered ineffectual by the first stanza, especially by the abstract and stilted line "To the good things, out of these ill." Such a line makes it difficult to feel the attraction of "Come, I shall lead you away." It is not that the theme of escape from the mundane world lacks appeal; the pastoral tradition suggests the opposite. It is rather that on taking up poetry again after college, Stevens had to make a second start toward overcoming the limitations of the generally dominant poetic style, stultifying in its standardized poeticisms and vague yearnings for a transcendent beauty. At Harvard he had achieved a fresher effect in his prose sketch "The Nymph"; its escapist air was intensified by its graceful whimsy and sophistication and controlled by comic deflation. He had then gone on to write the undergraduate poem "Outside the Hospital," so superior to "Noon, and a wind on the hill" in its handling of the triumph of the imagination over negation.

Two other manuscript poems are similar to the two just

discussed, but these are more transitional in Stevens' development; within their basically twilight-interval style they include a few anticipations of the later poet. "Ancient Rendezvous" (1908, "Winter Melody") is one of these.

I went into the dim wood
And walked alone.
I heard the icy forest move
With icy tone.

My heart leaped in the dim wood
So cold, so bare;
And seemed to echo suddenly
Old music there.

I halted in the dim wood
And watched; and soon
There rose for me, a second time,
The pageant moon.

The experience of the speaker brings him to a subjective relationship with nature which overcomes his sense of isolation. This sounds very close to Romantic doctrine. "And seemed to echo suddenly / Old music there" recalls Wordsworth's "The music in my heart I bore / Long after it was heard no more" in "The Solitary Reaper." In a way the poem expresses its Wordsworthian exaltation in the melancholy dim wood of much nineteenth-century poetry. On beholding "a rainbow in the sky," Wordsworth's heart leapt up with a freshness, but by the time Stevens' heart leapt, the figure was less convincing. If "Ancient Rendezvous" indicates some of what Stevens' outlook owed to the Romantics, it also contains stylistic qualities which he found increasingly inadequate for making the Romantic point of view viable in the twentieth century. Although his interest in moonlight did not diminish, he came to see the need for more original imagery than "pageant moon."

The poem does, however, move toward some of the poems in *Harmonium*, for here he endeavored to compose a music out of negation. The lines "I heard the icy forest move / With icy tone," are not only more specific and penetrating than "the good things, out of these ill" but they also prepare for poems such as "Domination of Black" or "The Snow Man": "One must have a mind of winter / To regard the frost and the boughs / Of the pinetree crusted with snow. . . ." Also, in "Ancient Rendezvous" the variations of rhythm, within a fairly tight structure, help to convey the tone. Further, the meaning of the poem is not declared explicitly; Stevens apparently wanted to dramatize the elusive yet immediate sense of the experience which culminates in the reappearance of the "pageant moon," with the actual moonrise evidently fulfilling his imaginative conception of the event and thus becoming pageant.

"Tides" (1908), the other of the two transitional poems, also attempts to convey an elusive reality. It focuses on the symbolic correspondence between nature's "infinite green motions" and "the secretive oceans," the latter presumably man's inner or imaginative oceans—a correspondence which leads to such a line as "In an interior ocean's rocking," in "Jasmine's Beautiful Thoughts Underneath the Willow" (first published in 1923 in *Harmonium*) or to the passage in "Peter Quince at the Clavier" (1915): "In the green water . . . , / . . . / She searched / The touch of springs, / And found / Concealed imaginings." Here is the poem:

> These infinite green motions
> Trouble, but to no end,
> Trouble with mystic sense
> Like the secretive oceans,

Or violet eve repining
Upon the glittering rocks,
Or haggard, desert hills,
Or hermit moon declining.

It is likely that Stevens, in observing an underlying "mystic sense" that relates by correspondence the tides and the secretive oceans, was tentatively drawing on the technique as well as mystique of the French Symbolists. The poem, however, is just as much an echo of Victorian elegiac poems like Arnold's "Dover Beach," with its brooding on nature's mystery and the "eternal note of sadness." Whatever his sources, one is struck by this early instance of Stevens' fondness for the word "motions," an abstract word for the flux of the physical world as well as for the sympathetic movement of the mind. It appears later in "no sweet land gave / Large-mannered motions to his mythy mind" in "Sunday Morning" and in "She made of the motions of her wrist / The grandiose gestures / Of her thought" in "Infanta Marina" (1921), and in several other poems. Also noteworthy in "Tides" is the series of examples which define an emotion. This device reflects Stevens' search for resemblances or correspondences which by their power to identify give us a feeling of control over, and reconcile us to, the indifferent and changing reality—a reality from which we feel alienated despite our physical ties to it. It is a device he later used frequently as in "Sunday Morning": "We live in an old chaos of the sun / Or old dependency of day and night, / Or island solitude . . ."; and in "The Curtains in the House of the Metaphysician" (1919), where again the word "motions" plays its part: "the drifting of these curtains / Is full of long motions; as the ponderous / Deflations of distance; or as clouds / . . . / Or the changing of light.

54

..." In "Tides," however, the series falls back on tired poetic figures: "violet eve," "haggard desert hills," and "hermit moon."

While the virtues of these poems as specimens of the Romantic and Victorian tradition should not be overlooked, they cannot be judged except as Stevens evidently came to judge them when he rebelled against the current lyric modes and began writing the poems of *Harmonium*. He could not easily rebel against modes so firmly established and so obviously poetic, despite his apparent acquaintance with the work of the Symbolists; but once he recognized the full range of opportunities opened to him by the revolution in the arts—the many exciting ways of making old things new—his development was rapid.

LATER IN his life, Stevens was to say in "Adagia" (*Opus*) that "Nothing could be more inappropriate to American literature than its English source since the Americans are not British in sensibility." Nonetheless, the English source did maintain an influence on his poetry and will be discussed in a later chapter. Further, one can argue that Americans are not French in sensibility, either; yet it is in this direction that Stevens turned for much of his inspiration. Yeats, at a 1914 Chicago banquet given in his honor by Harriet Monroe on behalf of *Poetry*, expressed the view that American poetry at that time was generally characterized by the sentimentality, rhetoric, and moral uplift of the Tennysonian era. The lag in American poetry existed not "because you are too far from England, but because you are too far from Paris." And he added, "It is from Paris that nearly all the great influences in art and literature have come, from the time of Chaucer until now."[6] In 1914, such

[6] Harriet Monroe, A *Poet's Life* (New York, 1938), pp. 336-338.

advice could only confirm Stevens' well-developed devotion to the French poets.

In his introduction to *Opus Posthumous,* Samuel French Morse refers to the "obvious influence of Verlaine" in the manuscript poems, and he is right. Stevens was indeed deeply impressed by Verlaine; Charles Henri Ford quotes him indirectly: "Verlaine! How just one musical French phrase of that poet was exalting enough for the whole day!"[7] But as the poems just examined show, Stevens did not easily free himself from the influence of nineteenth-century English poetry. Even when in some of the manuscript poems he introduced what seems a more French quality, he did not always avoid some of the elements seen in the poems already cited, as can be seen in this poem of 1909:

> He sang, and in her heart, the sound
> Took form beyond the song's content.
> She saw divinely, and she felt
> With visionary blandishment.
>
> Desire went deeper than his lute.
> She saw her image, sweet and pale,
> Invite her to simplicity,
> Far off, in some relinquished vale.

In theme (the relationship of music, feeling, and spirit) and somewhat in style, especially in lines three and four, this poem is a precursor of "Peter Quince at the Clavier": "She felt . . . / The dew / Of old devotions." And the first two lines prefigure the singer in "The Idea of Order at Key West," who "sang beyond the genius of the sea." But even as Stevens was beginning to find some of the qualities of his later style in terms of this Verlaine-like Pierrot-woman

[7] Ford, "Verlaine in Hartford," *View,* 1 (September, 1940), 1.

situation involving music, he lapsed into the tone and phrasing of the Tennysonian last line. Indeed, the whole poem has a Tennysonian or Pre-Raphaelite cast; in the twilight interval, this sweet, sad escapist note often stood in the way of, or in place of, variety and uniqueness in poetic style. In the increasingly industrialized world, the "relinquished vale" or "continents drowned in the sea," or Ficke's poetic isle, seemed the only possible places where the imagination could persist; it was therefore difficult to relinquish the relinquished vale, to find a convincing poetic strategy for establishing the value of the imagination in the contemporary world.

In another of the unpublished poems (1909), Stevens turned more distinctly to a *fêtes galantes* setting. Like the poem already discussed, the one below is pretty but fragile and would at first seem of little consequence in the poet's development. It does, however, offer one way out of the relinquished vale and points to an important element in Stevens' style.

> Life is long in the desert,
> On the sea, on the mountains—
> Ah, but how short it is
> By the radiant fountains,
>
> By the jubilant fountains
> Of the rivers, wide-sailing
> Under emerald poplars,
> In round ivory paling!

Here, with the "radiant fountains," "rivers, wide-sailing," "emerald poplars," and "ivory paling," is a setting similar to those in the paintings of Watteau and Fragonard. One is reminded, too, of the setting and atmosphere of several of

Verlaine's poems in his *Fêtes Galantes*, with their parks, fountains, statues, marble, radiance, and the general combination of beauty and wistful regret.

At first, the idealized world of Stevens' *fêtes galantes* poems does not seem significantly different from that of his poems in the idiom of nineteenth-century English poetry. The same "decorous melancholy" which would be treated with amused irony in "The Comedian as the Letter C" prevails—"Ah, but how short it is"—but the differences, despite the sentimentality in both modes, held a host of possibilities for Stevens' poetry. In the formal gardens and parks of the *fêtes galantes* mode was the essence of elegance, refinement, order, and art; and this setting, as Stevens developed the possibilities, would prove for him more satisfactory than "Noon, and a wind on the hill." In the slight piece of verse "Life is long in the desert," Stevens has left the "dim wood," "violet eve repining," and the "relinquished vale" for the more radiant "rivers, wide-sailing / Under emerald poplars." In the *fêtes galantes* atmosphere, Stevens seemed to find a sanction for being exquisite. Such halcyon atmosphere is congenial to the arts, with its statuary, lutes, and associations with poetry and painting. The terraces, pavilions, sweeping lawns, serene blue skies, and courtly characters make this setting a very sophisticated arcady, emphatically suggestive of imaginative order and beauty.

The *fêtes galantes*, rococo world had a further advantage for Stevens in that it contained some of the qualities Romanticism tended to reject: a highly civilized, aristocratic order and a different sort of union of man and nature; that is, nature ordered and refined by the imposition of man's imagination. As Stevens expressed it in one of the 1909 poems (later, the sixth poem in "Carnet de Voyage," *Trend*): "Man from the waste evolved / The Cytherean

glade," and he went on very explicitly in the second stanza
(with its trite, wooden, cloying manner),

> The isle revealed his worth.
> It was a place to sing in
> And honor Noble Life,
> For white doves to wing in,
> And roses to spring in.[8]

Caught in its ideal form in the paintings of Watteau and
Fragonard, this was the kind of order, a harmony of man
and nature, which to a degree had actually existed as one
of the more benign manifestations of seventeenth- and
eighteenth-century aristocracy, and which, however faded,
still could elicit real nostalgia for that lost refinement and
serenity. Stevens wrote in his poem "Study of Images I"
near the end of his career (thus revealing how deeply the
fêtes galantes tradition affected him) of "the terraces of
mandolins, / False, faded and yet inextricably there." Here
was the marriage of earth and air, of this world and heaven,
of this "Terra Paradise," as Stevens called it in "Montra-
chet-le-Jardin," again later in his career: "A little while of
Terra Paradise / I dreamed, of autumn rivers, silvas green,"

---

[8] The complete poem, "Carnet de Voyage," vi, is as follows:

> Man from the waste evolved
> The Cytherean glade,
> Imposed on battering seas
> His keel's dividing blade,
> And sailed there unafraid.
>
> The isle revealed his worth.
> It was a place to sing in
> And honor Noble Life,
> For white doves to wing in,
> And roses to spring in.

aware, though, that "in that dream a heavy difference /
Kept waking. . . ." That Stevens had already in the *Advocate* touched briefly on this world in "Ballade of the Pink
Parasol" and in the description of the garden fête in the
last sketch of "Four Characters" shows the persistence of
this interest during his career, but in the manuscript poems
he began to pursue more fully all that the *fêtes galantes*
tradition offered.

Very much a part of this tradition is Pierrot, tender lover
and aesthete, who observes the irony of his situation with
sadness, with wry self-mockery, and a humor that at times
becomes mordant. His voice not only adds a range of tonal
subtleties to Stevens' work but heralds the more adventurous irony and the boisterous humor in *Harmonium*, though
the exquisiteness of the voice would remain. "I lie dreaming" (1909, "Pierrot"; this title erased on the copy I used)
is a manuscript poem which shows one of the ways Stevens
during the early years of his development, was putting this
fellow to use.

> I lie dreaming 'neath the moon,
> You lie dreaming under ground;
> I lie singing as I dream,
> You lie dreaming of the sound.
>
> Soon I shall lie dreaming too,
> Close beside you where you are -
> Moon! Behold me while I sing,
> Then, behold our empty star.

Its basic situation, its touch of the macabre, and its element
of melancholy recall Verlaine's "Serenade":

> Comme la voix d'un mort qui chanterait
> Du fond de sa fosse,

> Maitraisse, entends monter vers ton retrait
> Ma voix aigre et fausse. . . .

In "I lie dreaming," the gentle, almost reverent address to the women and the theme concerning mortality and music make it another poem which takes the poet toward "Peter Quince."

The speakers in two other manuscript poems are somewhat more spirited than the one in "I lie dreaming." One of them (1909), presumably another Pierrot with his stringed instrument, desires a rich aesthetic and sensuous atmosphere favorable to art and the imagination:

> An odorous bush I seek,
> And lighted clouds around,
> To make my golden instrument's
> Wild, golden strings resound;
>
> Resound in quiet night,
> To an Arab moon above,
> Easing the dark senses need,*
> Once more, in songs of love.

Somehow, the music inspired by the beauty of the natural and sensuous setting must ease the speaker's dark sense of desire or death. The poem has glints of the later work, especially in the line "Wild, golden strings resound," a line which attempts the kind of exuberance and force Stevens would achieve, for example, in "The Man With the Blue Guitar" (1936):

> To bang it from a savage blue,
> Jangling the metal of the strings . . .

. . . .

* No apostrophe indicated for "senses."

> In a chiaroscuro where
> One sits and plays the blue guitar."

In "An odorous bush," however, the effect is dissipated in the bland poeticisms of "Arab moon" and "songs of love."
The other speaker is similar in his aestheticism:

> Hang up brave tapestries,
> Huntsman and warrior there.
> Shut out these mad, white walls.
> I hate a room so bare.
>
> And all these neighbor roofs
> With chimney and chimney above—
> Oh! Let me hear the sound
> Of soft feet that I love.
>
> Then fetch me candles tall.
> Stand them in bright array;
> And go. I need such lights
> And shadows when I pray.

This manuscript poem, equating art and religion, has an imperative note as well as the slightly absurd and bizarre effect of overstatement. When it comes to decor, the speaker is as finicky as Carlos in the one-act play "Carlos Among the Candles," published in *Poetry* in December 1917 (and reprinted in *Opus*); and his delight in ritual anticipates Carlos' symbolist ritual among his twelve candles. The manuscript version I used is improved by the omission of the second stanza, which was part of the 1908 June Book version.

The dated charm of most of the poems of this period is particularly marked in the following poem (1909), which became the fifth poem of the "Carnet de Voyage" group in

1914. The speaker, evidently a disenchanted Pierrot, limply expresses a *fin de siècle* world-weariness:

> I am weary of the plum and of the cherry,
> And that buff moon in evening's aquarelle;
> I have no heart within to make me merry.
> I read of heaven and sometimes fancy Hell.
>
> All things are old. The new-born swallows fare
> Through the Spring twilight on dead September wing.
> The dust of Babylon is in the air,
> And settles on my lips the while I sing.[9]

These poems led, nevertheless, to the grace and finesse of "Sunday Morning," which was completed by June of 1915.[10] Here he was to convert a similar boredom into the gently mocking description of the negation inherent in a changeless heaven divorced from earth:

> Alas, that they should wear our colors there,
> The silken weavings of our afternoons,
> And pick the strings of our insipid lutes!

Earlier in this poem, incidentally, he creates a lustrous courtly scene, with some of the atmosphere of a *fêtes galantes* setting:

> She [Death] makes the willow shiver in the sun
> For maidens who were wont to sit and gaze
> Upon the grass, relinquished to their feet.

[9] As the poem appears in *Trend*, line four of the first stanza reads "I nod above the books of Heaven or Hell."

[10] It is becoming generally known that Stevens had written all eight sections of "Sunday Morning" by this date, even though only five of them were published in *Poetry*. See Stevens' letter to Harriet Monroe advising her about the order he found best for the five sections she had chosen; this appears in Chapter ix, p. 237.

She causes boys to pile new plums and pears
On disregarded plate. The maidens taste
And stray impassioned in the littering leaves.

This is not in heaven but in a vital, earthly Eden, and is just one example of the way Stevens transformed the more attenuated qualities of the *fêtes galantes* mode into a serene, moving intensity.

His poems would also become gradually less cluttered with rococo embellishments—fussy decor, silks, and fans—but not before his reliance on them had contributed to his fastidiousness of manner as well as to the excesses of the finical so often justly rebuked by his critics. If the trappings of the *fêtes galantes* world could too easily seem merely antique and contribute to a mannered, arch style, Stevens could turn to other related sources. It was not an abrupt transition from Watteau and Fragonard to Renoir, who indeed, had converted some of the qualities of these very painters (whom he admired) into his own idiom. "Here there will be silks and fans . . . the movement of arms . . . rumors of Renoir . . . coiffures . . . hands . . ." (the punctuation is Stevens'), says Carlos in "Carlos Among the Candles" as he conjures one of the many possible worlds the imagination can conceive. However precious, the passage does point to Stevens' widening horizons.

MEANWHILE, Stevens' imagination had been captivated by oriental art—and by oriental literature as well. Much of his interest appears to have been inspired by the exotic content of this art and literature, as was the case with many of his contemporaries during this current wave of Western enthusiasm for oriental thought and art. While Stevens was in college, the *Harvard Advocate* and the *Harvard Monthly* were running ads by the import firm Yamanaka & Company, mainly for *objets d'art* from Japan; and in the early 1900's American literature was beginning to show the impact of this wave. Stevens eagerly participated, along with other poets, including his college friends Witter Bynner and Arthur Davidson Ficke.[11] With their parallels to the *fêtes galantes* mode, Chinese and Japanese prints and poetry offered exotic landscapes, idyllic settings, and quietly evocative scenes of courtly elegance, with aristocratic ladies and lords in colorful costumes.

The "steadfast Lady" in "Chinese Rocket" (1909; the seventh poem of "Carnet de Voyage"), with the light of her "curious lantern," discovers an underlying order in nature, despite the threat of chaos, and maintains her aristocratic imperturbability:

> There, a rocket in the Wain
> Brings primeval night again.
> All the startled heavens flare
> From the Shepherd to the Bear—
>
> When the old-time dark returns,
> Lo, the steadfast Lady burns
> Her curious lantern to disclose
> How calmly the White River flows!

While Stevens' idea that the imagination (which ordered the constellations) gives order to reality is apparent here, the Chinese rocket and lantern, mingled with Western names for the constellations, remain exotic details rather than becoming effective symbols. Like some of the language of the poem—"old-time dark" and "Lo"—they do not measure up to the poet's subtle aims.

[11] Holly Stevens has called my attention to the orientalism in Ficke's and Bynner's poetry.

Later, in the play "Three Travelers Watch a Sunrise," which first appeared in *Poetry* in July 1916 (reprinted in *Opus*), Stevens achieved a more consistent effect. The second Chinese, evoking the blissful calm of the ideal world of the imagination, says,

> Such seclusion knows beauty
> As the court knew it.
> The court woke
> In its windless pavilions,
> And gazed on chosen mornings,
> As it gazed
> On chosen porcelain.

The use of chinoiserie here—chinoiserie so similar in quality to that of the *fêtes galantes* and rococo details Stevens delighted in—is less obtrusive than in "Chinese Rocket," partly because within the free verse the control of language and cadence supports the effect. The passage is similar to the one in the Imagistic poem "Six Significant Landscapes," which was first published in *Others* in March of 1916:

> An old man sits
> In the shadow of a pine-tree
> In China.
> He sees larkspur,
> Blue and white.

No doubt, Stevens' fascination with orientalism prepared him to contribute enthusiastically to the surge in poetry generated by the Imagists, who were themselves strongly attracted by the art and literature of China and Japan. He did not, however, have to wait for the Imagist movement to take shape and thrust itself into the center of poetic activity; some of his own experiments were carrying him toward that center.[12]

A case in point is a manuscript poem (1909) which relates the sophisticated courtesans of France and Japan through the implication that the beauty of both must succumb to death, the leveling force which intensifies the sense of their beauty:

> She that winked her sandal fan
> Long ago in gray Japan—

[12] In a letter to Earl Miner, Stevens expressed his interest in Japanese prints and oriental art and said that he possessed six or so books of Japanese and Chinese poetry; see Miner's *The Japanese Tradition in British and American Literature* (Princeton, 1958), p. 190. Miner says that titles like "Six Significant Landscapes" and "Thirteen Ways of Looking at a Blackbird" recall "such series of Japanese prints as Hiroshige's 'Eight Views of Ōmi,' Hokusai's 'Thirty-six Views of Fuji,' or Utamaro's 'Seasons.' These poems are closest to the Imagist method and haiku technique, and are especially reminiscent of Amy Lowell's 'Twenty-Four Hokku on a Modern Theme' " (p. 194). Earlier (p. 190), Miner reports Stevens as saying "that while he knew about haiku, he could not ever remember writing with them in mind, and professed a greater interest in Japanese prints and Oriental art." Setting aside Stevens' "disclaimer" as characteristic of his reticence, Miner goes on to show marked parallels between the *Harmonium* poems "Thirteen Ways of Looking at a Blackbird" and "The Death of a Soldier" and haiku by Bashō (pp. 194-196). Whether Stevens was more inspired by oriental art, as he insisted, or by haiku, as Miner insists, the objectivity, indirectness, and condensation of the haiku technique seem to have had a more beneficial and lasting effect on his style than the merely ornamental details of orientalism. Still, oriental art and prints, often marked by stylistic economy, held fresh, unsentimental, non-rococo values for Stevens' sensibility, too. His uses of Imagism will be discussed in Chapter v.

> She that heard the bell intone
> Rendezvous by willowed Rhone—
>
> How wide the spectacle of sleep,
> Hands folded, eyes too still to weep!

In 1914 this became the fourth poem in "Carnet de Voyage," with one change: the more alliterative "rolling" was substituted for "willowed" in the second stanza. Appearing in print just when the Imagists were beginning to dominate *Poetry* and to publish their own collections—like *Des Imagistes* in 1914—this poem, I had thought when I found it in *Trend* before I knew about the June Books, must have been composed under the specific example of the Imagists. It begins with an Imagistic comparison of the flicking of a fan with the winking of an eye, and in its compression it approaches the economy and understatement of Pound's haiku-like "Fan-Piece for Her Imperial Lord" in *Des Imagistes*:

> O fan of white silk,
> Clear as frost on the grass-blade,
> You also are laid aside.

But learning that it was in the 1909 June Book dramatized for me Stevens' independent discovery of Imagistic techniques. The delight in sound, the wit of the alliteration and assonance, the appropriate shift of rhythm and pace in the last stanza of Stevens' poem—these hint at his later metrical virtuosity and are surely in tune with the Imagists' insistence on incisive command of prosody.

Another poem which is like the work of the Imagists is "Here the grass grows" (1909, "Concert of Fishes"), which later became the third poem of "Carnet de Voyage." Framed by the grass and wind at the beginning and end, the vivid description of the fishes suggests perhaps the beauty and depth of life within the flux of nature:

> Here the grass grows,
> And the wind blows,
> And in the stream,
> Small fishes gleam,
> Blood-red and hue
> Of shadowy blue,
> And amber sheen,
> And water-green,
> And yellow flash,
> And diamond ash.
> And the grass grows,
> And the wind blows.

This Impressionistic use of color is similar to what some of the Imagists were up to, again concurrently with Stevens, though unlikely to have influenced him directly. F. S. Flint's "The Swan" and Allen Upward's poem "The Gold Fish," both included in *Des Imagistes*, are examples of this; here is a stanza from "The Swan":

> Under the lily shadow
> And the gold and the blue and mauve
> That the whin and the lilac
> Pour down on the water,
> The fishes quiver.

followed by "The Gold Fish":

> Like a breath from hoarded musk,
> Like the golden fins that move
> Where the tank's green shadows part—
> Living flames out of the dusk—
> Are the lightning throbs of love
> In the passionate lover's heart.

Stevens must certainly have been discovering some of the same sources that inspired these poets.

One such source, at least for Stevens, was Japanese color prints; an entry in his journal for May 1909, reads: "Kakuzo Okakura is a cultivated, but not an original thinker. His 'Ideals of the East' was interesting." Then, shortly thereafter: "Japanese color prints: Pale orange, green and crimson, and white, and gold and brown. / Deep lapis-lazuli and orange, and opaque green, fawn-color, black and gold." Earlier (March 18, 1909), he had written a letter to Elsie Moll in which he referred to Okakura and then listed the colors above plus these: "lapis blue and vermilion, white, and gold and green."[13] From these lists emerged, following the order of colors in the journal entry, this manuscript poem:

Colors

◊ I ◊

Pale orange, green and crimson, and
White, and gold and brown.

◊ II ◊

Lapis-lazuli and orange, and opaque green,
faun-color, black and gold.

Stevens seems to have followed two prints with different scenes or perhaps two prints of the same scene under different conditions. At any rate, in the poem the first part possibly suggests a day scene, the other a night scene, for a greater degree of light is apparent in I than in II; in II a subtle shift occurs, a darkening in tonality to something slightly more mysterious and romantic: the pale orange

[13] These quotations are from a letter to me from Holly Stevens.

becomes orange; the green, opaque green; the white, faun-color; the brown, black; and the crimson, lapis-lazuli. In "Colors," as in "Here the grass grows," Stevens aimed at an orchestration of color values, with a vital clarity of description evident in the latter, and a contrast of overtones in the former.

It is this sensitivity to color and light which would help make Stevens' response to modern painting—the work of the Impressionists and later artists—a profound part of his experience. Indeed, "Colors" is curiously like a pair of abstract paintings transposed into words on the page. Or looked at another way, "Colors" is like a compact version of one of John Gould Fletcher's color symphonies which would be published a few years later. Like Fletcher, Flint, Amy Lowell, and other Imagists, who borrowed more than Pound approved from Symbolism and Impressionism, Stevens looked to France as well as to the Orient. If by 1909 Stevens had not yet become familiar with paintings by the Impressionists—though it is very possible he had—it is unlikely that he had not noticed the use of color by the French poets, Gautier, for example, the French and English Parnassians generally, or the Symbolists. Or he may have observed the color impressionism in the poetry of Bliss Carman, one of the first American poets to import the technique.[14]

Whatever the sources, he seems at first to have been

[14] Carman's "In Gold Lacquer" and "The Eavesdropper" are good examples of his color impressionism, which Holly Stevens pointed out to me. Odell Shepard in *Bliss Carman* (Toronto, 1923), p. 87, has recorded that "under the tutelage of his friend T. B. Meteyard, a pupil of Monet and illustrator of the Vagabondia books, the poet learned to make use of more delicate color distinctions."

charmed by the technique in much the same way that Amy Lowell was charmed, and with results similar to those in the poems she would write. The two following manuscript poems are good examples of Stevens' color impressionism. The first, "The Lilac Bush," appeared untitled in the 1909 June Book, and there included the fourth line printed below, a line sensibly omitted in the manuscript version I used:

> This is the lilac-bush,
> Full of the cat-bird's warble—
> The singer drunken with song,
> Of his heart's distillation,
> Falling from azure tuft
> From violet spray, and jade,
> Down through the dusk of the bush,
> To rest in a grassy shade.
>
> Soon again the happy sound
> Will enchant the purple ground.

The second manuscript poem also appeared in the 1909 June Book (at that time with the inclusion of a hyphen in "water mist"):

> Shower
>
> Pink and purple
> In water mist
> And happy leaves
> Of amethyst;
> Orange and green,
> And gray between,
> And dark grass
> In a shimmer
> Of windy rain.

Then the robin's
Ballad of the rain.

These poems are marked by the subject matter, lush sentiment, and color characteristic of much of Amy Lowell's
poetry; by the time she had put her Keatsian period behind
her, however, and had begun to write this kind of verse,
having discovered oriental poetry and the Impressionistic
qualities in the French Parnassians and Symbolists, Stevens
had gotten well beyond her sugary impressionism and was
pursuing the implications of the revolution the Impressionist painters had wrought. At the same time, he was rigor-
ously exploring the full range of possibilities that Imagism
opened to him, without in any way becoming a poet limited
to or by Imagism. With a little historical perspective, we
can appreciate how striking and new some of the techniques
of Impressionism and Imagism were in 1908 and 1909, but
Stevens was only temporarily seduced into creating superficial effects that were to date very rapidly.

As for Stevens' fascination with orientalism, it seems inevitable in retrospect that in his search for exotic details and
different techniques he would be attracted to this mode, as
well as to the arabesque—"The desert pool / Turns gaudy
turquoise for the chanting caravan ("Carnet de Voyage,"
II). But the *Trend* title "From a Junk" (one of "Two
Poems") suggests the orientalism he would soon reject;
"Wrong as a divigation to Peking" says Stevens in "The
Comedian as the Letter C." Toward the end of his life, he
wrote emphatically to Mlle. Paule Vidal, "I hate orientalism" (in a letter dated August 19, 1953). Purging the excesses of this mode from his verse, he became attracted to
the dazzling color and exotic qualities of the American
South, the Caribbean, Latin America, and modern French

painting. Even so, orientalism left its mark on *Harmonium*, in delicacy of effect and in such details as "Utamaro's beauties," "umbrellas in Java," and "a woman of Lhassa." Moreover, it was another way out of the relinquished vale, and it helped bring him into the mainstream of poetic experiment.

WHATEVER elegance Stevens acquired in his mental voyaging, his American background remained an intrinsic part of his outlook. Even "Three Travelers Watch a Sunrise," the last instance of Stevens' unguarded indulgence in chinoiserie, places the exotic Chinamen in the midst of Pennsylvania; the fact that a few years before the play appeared, a Chinese pagoda was erected on Mount Penn, overlooking Reading, does not make the combination of chinoiserie and the Pennsylvania setting any more convincing, but as Stevens became adept at using native details his poetry became less deliquescent.

This is not the case, however, in "Home Again," a 1908 manuscript poem later published as the second of "Two Poems" in *Trend* (November 1914):

> Back within the valley,
> Down from the divide,
> No more flaming clouds about,
> O! the soft hillside,
> And my cottage light,
> And the starry night.

The scene is presumably the American West—note the "divide"—not a relinquished vale, a Cytherean glade, or an oriental setting; but the poem demonstrates that a change of scene was no guarantee against a fatal softness. Here Stevens apparently wanted to symbolize the distinction between the human fear of the chaotic aspect of reality (the "flaming clouds") and the human need for order, defined by the "cottage light" and the patterned "starry night." In theme the poem is similar to "Chinese Rocket," with its use of the lady's lantern "to disclose / How calmly the White River flows." But "Home Again" acquires no greater intensity from its western setting, and the poem ends on a note of mere coziness. Skipwith Cannéll's "The Mountains," appearing in *Poetry* for August 1913, achieves the same innocuous result despite a potentially vigorous setting:

> The mountains
> Were sunk in the sea,
> But now they are risen
> High and more high:
> I will climb my mountains,
> I will rest in their winds:
> At night . . . I will descend . . .
> Wearied . . . to the valleys . . .
> In the warmth of my valleys
> I will sleep till the dawn.

Both poems would appear to have their legacy in the work of Joaquin Miller, Richard Hovey, and Carman Bliss, poets who had been intrigued by the romantic aura of the West. Indeed, the genteel bohemianism of Carman's and Hovey's very popular *Songs from Vagabondia* (1894), *More Songs from Vagabondia* (1896), and *Last Songs from Vagabondia* (1900) seem in particular to have stirred Stevens to emulation, for in two letters to Elsie Moll—one in 1907, the other in 1908—he mentions some verses of his for a first Vagabondia Book.[15] Perhaps "Home Again" was one of these. Feeble though it is, it was a first step toward such

[15] Reported to me by Holly Stevens in a conversation.

successful poems with western settings as "Earthy Anecdote" (1918), which concerns a "firecat" in Oklahoma: "Every time the bucks went clattering / Over Oklahoma / A firecat bristled in the way. . . ."

Gradually, Stevens would balance the aestheticism to which he was so strongly attracted with earthier, native details. Even in the rarefied atmosphere of "The Lilac Bush," quoted a few pages earlier, Stevens found the unglamorous, native catbird a fitting source of music, even if he describes it as a "warble." "L'Essor Saccade," an undated manuscript poem, seems also to have an American setting, a rural one:

> Swallows in the elderberry,
> Fly to the steeple.
> Then from one apple-tree
> Fly to another.
>
> Fly over the stones of the brook,
> Along the stony water.
> Fly over the widow's house
> And around it.
>
> Never mind the white dog
> That barks in the bushes.
> Fly over the pigeons
> On the chimney.

This poem, on a theme reminiscent of the undergraduate "Street Songs," shows promise, if not fulfillment; the swallows, like the pigeons in the earlier poem, are in splendid contrast to the negation beneath them. The speaker with his series of imperatives is more robust than most of the speakers encountered so far, and the rhythm tends to be in accord with that of actual speech; perhaps the absence of a rhyme scheme allowed for a more natural voice. The negation is defined by ordinary but concrete details: the "widow's house" and the "white dog / That barks in the bushes." The widow who owns the house would not appreciate the flight of symbolic swallows—as Stevens put it in "A High-Toned Old Christian Woman," "fictive things" make "widows wince." Such women, like the beggar woman on the steps of the cathedral in "Street Songs," are part of a long list of ordinary women in his poetry.

The title warrants comment: undoubtedly Stevens wanted the "lightness, the grace, the sound and the color of the French"[16] to stress the transcendence of the swallows' "sudden flight," though unfortunately the French remains too detached and exalted to enhance the effect. But Stevens would learn to fuse French elegance and grace with the native American idiom. He had achieved this aim to some extent at Harvard when he included the native wilderness of Massachusetts and the French sophistication in the prose sketch "The Nymph," or the earthy beer and the elegant crème de menthe in "Part of His Education"; later, for example, he would delight in such combinations as the American watermelon and the French pavilion in the *Harmonium* title "Hymn from a Watermelon Pavilion."[17] How appropriate for Stevens' theme to infuse, by such imaginative conjoinings, the earthy, vigorous reality of America

[16] The phrase is Stevens', taken from René Taupin's *L'Influence du Symbolisme Français sur La Poesie Americaine* (1910-1920), p. 276, where Taupin quotes from a letter to him from Stevens: "La légèreté, la grace, le son et la couleur du français ont eu sur moi une influence indéniable et une influence précieuse."

[17] William York Tindall also cites this title as an example of Stevens' practice of bringing French and American words together, and mentions the phrase "beau caboose" as well, in *Wallace Stevens* (Minneapolis, 1961), p. 20.

with the grace of the French words. By such means he was able to be richly aesthetic without sacrificing vitality.

DESPITE their anticipations of qualities in Stevens' mature style, however, most of the manuscript poems suffer from sentimentality and lack of vigor. They often lack certainty in versification, or become pastiches of ill-sorted elements. "Noon-clearing" (1909), for example, unsuccessfully brings together a description of brilliant serenity—whether influenced by the *fêtes galantes* mode or the Impressionists—with a Housman-like concluding couplet. The June Book version contains the third stanza printed here, while the manuscript version happily omits it. Also, "Flash" in the June Book version became "Brings" in the last line of the manuscript version I used.

> Now, the locust, tall and green,
> Glitters in the light serene.
>
> Leafy tremors shake around
> Brilliant showers to the ground.
>
> At a dart, an oriole sings,
> The fluttering yellow wings!
>
> Sunlight in the rainy tree,
> Flash two-and-twenty-back to me.

Radiant and delicate on the surface, the poem is undermined by its technical flaws: the rhythm, mechanical and singsong, does not help carry the ecstatic tone; the rhyme-scheme is a direct hindrance, leading to the poetic inversion of "light serene" and the awkwardness of "shake around." Evidently, Stevens needed freedom from set rhythms and rhyme-schemes in order to work out successfully his own conceptions.

"Afield" also illustrates dramatically the gap between the majority of the manuscript poems and the command of style and technique apparent in the work published after 1914.

> You give to brooks a tone,
> A melody to trees.
> You make the dumb field sing aloud
> Its hidden harmonies.
>
> An echo's rumor waits,
> A little while, and then,
> I hear the water and the pine
> Take up their airs again.

Concerned with love, music, beauty, and their relationship to nature, "Afield" just barely sketches out what would be a more complex treatment of similar thematic material in "Peter Quince at the Clavier," or in the much later "The Idea of Order at Key West." But how pallid, how thin this manuscript effort is when compared with the richness, control, and depth of these later poems! In the later work Stevens gives a poetic immediacy to the "hidden harmonies"; he does not simply express a sentimental exaltation which the prosody fails to sustain. As the new era burst forth with its innovations in all the arts and its reassessment of the achievements of the past, Stevens seized upon a great variety of new and old techniques for rendering both his conceptions and their attendant emotions. "A change of style is a change of subject," he would say in "Adagia" (*Opus*). His style changed and developed, and if he did not change his subject, he explored it more intensively and found poetic means for rendering its increasing complexity.

III. Rogues and Exquisites

*N*O REALLY serious reaction against twilight-interval poetry set in until about 1912, when the most advanced of the American poets, belatedly struck by the work of the nineteenth-century French poets and the paintings of the Impressionists, began to experiment with new forms and techniques. At the same time, a native literary energy was arising in the Midwest. The Chicago poets, who saw much to emulate in Whitman; the innovations of Eliot, Pound, and the Imagists; Amy Lowell's campaign for free verse; *Poetry* and the other little magazines which came into being in order to champion the new poetry—these are the obvious instances of the new life in American poetry at the time. The additional excitement of discovering Debussy's and Stravinsky's music and the paintings of the post-Impressionists and Cubists, which most Americans saw for the first time at the Armory Show of 1913, further convinced the new poets that the twilight interval was at an end, whatever the general public and many critics made of the new art and the new poetry. All this clamor over the arts—particularly in the years 1912-1915—is reflected in Stevens' own development, as he discovered the poetic techniques congenial to his temperament and brought his experiments to the point of a daring, fluent, diversified, and distinctive style.

More specifically, Stevens was caught up in the atmosphere of Greenwich Village, where he became associated with a group which seems by its interests and example to have whetted his impulse to poetry.[1] One of his Harvard

[1] See Michael Lafferty, "Wallace Stevens: A Man of Two Worlds," *Historical Review Of Berks County*, xxiv (Fall 1959),

friends, Pitts Sanborn, had joined the staff of *Trend* in the spring of 1914, whereupon its policy became aggressively modernist; it began presenting the work of such writers as Donald Evans, Walter Conrad Arensberg, Carl Van Vechten, Djuna Barnes, Mina Loy, and Stevens, among others.

Since Arensberg seems to have been at the center of this group, it is worth noting his interests as they have been described by Alfred Kreymborg:

> [In New York City the Arensbergs] gradually began to collect [paintings], and to keep open house for all the artists and writers of modernist tendencies. . . . Arensberg, an intimate friend of Donald Evans, of Stevens, of the Sanborns, of the *Rogue* group in the Village [Allen and Louise Norton were its editors], and the latest foreign painters and composers to visit our shores, conducted a sybaritic salon. . . . A profound classical scholar and reticent aesthete, he made each new movement his own, tried it awhile and then dropped it: Symbolism, Imagism, Vorticism, Cubism, Dadaism. Though he wrote fine poems in free verse, "Voyage à L'infini," "The Voice of One Dead," "For Forms that are Free," . . . Arensberg was radical solely in theory.[2]

In a letter, Stevens refers to some other friends of Arensberg's: Carl Van Vechten, the Walter Pachs, John Macy, and John Quinn, and says of Arensberg, "He liked to give

---

113, 130, and William Van O'Connor, *The Shaping Spirit* (Chicago, 1950), pp. 14-22, for other details of Stevens' relationship with this group, many of them old Harvard friends, after he moved to Greenwich Village in 1909.

[2] Kreymborg, *Our Singing Strength, An Outline of American Poetry, 1620-1930* (New York, 1929), p. 467.

parties for people in whom he was interested, although the only one I can remember at the moment is one which was attended by Amy Lowell. . . . His interest amounted to excitement." Stevens also says, "I don't suppose there is anyone to whom the Armory Show of 1913 meant more than it did to him."[3] Indeed, it meant so much that soon after, at other shows given by the same men who were responsible for the Armory Show, Arensberg, according to Walter Pach, bought a Matisse, a La Fresnaye, and "also, if I remember, a Picasso."[4] Stevens does not mention his own degree of interest in the art world of 1913, but his daughter reports that he, too, attended the Armory Show, which no doubt intensified his response to modern painting. Through the Arensbergs he got to know Alfred Kreymborg, William Carlos Williams and the *Others* group,[5] but in the beginning, Stevens seems to have been closest to the Arensberg circle—a world of avant-garde excitement, poetry, painting, and music.

IN HIS *On Native Grounds*, Alfred Kazin discusses a group of novelists, among them Carl Van Vechten, in a chapter called "The Exquisites." The epithet is appropriate for those in the Arensberg coterie too, since they were reacting

[3] Stevens' letter quoted by Fiske Kimball, "Cubism and the Arensbergs," *Art News Annual*, XXIV (1955), 176.

[4] Pach's letter quoted by Kimball, pp. 176-177.

[5] Kreymborg, in *Troubadour, An Autobiography* (New York, 1925), pp. 218-220, discusses Stevens' relations with this group. Also, S. F. Morse has written me to say that Stevens appears as the character "Fastidious" in Kreymborg's "At the sign of the Thumb and Nose, An Unmorality Play," from *Plays for Merry Andrews* (New York, 1920). See esp. p. 31. See also Carl Van Vechten's delightful memoir concerning Stevens and this group, in "Rogue Elephant in Porcelain," *Yale University Library Gazette*, XXXVIII (1963), 41-50.

against the vulgarity of the American environment. Their attitude, as seen in their writings, was urbane and aristocratic; their manner was often extravagant, elegant, dandified, ironic. But, serious in their frivolity, they formed a cult of beauty in the midst of American philistinism, though in retrospect they appear as mere dilettantes of the imagination. Much of their outlook and manner derived from the English Decadents, yet they also drew on the example of the French Symbolists and ironists and were alert to most of the new currents in the arts. A good notion of their exquisiteness and dandyism can be gained from the following passage by Donald Evans, part of a prefatory letter in the 1918 reissue of his *Sonnets from the Patagonian*:

> If we could purge ourselves of our fear of Germany we should capture Berlin. Could I enlist a Battalion of Irreproachables, whose uniforms should be walking suit, top hat and pumps and their only weapon an ebony walking stick and sail tomorrow, we should march down Unter den Linden in a month, provided wrapped in our kerchiefs we carried the Gospel of Beauty, and a nonchalance in the knot of our cravats.

In all its preposterous exaggeration the statement reveals a serious, almost desperate, sense of the need for beauty in a world of mechanized chaos. But unfortunately, such dandyish devotion to beauty in the manner of the Nineties was just as ineffectual in the modern world as the dying genteel tradition in American letters.

The extremes of effete artiness this group indulged in are epitomized by Louise Norton's one-act farce, *Little Wax Candle* (1914), an esoteric, symbolic play about art and love in the midst of marital and extramarital cavortings. This is the setting:

The Bedroom: It is hung in mist-colored grey shot with silver. . . . [The] carpet is the shade and texture of Florida moss and lies on an agate floor. The doors are mullioned mirrors. Over the silver mantle with a hearth of mother-of-pearl . . . hangs a mirror in a silver frame that reflects the room. There are two pictures on the walls, a grey Whistler and a Chinese dragon . . . ; the oval head and foot [of the bed] are mirrors in silver frames. From a crown a canopy falls in diaphanous, sinuous folds and pendent over the pillows swings a cut crystal ball of electric light . . . silk sheet . . . white spread, embroidered in silver; the pillows of crèpe de chine are frilly with ruffles of chiffon. NANCY's nightgown of pale grey chiffon is laid out with boudoir gown and slippers of coral colour worked in silver. . . . [The] telephone [is] . . . half-hidden by a bowl of green orchids. . . .

As one imagines the effect of this bedroom on the stage or, worse, in reality, he also notes the extravagant attention paid to the details of the set. It is no doubt meant to convey the height of tasteful luxury and beauty at the same time that it symbolically reflects the cold narcissism in Nancy. The grey, silver, and white are perfectly in keeping with the "grey Whistler" on the wall; the suffocating artificiality, so insistently divorced from the mundane world, establishes a Decadent atmosphere in which Des Esseintes and Dorian Gray would feel quite at home; and the Chinese dragon proclaims the era's addiction to chinoiserie.

In his poem "Gray Room," printed in *Others* in December 1917, and never reprinted, Stevens, while revealing his closely shared interest in the same effects, is more restrained; he avoids cut-crystal balls of electric light and telephones half-hidden behind green orchids, but the poem reminds one of Whistler, and its decor, with its oriental note and the similarity of basic colors, is very close to that of Nancy's bedroom.

> Although you sit in a room that is gray
> Except for the silver
> Of the straw-paper,
> And pick
> At your pale white gown;
> Or lift one of the green beads
> Of your necklace,
> To let it fall;
> Or gaze at your green fan
> Printed with the red branches of a red willow;
> Or, with one finger,
> Move the leaf in the bowl—
> The leaf that has fallen from the branches of
> > the forsythia
>
> Beside you . . .
> What is all this?
>
> I know how furiously your heart is beating.

One can see why Stevens left this poem a fugitive piece—like several of the poems discussed in the previous chapter, its style does not transcend the period's passing vogue for chinoiserie and ornamental impressionism. At the same time, however, Stevens was working within the free verse toward grace and subtlety of effect.

Complementing this group's delight in the precious and arty was its refined roguery, its sophisticated mockery of bourgeois attitudes. Louise Norton's *Little Wax Candle*, for example, conveys its theme—the difficulty of unifying flesh and spirit—with arch humor and with the bizarre and ironic details that the group as a whole favored. She describes the hero:

> Michael's appearance is bizarre, a grey squirrel coat and boots [it is summer], combined with soft summer hat that is trimmed with a scarf and quill. He is boyish and beautiful and his beauty is his boyishness.

He also wears coral-colored pajamas underneath his squirrel coat. Just as bizarre, and presumably closer to Stevens' taste, is the following passage in which Peter, one of the characters in the play, soliloquizes while examining the bedroom and quotes from Aubrey Beardsley's "The Barber of Meridian Street" (a poem which had appeared in the English periodical *The Savoy* in July 1896):

> Curling irons, curls, puffs! How unromantic are the accessories of romance! Only a Beardsley could put poetry into that (holding up curling tongs) or put it into poetry. (sighing) Ah! for the barber of Meridian Street:
> > Such was his art, he could with ease
> > Curl wit into the dullest face.
> > . . . But then, he used only silver tongs.

Stevens' fondness for just such details is evident in his later use of barbers and curls in "Le Monocle de Mon Oncle" (1918).

Allen Norton also delighted in taking a roguish stance while at the same time paying tribute to Oscar Wilde in his *Saloon Sonnets: With Sunday Flutings* (1914; the Sonnets were dedicated to Donald Evans, founder of the Claire Marie Press which published them, and the *Flutings* were dedicated to Louise Norton). In "Profoundest Beating

Star," Norton uses a grotesque Satan to express a pleasantly sinful union of a poetic paradise with the sensual life:

> And Satan winks at me in weird neckties.
> Yet when the poets plan their paradise
> O promise we take passage on that ship—
> And I still muted to your magic thighs.

In the same collection, his ironically titled "The Last Supper," with the simile "We danced the Turkey Trot like centipedes," shows again the group's interest in the irreverent and the bizarre. Stevens too would make humorously morbid use of insects in his work, as he did in "Six Significant Landscapes," first printed in *Others* in March 1916: "Nevertheless, I dislike / The way the ants crawl / In and out of my shadow." Norton uses ants for similar effect in "Chee Toy: From the Theatre" in his *Saloon Sonnets*:

> The white ants creep across the rotting wall
> And here hourly, inside my garden small
> The flowers harden and the days grow cold;
> I in my twenty years am more than old!
> And yet tonight in the worm-eaten grass,
> Like little fingers, comes a thing of glass.

Although Stevens went far beyond the experiments of the Nortons, this community of interests must have contributed to his taste for the exquisite as well as to his penchant for wit, irony, the bizarre, and the grotesque. It is appropriate that his first two poems which successfully combine wit and elegance, the earliest poems to be collected later in *Harmonium*—"Tea" and "Cy Est Pourtraicte"—appeared in the Norton's little magazine, *Rogue* (March 15, 1915).

Pitts Sanborn also took part in the general interests of the group. He moved from a *fin de siècle* interest in "Salome" (the title of one of his poems) to an interest in French irony, apparent in the title of his Laforgue-like poem, "Vie Bordeaux, Sauce Supreme (To E. L.)" (*Trend,* April 1914):

In my upper room I sat in the half-light
Looking out on the drab roofs,
Tiling, gutters, chimneys, chimney-pots—
Everywhere behind the clay tremulous sapphire deepening.

. . . .

Oh—
I was full of God that day,
The droll,
The secret
God!

Sanborn exemplifies the minor poet who keeps up with current trends.

But of this group of minor poets, Arensberg and Evans are the most important. Warren Ramsey mentions them in his *Laforgue and the Ironic Inheritance,* and Pitts Sanborn, in an August 1914 *Trend* essay, "Some Recent American Poetry," extolled them for qualities which suggest their importance in the background of Stevens' development. Of four Harvard poets, Sanborn quickly dismisses Arthur Davidson Ficke, John Hall Wheelock, and Herman Hagedorn for their conservatism.[6] He then credits Arensberg for

[6] As a result of such criticism of his beliefs about poetry, Ficke invented, along with Witter Bynner, a "Spectrist" school of poets, all of whom, under pseudonyms, were Ficke and Bynner and their confederates. Their new poetry was accepted by *Poetry* and *Others* and was anthologized in *Spectra: A Book of Poetic Experiments* in 1916; the ruse was admitted in 1918. See William Jay Smith, *The Spectra Hoax* (Wesleyan, 1960).

his fastidiousness, for not letting freedom go to his head, and for combining whimsy and the spiritual. He cites Arensberg's debt to the French, especially Laforgue and Verlaine. Then after ridiculing "the vociferous proclamations of the noisemakers—I mean Mr. Nicholas Vachel Lindsay, Mr. Louis Untermyer [sic], and Mr. Arturo Giovanitti," Sanborn praises Evans, and refers to the influence of Laforgue and Gertrude Stein on his work. He adds, "There is the essential fact that in the fantasticalness, the bizarrerie, of these sonnets are poetry and a finely ironic, a grimly jaunty criticism of life." He concludes by defending Evans' "Her Smile," in *Sonnets from the Patagonian* (1914), against accusations of meaninglessness.

Evans has been almost totally obscured by more important poets. His career can be summed up briefly by saying in a phrase from his "En Monocle" (one of a number of "Portraits of Allen Norton" in *Sonnets from the Patagonian*), that he fought "brief lost battles with banalities." Underlying his esprit and dandyism there is a sense of futility and disillusionment that led, after his small but important contribution to American poetry, first to the mordant irony of many of the poems in his *Two Deaths in the Bronx* (1916) and *Ironica* (1919), and eventually to his suicide. But before that, he experimented in ways that have a bearing on this study.

Although Evans' work is often as fantastical, bizarre, jaunty, and ironic, as Pitts Sanborn claimed, it tends to be conventional in cadence and form. Frequently his poems bring together various influences into a pastiche, as in "Buveuse d'Absinthe," one of his "Portraits of Louise Norton" in *Sonnets from the Patagonian*. In this sonnet the imagery based on synesthesia, which seems derived from French Symbolism, is not quite brought into harmony with the *fin de siècle* quality in the sestet, with its echo of Ernest Dowson's "Non Sum Qualis . . . Cynaræ."

> Her voice was fleet-limbed and immaculate,
> And like peach blossoms blown across the wind.
> Her white words made the hour seem cool and kind,
> Hung with soft dawns that danced a shadow-fete.
>
> A silken silence crept up from the South,
>   The flutes were hushed that mimed the orange moon,
>   And down the willow stream my sighs were strewn,
> While I knelt to the corners of her mouth.
>
> Lead me afar from clamorous dissonance,
>   For I am sick of empty trumpetings,
> And all the streets are sad with dusty noise.
> Here I have found her sweet sheer utterance,
>   And now I seek the garden of the wings
> Where I may bathe in sounds that life destroys.

Though the effeminate languor is thin and faded now, the poem made radical departures from the genteel tradition in 1914. The concern with the transciency of beauty amid the "dusty noise" of life, the exquisite, aesthetic point of view, the emphasis on color and music, the French title, the elegance of diction, imagery, and sound place the poem in the area of Stevens' own interests during this period. Compare, for example, the beginning of Evans' poem with the beginning of one of Stevens' manuscript poems, "To Madame Alda, Singing a Song, in a White Gown":

> So much sorrow comes to me out of your singing.
> A few large, round leaves of wan pink
> Float in a small space of air,
> Luminously. . . .

90

Both poets were enchanted with highly civilized, even rococo, ritual in an atmosphere of feminine beauty and gorgeous decor. In Evans' "Placide Pours Tea" (*Discords,* 1912), a gracious creature "Makes of her drawing-room the great good place," while in Stevens' "Tea," the speaker recalls his visit when "Your lamp-light fell / On shining pillows." The poems differ markedly, though: Evans' turns in the direction of irony and disillusionment: "And the night as it comes puts final seal / On an hour's joy that was almost real." Stevens' poem, with wit, humor, and Imagistic precision, carries the conviction that beauty and elegance can indeed be sustained within the negations of existence.

And actually, in many ways Evans' work is closer to Eliot's than to Stevens'. His "Portrait of Nancy Trevors" (*Trend,* May 1914), presents an empty, restless sophistication within an aristocratic situation reminiscent of some of Eliot's early poems, though Evans' treatment is more brittle and arch:

> They sat in her drawing room amid easeful silence in
>   tolerant enmity—
> The men were three, and her husband was the third.
> This in its way intensified his urbanity.
> His suavities were of ivory.
> He was more irreproachable than her virginal teacups.
>
> . . . .
>
> And then she wrapped herself in the soothing nerves
>   of excitement.
> The three were lost in the pursuit of fragrance. . . .

Eliot, of course, would never merely describe the scene and tell us it was urbane and suave—he would render that suavity. And he would never be guilty of the remainder of the poem:

Archly then her voice dared:
"Will you have another cup, my beloved?"

It was three cups that rang to her, and her husband's
was the third.
She smiled over her adroit and ample confession and
it was enough.
She had done with the hour
And she let the uneasy hush turn to hodden-gray.

All too often Evans, like most of the group, expressed a
merely flippant joy in naughtiness. This is apparent, again,
in his "Dinner at the Hôtel de la Tigresse Verte," printed
in *Trend* in December 1914: two sophisticated purposeless
beings surrounded by luxury are conversing; one asks the
other, "In which room shall it be tonight, darling?" The
reply is, "In every room, my beloved!"

Stevens treats sex wittily in "Le Monocle de Mon
Oncle" but in a larger, more significant context. Nonetheless, Evans' poetry contains many elements for which Stevens must have felt an affinity. Kreymborg saw this when
he said of Stevens' "Le Monocle de Mon Oncle" that his
indebtedness to Evans' "En Monocle" was "unmistak-
able."[7] In Evans' adoption of a Laforgue-like dandyism in
"En Monocle"—"His calm moustache points to the ironies"
—Stevens must have seen possibilities for his own verse, and
the title, along with a large number of other titles culled
from Evans' 1912 volume, *Discords*, would not be out of
place in a list of Stevens' titles: "Somnambulist," "Nocturne

[7] See Kreymborg, *Troubadour*, pp. 408, 332-333, for a description of a party Stevens attended at which Evans read his "En
Monocle" and for Kreymborg's comment. Nevertheless, I think the
indebtedness is restricted almost entirely to the title and the general irony.

in Red," "Tristesse," "Tout Passe, Tout Casse, Tout Lasse," "Cette Maladie Qui S'appelle la Vie," "Snow Touching Woman," and a title after Verlaine, "Jadis et Naguère." Also, in both poets one finds a fondness for aesthetic details, as in Evans' "Flaunt . . . the glitter of a new brocade." His poem "The Jade Vase (Pittsburgh)" ("Still the vase was there [in Pittsburgh], and that was everything") is like Stevens' "Anecdote of the Jar" ("I placed a jar in Tennessee") to the extent that the aesthetic object is in a nonaesthetic setting. Some of Evans' exquisite and witty diction would have appealed to Stevens' taste too: "flash fanfaronade," and "pensive promenade," for instance. The two occasionally use similar phrasing: Evans' "crapulous hands," Stevens' "crapulous crow" in one of his manuscript poems; Evans' "fictive tear," Stevens' title "To the One of Fictive Music"; Evans' "They sat sipping their glasses," and Stevens' "They sip the glass" in "Phases."[8] Evans, however, was unable to synthesize the elements of his poetry into a controlled style; the exquisiteness conflicts with his irony, his despair and disillusionment. Stevens, without losing sight of the causes of despair in the modern world, would make these contrasting elements cohesive parts of a compelling style that he could modulate in accord with the range and the nuances of his ideas, feelings, and attitudes.

[8] "Flaunt . . . ," "Flash fanfaronade," and "crapulous hands" from Evans' poem, "Extreme Unction"; "pensive promenade" from "En Monocle"; "fictive tear" from "The Noon of Night," all three of which are in *Sonnets From the Patagonian* (1914); "They sat sipping their glasses" from "Dinner at the Hôtel de la Tigresse Verte," *Others Anthology for 1919* (first in *Trend*, December 1914). Stevens' "They sip the glass" is from a section of "Phases" that was printed in *Opus Posthumous* (New York, 1957) and first appeared in *Poetry* (November 1914).

Arensberg was another, who, like Evans, did not bring his experiments to any really satisfactory fruition; for one thing, he could all too easily fall into the insipid sentimentality of "Vain Excuse," his first *Trend* poem (April 1914):

> Be patient, life, when love is at the gate,
> And when he enters let him be at home.
> Think of the roads that he has had to roam,
> Think of the years that he has had to wait. . . .

Or he would confect such examples of coy wit as these in the June 1914 *Trend*:

An Epitaph

> Perhaps it doesn't matter that you died,
> Life is a *bal masque* which you saw through.
> You never told on life—you had your pride;
> But Life has told on you!

To a Garden in April

> Alas, and you pleading now for pardon?
> Spring came by night—and so there was no telling?
> Spring had his way with you, my little garden . . .
> You hide in leaf, but oh! your buds are swelling!

The term "whimsy," which Sanborn used in his *Trend* essay, is accurate for such verse, but Arensberg could not usually combine the whimsical and the spiritual as successfully as Sanborn claimed he could. In fact, his poems tend to vacillate between sophisticated whimsy and the flat earnestness of "Vain Excuse." Stevens' manuscript poem "Testamentum" is similar in quality to the poems above, although its whimsy is more understated.

> Plant the tea-plant on my grave,
> And bury me with funerary cups,

Of which let one be such
That young Persephone will not resist.
["That" substituted for "As" erased.]

Arensberg, on occasion, however, produced work that makes one think he could have become a more important poet than he actually was. "Voyage à L'Infini," first printed in *Others* (September 1915), is such a poem; it is one of his best, no doubt growing out of his interest in French Symbolist poetry. He had spent a year translating Mallarmé's "Après Midi d'un Faun,"[9] but also significant from our point of view are his translations of Nerval, Baudelaire, Verlaine, Laforgue, and Mallarmé in his *Poems* (1914), and his attempts to draw into his own poetry some of the qualities of these poets. Hi Simons called attention to this fact and suggested his possible influence on Stevens. He mentioned particularly Arensberg's "Voyage à L'Infini," with its Mallarméan derivation, its thematic concern with imagination and reality, and its fluent style, as one of the possible inspirations for Stevens' "Sunday Morning":

Voyage à L'Infini

The swan existing
Is like a song with an accompaniment
Imaginary.

Across the glassy lake,
Across the lake to the shadow of the willows,
It is accompanied by an image,
—As by Debussy's
"*Reflets dans l'eau.*"

[9] See letter by William Ivins, quoted by Kimball, *Art News Annual*, p. 177.

95

The swan that is
Reflects
Upon the solitary water—breast to breast
With the duplicity:
"The other one!"

And breast to breast it is confused.
O visionary wedding. O stateliness of the procession!
It is accompanied by the image of itself
Alone.

At night
The lake is a wide silence,
Without imagination.

Simons pointed to the first section of "Sunday Morning," with its "procession of the dead, / Winding across wide water, without sound," and to the last section, with "that wide water, inescapable," as evidence that Stevens quite possibly knew Arensberg's poem when he wrote "Sunday Morning"; but the dates of publication of the two poems would make it difficult to say who knew whose poem first.[10] It is perhaps more important to stress that the evidence shows the extent of the rapport between the two poets.

Arensberg did not often capture this degree of musical fluency and emotional refinement, but a few other poems of his show the possibility of his and Stevens' influence on

[10] See Hi Simons, "Wallace Stevens and Mallarmé," *Modern Philology*, XLIII (May 1964), 257-258. Arensberg's "Voyage . . ." was first published in *Others* (September 1915), according to W. S. Braithwaite, *Anthology of Magazine Verse for 1915* (New York 1915), p. 188. Five stanzas of Stevens' "Sunday Morning" first appeared in *Poetry* (November 1915), but he had submitted all eight stanzas to Harriet Monroe before June of that year. See Chapter IX, p. 237.

each other. One is "For a Picture of a Saint," from *Poems*
(1914):

> She was a girl who waited on the Lord,
> And years becalmed were hers that she might pray,
> For He had pleasure in the simple way
> She spake, and when before the Throne she poured
> The patience of her gaze she made accord
> With all the viols that in Heaven play,
> And from the hymn on high the Will would stray
> Earthward to her for some enchanted word.
>
> Fountains were like the service of her thought,
> And on her soul, for sooth, her senses fell
> Like April rains at night that waken not.
> But if she ever loved I cannot tell,
> Or if the soul that has to Heaven been caught
> Had dared to tarry with a soul in Hell.

Stevens' "Cy Est Pourtraicte," which originally appeared in
Rogue on March 15, 1915, also has a girl who served the
Lord, but with an offering of "radishes and flowers." The
good Lord "heard her low accord, / Half prayer and half
ditty, / And He felt a subtle quiver, / That was not heavenly love, / Or pity." Stevens' wittier poem followed Arensberg's, if publication dates are any clue, and may well have
been prompted by "For a Picture of a Saint."

Also, Arensberg's "Music to Hear" (*Poems*, 1914) might
have offered a possible suggestion for "Peter Quince at the
Clavier," although the notion could have come to Stevens
directly from the French.

> A little longer let thy fingers fall
> Upon the keys. Oh cease, oh cease not yet!
> But still, oh very gently, touch and fret
> The sleep of an enchanted madrigal!

In "Peter Quince at the Clavier" (first printed in *Others*, August 1915) Stevens says:

> Just as my fingers on these keys
> Make music, so the selfsame sounds
> On my spirit make a music, too.

It is possible that the notion of the fingers falling on the keys derives from Verlaine's "Romances Sans Paroles," v: "Le piano que baise une maine frêle. . . ." Robert de Montesquiou (Fezensac) was also fond of the conception, and there are several uses of it in his *Les Hortensias Bleus*. Stevens and Arensberg were surely drawing from the same sources, if not directly from each other.

Arensberg's "Voyage à L'Infini" shows us that Stevens was not alone in his concern with the theme of imagination and reality. Other poems in Arensberg's 1914 collection reveal this interest, for example "The Poet": "Of life he wants to live the whole! / . . . Poor fellow, he must make things *seem!*" "The Masterpiece" contains a more daring conception which must have struck a sympathetic chord in Stevens ("This happy creature—It is he that invented the Gods," he would assert in "Adagia," *Opus*):

> I think ere any poet awed
> Men with a haunted image of Mankind
> They buried in a grave gone out of mind
> The supreme poet who imagined God.

Of particular interest is Arensberg's quatrain "To a Poet," from his 1915 collection, *Idols*.

> What are you doing like a naughty child
> To the original NON-ENTITY,
> Without a wedding and a little wild
> Those moments when you say of beauty: "Be"?

A typescript version of this poem, with a slightly different second line ("Upon the cosmical Nonentity") is among the manuscript poems left by Stevens, and until I came upon the poem in Arensberg's *Idols* and in *Rogue* (June 15, 1915), where the second line reads, "To the great Cosmical Nonentity," I had assumed it to be an early Stevens experiment in Laforguian concept and irony ("Jonglons avec les entités . . . ," says Laforgue in "Complaint de Lord Pierrot"). The theme of poetic beauty (as opposed to bourgeois order: "Without a wedding") created in the midst of cosmic emptiness is surely in keeping with Stevens' concerns. By whatever means a version of the poem came to be among Stevens' papers, "To a Poet" is a good indication of the similar interests and the close friendship of the two poets at this important time in Stevens' career. But Arensberg, basically more of a scholar than a poet, was to drop the writing of poetry shortly, maintaining, however, his dedication to modern painting, of which he made a notable collection now housed in the Philadelphia Museum of Art, and becoming involved in the Shakespeare-Bacon controversy, using cryptography to prove Bacon's authorship.[11]

STEVENS, of course, was responding to other influences in his milieu, but his association with these rogues and exquisites put him at one of the centers of enthusiasm for modernist trends in literature, music, and painting. Furthermore, it was no small matter that his first published poems appeared in *Trend,* shortly after Pitts Sanborn joined its staff, and in *Rogue.* This may have helped him to overcome

[11] "The conclusive evidence that William Shakespeare is the pseudonym of Francis Bacon is incorporated in the original editions of the Shakespeare plays and poems." *The Cryptography of Shakespeare*, Part 1 (Los Angeles, 1922), p. 3.

some of his reticence about publishing,[12] and have increased his confidence. Soon he was sending work to *Poetry* and then to a number of other little magazines, including *Others*, which had been started by Arensberg and Kreymborg and edited during part of its existence by William Carlos Williams. More important, his association with this group occurred during a crucial, formative period of his poetic career. With the reassurance of being part of a group which was striking out in new directions—even at the risk of appearing absurd—and which shared his interests, he must have felt encouraged to make more daring experiments of his own. Perhaps, too, within this circle he began to take the measure of his own potential and feel a challenge to surpass his friends at their own game. Arensberg, as Kreymborg has said, was more radical in theory than in practice, and Stevens went beyond Arensberg in absorbing into his verse the possibilities offered by the example of the French Symbolists and ironists and beyond the generally effete and often *fin de siècle* tone of the exquisite group as a whole. More than a dilettante of the imagination, he was obsessed with the power of the imagination to enrich and order life. He wanted more than to escape from banality and to affront the philistines. Though an amateur ("It is necessary to any originality to have the courage to be an amateur," Stevens said in "Adagia"), and perhaps because

[12] Kreymborg reports in *Our Singing Strength*, p. 500, that Stevens finally let Van Vechten persuade Knopf to publish *Harmonium*. One explanation of his reticence comes from his daughter, who says that Mrs. Stevens—at least in the beginning—regarded Stevens' poetry as a private affair between the two of them, not to be made public.

he was, he became increasingly absorbed in his search for techniques and forms that would give poetic embodiment to his deepening conviction that the actual world is apprehended and shaped by the imagined one at the same time that the imagined is dependent on the actual.

IV. An Odor From A Star

"CARNET DE VOYAGE," the group of poems which appeared in *Trend* in September of 1914 and the first of Stevens' work published after he left Harvard, must have struck its readers as innovative, arty, and a touch obscure; however jaded it strikes one now, it very much accorded with the advanced taste of the period. These eight poems are essentially a pastiche, ranging from the use of Shakespearian song refrain ("With a hey and a ho" and "Hey nonino!")[1] to chinoiserie, *fêtes galantes* and Imagistic elements, but including also some derivations from the Symbolists, Mallarmé in particular; the predominant tone is an 1890's despondency. Yet the group marks an important point in Stevens' poetic career, for it provides a good sample of his work just at the time when he was stirred by influences then coming into vogue in America, when he was

[1] The poem, "On an Old Guitar," VIII, follows:

> It was a simple thing
> For her to sit and sing
>   "Hey nonino!"

> This year and that befell,
> (Time saw and Time can tell),
>   With a hey and a ho—

> Under the peach-tree, play
> Such mockery away,
>   Hey nonino!

See the song at the beginning of Scene III, Act V, of *As You Like It*; it has the refrain, "With a hey, and a ho, and a hey nonino." The second stanza of Stevens' poem has a trace, despite the coyness of the second line, of the sadness that pervades Feste's song at the end of *Twelfth-Night*, but none of the moving depth of that song.

incorporating new techniques in his poetry but without as yet making these techniques his own. Very soon, however, as he passed through this transitional stage, these would become effective strands in the early *Harmonium* style.

The eight poems of "Carnet de Voyage" are a series of statements or—to follow the title—a notebook concerning man's desire for beauty, order, and nobility, values which can never be more than transitory in a world of time, change, and death. Despite their prevailing tone of despondency, a few of the poems express an acceptance of and satisfaction with the beauty that is a part of change, and they praise man's endeavor to identify that beauty and live in accordance with it. In short, "Carnet de Voyage," for all its stylistic uncertainty, plays its part in the progression of poem sequences in Stevens' career that began with the undergraduate "Street Songs" and led to "Notes Toward a Supreme Fiction" and other later sequences.

BUT IT is the opening poem in "Carnet de Voyage"—in a way its showpiece—that serves as a point of departure for observing Stevens' response to the Symbolists and his rapidly developing resourcefulness in fitting many of their techniques to his needs.[2]

[2] The most perceptive study of Stevens' work in relation to the Symbolists is Michel Benamou's "Wallace Stevens and the Symbolist Imagination," *ELH*, 31 (March 1964), 35-63. See also his "Beyond Emerald or Amethyst—Wallace Stevens and the French Tradition," *Dartmouth College Library Bulletin*, IV (December 1961), 60-66. While Benamou is concerned with Stevens' whole *oeuvre* and I with the early development, his essays have provided me with many insights, confirming, preceding, and going beyond several of my own conclusions in the present chapter. Particularly useful is Benamou's analysis of Stevens' points of similarity and difference with Mallarmé and Baudelaire. I would qualify only one

An odor from a star
Comes to my fancy, slight,
Tenderly spiced and gay,
As if a seraph's hand
Unloosed the fragrant silks
Of some sultana, bright
In her soft sky. And pure
It is, and excellent,
As if a seraph's blue
Fell, as a shadow falls,
And his warm body shed
Sweet exhalations, void
Of our despised decay.

The fancied scene between the seraph and the sultana symbolizes an ineffable reality, "void / Of our despised decay," which remains undisclosed to ordinary sense perception but reveals itself to imaginative insight. The poem is, in fact, one of Stevens' very early "Seraphic proclamations of the pure," to take a phrase from "The Comedian as the Letter C," and appears to owe much to the example of Mallarmé, who through the refinements of art would convey the essence of the infinite, the absolute stripped of all its disguises. Looking beyond the coyness of the rarefied but stagy disrobing in "An odor from a star," one notices several stylistic elements in the mode of that French poet. It is more than likely that Stevens had read such poems as Mallarmé's

---

of his statements—that Mallarmé's "influence on Stevens was exercised mostly from 1931 on" (*ELH*, p. 50). The influence was surely strong and continuous, from at least as early as 1914, though Stevens seems to have moved from the lush, shimmering qualities in Mallarmé to Mallarmé's insistence on absolute purity, the "ideally transparent and visible," as Benamou defines it.

"Apparition," with its "Neiger de blancs bouquets d'étoiles parfumées," "séraphins en pleurs / Revant," "glissant sur l'azur des corolles," "la fée au chapeau de clarté," and "Sans regret et sans deboire." Mallarmé's "Herodiade," with its star symbolism, may also have prompted some of the details in "An odor from a star," though of course Stevens' poem places less emphasis on cold chastity:

> selon qui, des calices
> De mes robes, arôme aux farouches délices,
> Sortirait le frisson blanc de ma nudité
> Prophétise que si le tiède azur d'été,
> Vers lui nativement la femme de dévoile. . . .

Note also the resemblance between "l'azur / Seraphique," a phrase which occurs later in "Herodiade," and "seraph's blue" in "An odor from a star."

Clearly, Mallarmé's seraphic blue realm, pure and exotic, offered Stevens one more model for his abodes of the imagination, and although his fondness for sultanas and seraphs diminished, such Mallarméan details contributed much to the exquisite imagery characteristic of his later poetry: an imagery of stars, jewels, fragrances, and delicate sensations which creates an aura of beauty that is as celestial as it is sensuous. At one point in "Sea Surface Full of Clouds," for example, the clouds are likened to "damasks that were shaken off / From the loosed girdles in the spangling must." Such evocative imagery helps to define the indescribable, but it also can fail to become anything more than the effete adornments of an otherworldly boudoir. Alone, it does not signify a major turn in Stevens' development; it is merely another manifestation of the arabesque, appealing to aesthetes. In the versification of "An odor from a star," however, the poet, by trying to create an artful music in accord with the atmosphere and import of the poem, was making a more decisive addition to his repertoire of poetic effects. The delicate rhythmic variations and pacing in addition to the patterns of alliteration and assonance—the poem is a veritable orchestration of sounds—produce an exquisite and exalted music, also apparently inspired by Mallarmé. Here, in place of mere references to guitars and mandolins, is a quality in the verse itself that bears a close resemblance to music—something Debussy-like, soft and scintillant.

Instead of alluding to "Old music there" as he did in the manuscript poem "Ancient Rendezvous," Stevens was learning to convey a sense of music itself. Instead of setting down the metronomic trochees so disastrous to the effect of tremulous radiance sought for in "Noon-Clearing," he would create the "noble accents / And lucid, inescapable rhythms" he refers to in "Thirteen Ways of Looking at a Blackbird." The point is not simply that the sound should echo the sense, a part of poetics that he would certainly master, but that he was intent upon capturing the music of the imagination, shimmering, fine-spun, and inescapable. Gradually, under the tutelage of some of his French masters, chiefly Mallarmé, he was to achieve his desire. Verlaine also had pointed the way, calling for this sort of music in his "Art Poetique":

> De la musique avant toute chose,
> Et pour cela préfère l'Impair
> Plus vague and plus soluble dans l'air,
> Sans rien en lui qui pese ou qui pose
>
> . . . .
>
> Rien de plus chere que la chanson grise
> Où l'Indecis au Précis se joint.
>
> . . . .

Oh! la nuance seule fiance
Le rêve au rêve et la flute au cor!

This nuance of music and tone is prevalent in Verlaine's poetry, of course. And such music was one of the ways by which the Symbolists sought to express the inexpressible. As Rimbaud stated in "Alchimie du Verbe": "J'écrivais des silences, des nuits, je notais l'inexprimable."

Stevens, in "To Madame Alda, Singing a Song, In a White Gown," expresses the intangible feeling of sorrow by uniting color and visual details with the languorous, floating cadences of the poem:

> So much sorrow comes to me out of your singing.
> A few large, round leaves of wan pink
> Float in a small space of air,
> Luminously.
> A white heron rises.
> From its long legs, drifting, close together,
> Drops of water slide
> And glisten.
> It drifts from sight.

This is similar to the effect one finds in Mallarmé's "L'Après-Midi D'un Faune":

> Si clair,
> Leur incarnat léger, qu'il voltige dans l'air
> Assoupi de sommeils touffus. . . .

And something of the same ethereal quality in the final three lines of Stevens' "The Silver Plough-Boy" (1915; Opus), with the hushed diminuendo of their rhythmical fall, enhances the feeling of lament mingled with wonder:

A black figure dances in a black field.
It seizes a sheet, from the ground, from a bush, as if
    spread there by some wash-woman for the night.
It wraps the sheet around its body, until the black
    figure is silver.
It dances down a furrow, in the early light, back of a
    crazy plough, the green blades following.
How soon the silver fades in the dust! How soon the
    black figure slips from the wrinkled sheet!
How softly the sheet falls to the ground!

Stevens evidently grew uncertain about the worth of this poem, for he excluded it from the second edition of *Harmonium*. Perhaps he came to see in it too much precious aestheticism in the manner of Amy Lowell, who had high praise for "Plough-Boy" when it first appeared.[3] In the poem, though, Stevens aimed with symbolist techniques to present an ephemeral event as palpably as possible without any overt explanation. Undoubtedly it concerns the imaginative transformation of reality and negation: the black figure, the plough-boy, dances; the ordinary, matter-of-fact sheet becomes silver, a garment of the imagination. Mortality seems to triumph—"How soon the silver fades in the dust!"—but the poem leaves one's imagination to reflect on the softly falling sheet. The radiant movement is embodied in the poem, along with the wash-woman and the crazy

    [3] "Who is Mr. Stevens?" she asked Alfred Kreymborg in a letter congratulating him on the August 1915, issue of *Others*, in which "Plough-Boy" and "Peter Quince" appeared. "His things have an extraordinary imaginative tang. That 'Silver Plough-Boy' is quite delightful, though no better than 'Peter Quince at the Clavier.' " Quoted in S. Foster Damon, *Amy Lowell: A Chronicle* (Boston and New York, 1935), p. 316.

plough, and in that way the imagination triumphs. Further-more, the symbolic, bizarre action is supported by the or-chestration of black, green, and silver, and by the fluent and appropriate modulations in the movement of the verse: the reader is intended to see the scene and to feel the rhythms of it.

In "Peter Quince at the Clavier," companion piece to "Plough-Boy" in *Others* for August 1915, Stevens more fully realized this intention. The influence of Mallarmé, evident in the atmosphere characterized by the "blue-shad-owed silk" worn by the woman Quince addresses, is more pronounced in this poem; but at the same time, Stevens brought this influence into a unique fusion with other ele-ments, so that the poem, instead of being derivative in effect, is fully his own. In his essay on Stevens and Mal-larmé, Hi Simons called attention to important similari-ties in the two, particularly in their color symbolism and their imagery, and also discussed the similar paradoxes of "musicienne du silence" in Mallarmé's "Sainte" and "Mu-sic is feeling, then, not sound" in Stevens' "Peter Quince."[4] But just as important in the latter poem is its graceful, swaying music, at least partly in the mode of Mallarmé:

> She walked upon the grass,
> Still quavering.
> The winds were like her maids,
> On timid feet,
> Fetching her woven scarves,
> Yet wavering.

The command of cadence here is even more apparent when we compare "Peter Quince" with its manuscript prede-

[4] Simons, "Wallace Stevens and Mallarmé," *Modern Philology,* XLIII (May 1946), 246.

cessor, "He sang, and in her heart, the sound" (1909), the first stanza of which treats the theme in a rudimentary way:

> He sang, and in her heart, the sound
> Took form beyond the song's content.
> She saw divinely, and she felt
> With visionary blandishment.

This approaches the quality of "Peter Quince," but it misses, and the difference is in part a matter of rhythm, of the refinement in the later poem away from metrical stiffness toward a more sinuous, Mallarmé-like music:

> Upon the bank, she stood
> In the cool
> Of spent emotions.
> She felt, among the leaves,
> The dew
> Of old devotions.

Here, in creating Susanna's music, Stevens also achieves a poignant intensity that surpasses the soft and arabesque quality of "An odor from a star" and the more mechanical rhythms of "He sang, and in her heart, the sound."

STEVENS never came quite to the point of desiring to convert poetry to the condition of pure music, as did Mallarmé, so that Debussy was later moved to carry Mallarmé's verse to its final apotheosis in actual music. Stevens did, nevertheless, in following Mallarmé and the other Symbolists, further refine the Parnassian grace that became an important part of his style, a grace that he sought from his college years on. Now, however, he was turning to the original models, not to versions of these by the English aesthetes of the Nineties. The almost preternatural fluency of the Symbolists offered one means of presenting more intensely those ideal presences and spiritual feelings known by the imagination. And the Symbolists no doubt made Stevens more conscious of how every detail in the poem must function in the whole, so that the poem becomes a sacramental symbol justifying its own existence, shedding the radiance of its unique conception and feeling: the poem, finally, as icon, though for him the icon must render the phenomenal world and the emotions of human, earthly existence. The transformation of sounds into a music of exalted feeling is part of the process: "syllable / To blessed syllable affined" is the reverent way Stevens states it in "The Comedian as the Letter C." Another part of the process, color values and their appropriate use, is matter for a later chapter.[5]

The alchemy of words, referred to by Rimbaud (indeed, he attributes a magical power even to vowels in his famous sonnet, "Voyelles"), is yet another crucial part of the process; and surely Stevens was devoted to the Symbolists' mystique of the word, seeking those words that in their con-

---

[5] See George McFadden, "Probings for an Integration: Color Symbolism in Wallace Stevens," *Modern Philology*, LVIII, 3 (February 1961), esp. 187. He points out that over a forty-year period Stevens evolved a natural spectrum of colors, "natural in both the scientific and popular senses of the word. Besides black, the 'limit' or *terminus a quo* of color, and white, its completion or finality, this spectrum runs from red, the color of aging stars and of time as measured by the sun, through green, color of vital force and change, and blue, the color of nature composed by the imagination, to ultraviolet or 'total blue,' where the sounds of poetry are shaped out of the creative dark. This structure conforms to Newton's famous demonstration that the components of light are, in order, red, orange, yellow, green, blue, indigo, and violet, passing smoothly into each other in order."

111

texts reverberate with implications. The word "exhalations" in "An odor from a star," suggesting an aura of supreme physical, but at the same time heavenly, beauty, is an early example; it is a word that he would use again in "Academic Discourse at Havana" (which was first published as "Discourse in a Cantina at Havana" in *Broom* in 1923): "How pale and how possessed a night it is, / How full of exhalations of the sea." If the Symbolists set the example, Stevens had his own ear for language, a fine sensibility for choosing words and phrases that almost breathe with their effects. It was a virtuosity, in fact, that he on occasion carried to fault, indulging in words as a prestidigitator, making them the playthings of fancy rather than the instruments of the imagination. But this remained occasional. Even in the ironic context of "Le Monocle de Mon Oncle" where he says, "I quiz all sounds, all thoughts, all everything / For the music and manner of the paladins / To make oblation fit," the irony is only a thin veil over the deepest commitment. Again and again he found the fit words and sounds for his "great hymn," and when the English language failed him, he did not hesitate to appropriate a French word for its sound and its penumbra of meaning and emotion. "Yet you persist," he says in "Le Monocle," "To make believe a starry *connaissance*."

"An odor from a star" employs one further and obvious Symbolist technique for communicating this "starry *connaissance*"—the synesthesia of the opening line itself. Although the Symbolists did not invent such imagery (as is clear, for example, in Shelley's description in "The Sensitive Plant" of music that "felt like an odor within the sense"), they were particularly fond of deliberately confusing the senses in order to symbolize the possible union between man and the absolute. The synesthesia at the beginning of Stevens' poem, then, introduces the reader to a fusion of odor, sight, color, and "music" designed to render a corporeal sense of that union. Here, Stevens—and Mallarmé before him—were in effect following Baudelaire's assertion in his seminal poem "Correspondences" that "Les parfums, les couleurs, et les sons se répondent." These correspondences for Baudelaire suggested the mystery and the unity inherent in nature and revealed through an occult recognition. Nature, indeed, is a temple, a forest of symbols:

> La nature est un temple où de vivante piliers
> Laissent parfois sortir de confuses paroles;
> L'homme y passe à travers des forêts de symboles
> Qui l'observent avec des regards familiers.
>
> Comme de longs échos qui de loin se confondent
> Dans une ténébreuse et profonde unité, . . .

Symbolism was an almost desperate reaching for a spiritual union between man and nature in an age of growing materialism, scientific dominance, and religious atrophy, when traditional forms of spiritual discourse had collapsed. The isolated individual, particularly the artist, had then to become his own arcane interpreter of his relation to the universe. Of course the Romantics craved a similar union, and even though the Symbolists were generally more occult than they were (more like Blake than like Wordsworth), the difference in doctrine was not great. John Senior points this out and then goes on to make an important distinction:

> Historically, Symbolism was an arc within the great curve of Romanticism. According to its practitioners it is a better way of accomplishing what the romantics wanted to achieve. Briefly, and not at all crucially, the

113

difference between the two "kinds" of poetry are [sic] differences between the philosophical and the presentational. The world views are the same, but the Romantic poet tends to write about his ideas or to relate experience in which these ideas were acted out; the Symbolist poet tries to create the experience on the page.[6]

Certainly in terms of style the difference is crucial, as the final sentence suggests. And generally it is in the direction briefly outlined in this sentence that Stevens moved—not that in his mature poetry he never wrote "about his ideas." The techniques of Symbolism, though, gave him poetic means for imbuing these ideas and their attendant emotions with both mysterious depth and immediacy, and thereby enabled him to "create the experience on the page."

He learned from Mallarmé, as we have seen; he also learned from Baudelaire, as is rather tenuously apparent in a manuscript poem called "If only birds of sudden white" (1909), which with color, sound, and symbol expresses the desire for a transcendent beauty in nature:

> If only birds of sudden white,
> Or opal, gold, or iris hue,
> Came upward through the columned light
> Of morning's ocean-breathing blue . .
>
> If only songs disturbed our sleep,
> Descending from the wakeful breeze,
> And no great murmur of the deep
> Sighed in our summer-sounding trees.

[6] Senior, *The Way Down and Out: The Occult in Symbolist Literature* (Ithaca, 1959), p. 51.

The poem, with its radiance, color, and "summer-sounding trees," has some of the atmosphere of a *fêtes galantes* setting but with a quality of spaciousness and sweep added. Is it misleading to note intimations of Baudelaire here? If his "La Vie Antérieure" lacks birds, it abounds with sea imagery, columns, azure, and brilliances. Stevens discusses Baudelaire's poem much later in life ("Two or Three Ideas," *Opus*), and, interestingly enough, his imagination associates a flight of birds with it. Although the phrase "If only" contains the note of melancholy longing evident in many of the poems of the escapist, twilight-interval variety, the symbolic birds and the "columned light / Of morning's ocean-breathing blue" are partially successful in presenting a notion of the resplendent earthly beauty desired in place of the other quality in nature's duality, the "great murmur of the deep," mortality or the unknown. The adjective "columned" lends a visual concreteness to the ethereal light, but one cannot feel that the poem as a whole creates the experience on the page. The versification is not particularly subtle or effective; the colors are hardly more than ornamental. This poem, however, like the 1908 manuscript poem "Tides" ("These infinite green motions / . . . , / Trouble with mystic sense / Like the secretive oceans"), reflects some of the early, possibly indirect, effects of the Symbolists on Stevens' art, and perhaps of Baudelaire in particular. It is a transitional work, coming in his development between the undergraduate sonnet "Cathedrals are not built" and all the later poems which express his fascination with the sea's beauty and its disturbing power.

"Blanche McCarthy," probably written in 1915 or 1916 and first published in *Opus Posthumous*, bears more certain signs of Baudelaire's influence. It is an interesting exercise, but only partially successful as a symbolic poem. In the middle stanza, for example, the abstract term "symbols" itself is not given sufficient definition in the line following. The word "glare" seems exaggerated, and the procession of revelations is more like a heavenly spectacle in a stage pageant than the real thing;[7] the sense of awesome knowledge is insisted upon unconvincingly.

> Look in the terrible mirror of the sky
> And not in this dead glass, which can reflect
> Only the surfaces—the bending arm,
> The leaning shoulder and the searching eye.

> Look in the terrible mirror of the sky.
> Oh, bend against the invisible; and lean
> To symbols of descending night; and search
> The glare of revelations going by!

> Look in the terrible mirror of the sky.
> See how the absent moon waits in a glade
> Of your dark self, and how the wings of stars,
> Upward, from unimagined coverts, fly.

But this is a clear exposition of the Symbolists' position. Stevens' manuscript poem "Ancient Rendezvous" describes in Romantic terms an intimate relationship with nature: "There rose for me, a second time, / The pageant moon"; in "Blanche McCarthy," however, Stevens shows a positive recognition of both Symbolist concept and method. John Senior says, "The function of the Symbolist poet is the function of the magus—to provoke us into this different

---

[7] In discussing the quality of Baudelaire's paradise, Michel Benamou says, "Nature was dreamed from a room, the walls of which receded to the controlled depths of dioramas," pp. 40-41 in "Wallace Stevens and the Symbolist Imagination."

116

kind of perception, that is, to present to the ordinary eye an object so dazzling that the scales will fall."[8] And this is precisely Stevens' intention in presenting to Blanche the "terrible mirror of the sky." The import here is just that in Baudelaire's "L'Homme et la Mer": "La mer est ton miroir; tu contemples ton âme / Dans le déroulement infini de sa lame." Blanche is not quite in Baudelaire's "forest of symbols," but she is surrounded by the "symbols of descending night," something very similar, and in her soul lies a symbolic correspondence with nature if only she will recognize it: "See how the absent moon waits in a glade / Of your dark self." Further, she has the capacity to "search / The glare of revelations going by!" if she will use her imagination. Unfortunately, though, Blanche is the ordinary woman, limited to a concern for appearances, for surfaces. But as the terrible mirror makes clear, Blanche, in her dark self and in the obscure darkness of "descending night," could penetrate beyond her whiteness (suggesting deadness as does the "dead glass") to a profound enlightenment. The phrase "wings of stars" is an attempt to present the very thing itself, to create on the page the evanescent, invisible reality. It is illogical, like an odor from a star, and intended to produce a resonance of meaning and emotion.

It is hardly surprising that Stevens would become so consciously and definitely attracted to Symbolist techniques, spurred on as he was by the growing enthusiasm in America for the Symbolists. Even in his undergraduate writings he had a marked propensity for indirection and allusion and for avoiding the didactic and discursive. The triumph of beauty over vulgarity in the prose sketch "Pursuit" is presented as though it were simply a description of a butterfly

[8] Senior, *op.cit.*, p. 95.

chase. "Outside the Hospital" is ostensibly nothing more than a description of the handicapped at play. "Street Songs" would seem to be no more than a series of picturesque scenes; in fact, a student reviewer in the *Harvard Crimson* expressed the desire to see more of the work by the writer of "this light verse."[9] Finally, the butterfly in "Pursuit," the pigeons in "Street Songs," the parasol in "The Ballade of the Pink Parasol" are all symbols for conveying what is unstated otherwise. In these instances the young poet, evidently responding to Parnassian models in the Nineties, was trying to present an idea or emotion itself, without muffling it in tedious abstractions. But the undergraduate writings, despite their indirection, do not show any specific debts to French Symbolist doctrine and method; poems like "An odor from a star," "The Silver Plough-Boy," "If only birds of sudden white," and "Blanche McCarthy" do.

Obviously, Stevens' predilection for symbolic presentation was intensified by that doctrine and method. Between the young girl in the undergraduate story "The Nymph," and Susanna in "Peter Quince" there would seem to lie, for one thing, an assimilation of Mallarmé. Susanna, in her perfection (suggesting, as does the woman Quince addresses, earthly beauty, art, the imagination, and the immortality of the spirit within nature's change), is similar to Mallarmé's Herodiade, although she is hardly so frigidly chaste and is not waiting for the unknown beyond nature as Herodiade is. "Heavenly Vincentine," too, in "The Apostrophe to Vincentine" (1918), is a creature of nude perfection deriving at least in part from Mallarmé; the very phrase "white animal" in Stevens' poem seems to be a

[9] *Crimson*, XXXVII, 43 (April 1900), 1.

translation of the phrase "blancheur animale" in "L'Après-Midi d'un Faune." The example of Mallarmé was indeed tempting—dangerously so at times—to that side of Stevens' sensibility which yearned for an ideal beauty. Even though Vincentine is as earthly ("warm as flesh") as she is heavenly, an incarnation giving profound meaning to earth through her perfection, she tends to remain more a symbolic configuration, a pleasing aesthetic object, than a fully realized deity of both earth and heaven. This is even more true of the divine being in "To the One of Fictive Music" (1922), a poem which has points of resemblance with Baudelaire's "Hymne," particularly in the reverent address to the angel of immortal beauty. Despite her ability to give "motion to perfection" "out of our imperfections wrought," she fails to be convincing; she is too much a static figure of perfumed and bejeweled artifice.

Baudelaire, with his extreme sense of the opposition between the demonic and the angelic, between the corruptibility of the flesh and the perfection of an ideal world of jewels, perfumes, and timeless beauty, no doubt intensified Stevens' consciousness of the disparity between the known and the unknown. The American poet's distress over his Donna's insatiable lasciviousness (she is a "Virgin of boorish births") in "O Florida, Venereal Soil" (1922) is in keeping with Baudelaire's obsession with the rank, decadent particulars of life, although Baudelaire's much greater degree of morbid fascination and disgust is one measure of Stevens' difference from his predecessor. His Donna in this poem is too much a part of the physical world (of "our despised decay" as he says in "An odor from a star"), and so he would implore her to become the mysterious, bejeweled source envisioned by Baudelaire or Mallarmé, "Wearing a clear tiara / Of red and blue and red, /

Sparkling, solitary, still . . . ," "in indigo gown / And cloudy constellations." But for Stevens, the ultimate reality must be a combination of the physical and the ideal. Thus his Donna should be remote and concealed but at the same time disclose the tangible perfection of this world (not its "dreadful sundry"), disclose "A hand that bears a thick-leaved fruit, / A pungent bloom against your shade." She thus becomes the true mother of beauty. This is what the woman in "The Ordinary Women" (1922) apparently fail to comprehend as they shift from one poverty to another, from dry catarrhs to dry guitars; their coiffures glitter in "diamond point" and "sapphire point" for a moment, but this beauty divorced from the actual world is illusory; consequently they return dissatisfied to their dry catarrhs.

Baudelaire in "Le Reniement de Saint Pierre" complains of a world where "l'action n'est pas la soeur du rêve," yet he dreams of an immutable reality in nature, beyond appearances, beyond the ennui and hideousness of the modern city, and beyond the inescapable fact of mortality and putrescence—a reality that corresponds with man's deepest desires. Such poems as "La Vie Antérieure" and "L'Homme et la Mer" concern the kind of ultimate experience sought by the girl in Stevens' "The Paltry Nude Starts on a Spring Voyage" (1919): she is "Eager for the brine and bellowing / Of the high interiors of the sea"; the later "goldener nude" "Will go, like the centre of sea-green pomp, / In an intenser calm." Similarly, the "vivid apprehension" imagined by Jasmine in "Jasmine's Beautiful Thoughts underneath the Willow" (1923) will be "Of bliss submerged beneath appearance, / In an interior ocean's rocking." For Stevens, this bliss must always be perceived as a part of nature; dream and action are not separated when the imagination plays its true role. This is why the

120

dancer who unites dream and action in "The Silver Plough-Boy" is both farmer and aesthete and why Bonnie and Josie in "Life is Motion" (1919) celebrate "the marriage / Of flesh and air" in Oklahoma, refreshingly so when one thinks of the ornate, fanciful activity of the sultana and seraph in "An odor from a star." At supreme moments, according to Stevens, one apprehends vividly the fusion of nature and the ideal. This is the case in the post-*Harmonium* poem "The Idea of Order at Key West" (1934), where the girl symbolizes the union of nature's sound and the music of the imagination. Later still, in "Notes toward a Supreme Fiction" (1942), Stevens symbolized the ultimate unity in his "Fat girl, terrestrial," his "fluent mundo" who finally "will have stopped revolving except in crystal." Here, the hugeness of conception and the sense of a force as boundless as life itself is not far from Baudelaire's impression of an uncorrupted nature in "La Géante." But such perfection for Baudelaire was remote, before corruption entered the world, or as far away as the Malabar girl in his "A une Malabaraise." For Stevens, it was very much in the here and now, but perceived with a Mallarméan and Baudelairean eye in the absolute purity of art. The prototype for this symbol of perfect reconciliation— the fluent mundo in crystal—is the girl in "The Nymph," who exists in two worlds, undaunted by the flies in the jelly, making dream, action, and nature one. But as we can see, the nymph underwent an evolution, a series of mutations, on the way to becoming the semi-mythical creature of supreme fiction.[10]

[10] It is worth considering Stevens' "Romantic image," his green mundo revolving in crystal, and its evolution in the perspective of Frank Kermode's discussion of the dancer image in his chapter "The Dancer" in *The Romantic Image* (New York, 1957). Also,

Although she is the prototype, Stevens became more deeply conscious of the forces symbolized in her: the ordering power of the mind or the aesthetic principle on one hand and nature and mortality on the other. And as his transcendental leanings were turned in the direction of the dark and mysterious by his response to the ethos of the Symbolists, he became more urgently concerned with conveying the indefinable in the poem itself, where its reality would be distinguishable or at least intimated. As a result, many of his images and symbols combine clarity with an air of mystery. It is just this fusion which the woman in "Two Figures in Dense Violet Night" (1923) requires from her "puerile" companion: "Say that the palms are clear in a total blue, / Are clear and obscure." This is paralleled by the Mallarméan description of night in the second of "Six Significant Landscapes" (1916): "The night is the color / Of a woman's arm: / Night, the female, / Obscure, / Fragrant, and supple." Stevens would make us experience "the dropping / Of the silence, wide sleep and solitude / Of night" in "The Curtains in the House of the Metaphysician" (1919) as a felt ambience. The very adjective "hymeneal" in "Last Looks at the Lilacs" (1923) gives the air which it modifies a sensuous and ceremonious presence. This occurs in a humorous context, but at those supreme

---

Glauco Cambon, in discussing the Nanzia Nunzio and Ozymandias section in "Notes toward a Supreme Fiction," suggests the heritage of Stevens' "spouse beyond emerald or amethyst, / Beyond the burning body that I bear": "This is such a dance as Salome might have danced if holiness and not perversity had been her motive force," *The Inclusive Flame* (Bloomington, Indiana, 1963), p. 106. Stevens' dancer image, with its similarities to and differences from its predecessors, is thus one culmination within the Romantic-Symbolist-Decadent tradition.

moments of recognizing the unity of the physical and spiritual, Stevens rightly assumed a sacerdotal tone.

On other occasions, though, his tone was more vigorous and celebratory, for opposed to the obscure reality of night with its moonlight flickerings and dark emanations is the burning intensity of day with its Baudelairean brilliancies and splendor of the sun, the animal force, the inescapable male reality. Now, for Stevens, it is the function of the imagination to encompass both day and night and all they represent. Like the blank finality of snow or slate and the rich abundance of summer, and many other of his dichotomous details, they symbolize the poles of a total reality. "When my dream was near the moon," he says in the fourth section of "Six Significant Landscapes," it began to include the sunrise: "The white folds of its gown / Filled with yellow light. / The soles of its feet / Grew red." And he continued in poem after poem seeking to capture the essence of reality in all its shadings and shifting colors, its evanescent mystery and its tangible splendor. Neither Mallarmé nor Baudelaire alone was sufficient to his desires. Nor, indeed, was the inspiration of the two combined, for their influence was qualified by his assimilating the lessons of the Impressionist and post-Impressionist painters, by his Wordsworthian sense of nature, and by the integrity of his own observations of the real.

For all his debt to the Symbolists, and it was a debt that was reinforced and kept current by his interest in such poets as Fargue and Valéry, Stevens did not pursue an occult, mystical union with the absolute. He could strongly regret that the blue of the sky was a barrier to any final revelation, but when he says "Death is the mother of beauty," he is not, like Mallarmé, longing for a death-like perfection; rather, he is accepting the natural life cycle. This acceptance is spiritual in quality, and yet it often includes resignation to the quotidian—expressed in the comic, buoyant tone which differentiates his work from Baudelaire's and Mallarmé's. The Symbolists' conception of paradise depended on a rejection of this world, but to Stevens the atmosphere of such a paradise was either too rarefied or too richly perfumed; he would suffocate there. Stevens insisted that his paradise include the fresh air of earth, which for him was "all of paradise that we shall know." Still, although his interest in odors from stars lessened, the example of the Symbolists made available to him a number of techniques for defining his paradise with immediacy and depth.

V. What One Star Can Carve

$\mathcal{O}$F, AS Graham Hough says, Imagism was a "by blow from Symbolism," or "Symbolism without the magic,"[1] it nevertheless offered the compression, precision, and hard clarity that Symbolism often lacked. Chapter II dealt briefly with a number of Stevens' experiments, those poems in which he was working with some of the same techniques that the Imagists favored; like them, in their efforts to establish a new poetry, he was drawn to Chinese and Japanese art and poetry, and to Impressionism. But as the movement developed, neither he nor they were limited to these sources. They often, for instance, created metaphors like those of the French poets; compare Corbière's 'Crénelé comme la machoire d'une vieille," from "Le Poète Contumace," with Stevens' more exotic "Crenellations of mountains / Cut like strummed zithers," from a manuscript section originally intended to be the sixth of "Eight Significant Landscapes." Also, Stanley K. Coffman, Jr., in his study of the movement, suggests that Pound's program for *Imagisme* had its origins in his desire to get a hearing for H. D.'s poetry, which had been inspired by Greek lyrics rather than the Imagist doctrine. In fact, Amy Lowell, the leader of her own wing of Imagism (dubbed Amygism by Pound), said with some justification that Imagist principles were "not new . . . by any means . . . but fallen into desuetude."[2]

And yet, despite the individual explorations and differ-

[1] Hough, *Image and Experience: Studies in a Literary Revolution* (London, 1960), p. 9.

[2] Coffman, *Imagism, A Chapter for the History of Modern Poetry* (Norman, Okla., 1951); see p. 145 for suggestion about origin of Pound's program and p. 175 for Lowell quotation.

ences, the doctrine propounded by T. E. Hulme and disseminated by Pound and then Amy Lowell did concentrate the tendencies into a movement which effectively focused attention on the need for precise diction, concrete imagery, and exactness of cadence and sound. Stevens' association with Arensberg, who, according to Kreymborg, was "passionately fond of Pound and the imagists,"[3] and with William Carlos Williams, who remained in close touch with Pound, brought him near the vortex of Imagist theory and practice; and the Imagists' poetry generally, reaching its height in the years between 1913 and 1917, no doubt spurred his own experiments in this vein. Indeed, in some instances Stevens seems to have borrowed specific details and applied them in his own manner. Notice, for example, the similarity of H. D.'s "Do your roots drag up color / from the sand?" in "Sea Iris" (1915) and Stevens' later "The birch trees draw up whiteness from the ground. / In the swamps, bushes draw up dark red . . ." in "Primordia" (1917; *Opus*). Possibly, too, despite all the stylistic differences in Stevens' poem, some hints for his "The Paltry Nude Starts on a Spring Voyage" (1919) were derived from Amy Lowell's "Venus Transiens" (1915) and H. D.'s "Hermonax" (1914). Amy Lowell's poem, like Stevens', compares Botticelli's Venus with another manifestation of Venus:

> Was Venus more beautiful
> Than you are,
> When she topped
> The crinkled waves,
> Drifting shoreward
> On her plaited shell?

[3] *Troubadour, An Autobiography* (New York, 1925), p. 221.

126

Was Botticelli's vision
Fairer than mine;

. . . .

You stand poised
In the blue and buoyant air,
Cinctured by bright winds,
Treading the sunlight.

Stevens' more symbolic poem is not addressed to a woman,
nor is Botticelli explicitly mentioned; Venus heads not
shoreward but seaward, toward the "high interiors of the
sea."

But not on a shell, she starts,
Archaic, for the sea.

. . . .

She scuds the glitters,

. . . .

The wind speeds her,

. . . .

She touches the clouds, where she goes
In the circle of her traverse of the sea.

Further, he places his paltry nude, whose "heels foam," and
who is "Eager for the brine and bellowing," on the "first-
found weed." Such details are close to those in H. D.'s
"Hermonax":

Leaving warm meads
For the green, grey-green fastness
Of the great deeps;

. . . .

Broken by great waves,
The wavelets flung it here,
This sea-gliding creature,

127

> This strange creature like a weed,
> Covered with salt foam,

These comparisons do little more than suggest that Stevens was keeping up with the Imagists' verse. His own poetry makes clear, however, that he responded to much more than the subject matter and a few random details in Imagist poetry; he applied the tenets and techniques of Imagism with a deep sense of what they could do for his own poems.

VERY MUCH in the Imagist mode is a poem called "From a Junk," one of "Two Poems" in the November 1914, *Trend:*

> A great fish plunges in the dark,
> Its fins of rutted silver; sides,
> Belabored with a foamy light;
> And back, brilliant with scaly salt.
> It glistens in the flapping wind,
> Burns there and glistens wide and wide
> Under the five-horned stars of night,
> In wind and wave . . . It is the moon.

It exemplifies the Imagists' insistence that analogies be based on clearly perceived objects and Pound's advice that the poet "Go in fear of abstractions."[4] The adjectives in the poem are chosen from an Imagistic point of view: "Rutted," "foamy," and "scaly" all aim at visual precision; the "flapping wind" is made concrete by being compared with an unstated object—a sail; "five-horned" is a similar attempt to give the stars visual and physical definition, but the phrase tends to be a mere poeticism. This can be said of the poem as a whole, despite its particularity. The description of the fish is overdrawn; Stevens insists on too many points of

---

[4] "A Few Don'ts By an Imagiste," *Poetry,* 1, 6 (March 1913), 203.

analogy between it and the moon, so that the final revelation, which should strike a note of awe, comes as an anti-
climax. Nor is "From a Junk" strengthened by the chinoiserie of its title. But soon after this, Stevens, seizing upon
the innovations in the Imagists' verse and responding to
the very spirit of the poetic breakthrough, achieved a mastery of Imagism that would leave an indelible imprint on
his mature style.

"Tea," published in March 1915, only four months after
"From a Junk," is a good illustration of this; and interest-
ingly enough, Stevens thought it worthy of inclusion in
Harmonium a little over seven years later.

> When the elephant's-ear in the park
> Shrivelled in frost,
> And the leaves on the paths
> Ran like rats,
> Your lamp-light fell
> On shining pillows,
> Of sea-shades and sky-shades,
> Like umbrellas in Java.

Light, witty, rococo as the poem may be, it is charged with
its theme, and it has compression, concentration, and precision. It dwells only on details essential to its point and its
effect; only the title, suggesting elegance, order, ritual, and
civilization, defines the dramatic situation. The two images
in the first four lines incisively depict coldness and mortality. In "elephant's-ear" and "shrivelled" there is an exactness of diction; but more, "elephant's-ear" contains a hidden
Imagistic analogy: since the plant is metaphorically named,
the shrivelled or wrinkled quality of the leaves is intensified
by the comparison with an actual elephant's ear. With
equal economy, the last four lines set the world of civilized

order against the outdoor coldness, ending on a note of exotic beauty, color, and elegance which is clearly defined by the Imagistic comparison of the pillows and umbrellas. One sees in this poem how fully Stevens had sharpened the irony and wit which Coffman points out are implicit in Imagism.[5] One sees, too, in the first four lines the tightening of effect through the repetitions of sounds, the *r*'s in particular. Then the second half of the poem shifts appropriately to a grace and delicacy supported by rhythm and alliteration.

Imagism served Stevens well as a means of surprising the reader into sudden awareness. In miniature, the image dramatizes what the imagination can do: out of two things a third is created; or as Hulme said, "analogies . . . make another world."[6] Many of Stevens' images draw disparate qualities in nature or experience into unexpected relationships. For example, in "Primordia," I (1917; *Opus*), the raucous "syllables of the" ordinary "gulls and . . . crows" and the syllables of the rare and beautiful bluebird "Meet in the name / Of Jalmar Lillygreen. / There is his motion / In the flowing of black water." Here the name itself is by aural figuration Imagistic. Further, Jalmar Lillygreen seems to assimilate elements of nature into a unity of being, so that the fluency of his motion is comparable to that of the flowing water, another Imagistic conception.

Through such techniques, Stevens was able to present a fresh and immediate sense of the physical world. The eye

[5] Coffman, p. 71. Incidentally, Carl Van Vechten recalled seeing a version of "Tea" which included the phrase "teashades and seashades." See his "Rogue Elephant in Porcelain," *Yale University Library Gazette*, xxxviii (1963), 43.

[6] See Glen Hughes, *Imagism and the Imagists, A Study in Modern Poetry* (Stanford and London, 1931), p. 21.

focuses with utmost attention on an object, and the aesthetic result is a relationship of object and emotion, free of poetic vagueness. Instead of a locust glittering "in the light serene" (in the manuscript poem "Noon-Clearing"), the "light is like a spider. / It crawls over the water." It is by such visual precision in "Tattoo" (1916) that he renders a sense of the way light moves across the water. If the reader is of a disposition to suspend his literal-mindedness, both the light and the spider crawl into his mind's eye. But even the very literal-minded are given slight chance for evasion when, in the same poem, the following analogy suggests a close relationship between the subjective self and objective nature: "The webs of your eyes / Are fastened / To the flesh and bones of you / As to rafters or grass." Within the basic comparison of webs and eyes, the physical is further accentuated by the comparison of flesh and grass, bones and rafters. This poem is a good example of the resemblance between the metaphysical conceit and the Imagistic analogy, for it reminds us of Donne's "Our eye-beams twisted, and did thread / Our eyes upon one double string." And Stevens creates something like a metaphysical shudder in "It [the light] crawls under your eyelids / And spreads its webs there—." This is the kind of thing in Stevens' poetry that led Joseph E. Duncan to discuss Stevens in terms of the metaphysical revival.[7] More to the point, however, is the poet's use of Imagistic technique in "Tattoo" to stress the reality—as well as wonder—of our physical being. The poem suggests a subtle relationship between man and nature by a Whitman-like naming of physical details of man and earth. In response to the light and the beauty in nature, man's form—his natural architecture

[7] See *The Revival of Metaphysical Poetry, The History of a Style, 1800 to the Present* (Minneapolis, 1959), pp. 182-186.

(flesh and bones)—and his vision have developed to catch "the glare of revelations going by"—the patterns in nature stamped on our inner consciousness like tattoos.

Corollary to Stevens' using imagery to delineate the physical world is his using it to give concreteness to the imagined or abstract. In the fourth section of "Six Significant Landscapes" (1916), he gives a specific embodiment to his dream: "Its hair filled with certain blue crystallizations / From stars, / Not far off." And in the fifth section the star, symbolic of the romantic, the imaginary, the beautiful, carves out a place for itself. The techniques of Symbolism and Imagism complement each other in this poem:

> Not all the knives of the lamp-posts,
> Nor the chisels of the long streets,
> Nor the mallets of the domes
> And high towers,
> Can carve
> What one star can carve,
> Shining through the grape leaves.

In conception, though with conscious wit, irony, and exaggeration, the central image is very similar to Skipwith Cannéll's image, however unintentionally humorous, in one of his "Nocturnes" published in *Des Imagistes*: "For upon my head has the moonlight / Fallen / As a sword." Stevens' and Cannéll's images could not be more in the Imagist canon as set down by Hulme, who stressed sculptural hardness in poetry. This attitude is evident, too, in Pound's interest in Gautier, especially his *Émaux and Cameos*; reacting in this work against Romantic softness, Gautier made apparent his desire for hard clarity in poetry. Pound recommended that the symbol be in the object, and that is just what occurs in the case of Stevens' star. Like the Symbolists, the Imagists wanted to present a vivid illumination, but more sharply defined, without the vagueness they attributed to Symbolism. According to Pound, "An image is that which presents an intellectual and emotional complex in an instant of time . . ."[8] and yet, what they achieved, though vivid, was often static: their illuminations remained suspended in a vacuum. Nevertheless, they contributed greatly to Stevens' sense that "the romantic exists in precision as well as in imprecision" ("Adagia," *Opus*).

THIS concern for precision, as a few passing references to rhythm and sound have already indicated, extended to every detail of versification, the "minutiae" of the poet's craft as Pound put it. Paul Rosenfeld coined an epithet for Stevens which ought to have more currency than it does for describing this part of Stevens' Imagistic technique. He referred to him as a "musical imagist," commenting that "music remains the prime element of this diverting art."[9] Rosenfeld did not specify by example just what he meant by the term, but presumably he had in mind Stevens' use of the apt cadence which reproduces exactly the desired mood or emotion. That is what "musical imagist" means here, and it conforms to one of F. S. Flint's rules for the

[8] Pound's quotation is from "A Few Don'ts By an Imagist," *Poetry* (March 1913), p. 200. Pound's interest in Gautier is expressed in his "The Hard and the Soft in French Poetry," *Poetry*, XI, 5 (February 1918), 265-266 and is requoted by Coffman, pp. 85-86.

[9] Pound said in his "Don'ts": "Let the neophyte know assonance and alliteration, rhyme immediate and delayed, simple and polyphonic, as a musician would expect to know harmony and counterpoint and all the minutiae of his craft," *Poetry* (March 1913), p. 203. Rosenfeld's comment is from *Men Seen, Twenty-Four Modern Authors* (New York, 1925), p. 152.

Imagist, that regarding rhythm he "compose in sequence of the musical phrase, not in sequence of the metronome" and to Pound's injunction that he "behave as a musician . . . when dealing with that phase of your art which has exact parallels in music. . . ."[10] Such emphasis dovetailed with and reinforced the musical education Stevens gained from the Symbolists. "To Madame Alda, Singing a Song, in a White Gown" for example, is an ephemeral poem in the mode of Mallarmé, but Stevens very carefully controlled the movement of the free-verse lines in his desire to make the intangible feeling of sorrow palpable. The spondees and slow pace in "A few large, round leaves of wan pink / Float in a small space of air" produce a suspension, and the effect of floating is enhanced by the drawn-out quality of "Luminously," the sole word in the following line. Similarly, the sense of the white heron's flight has its rhythmic counterpart in the line, "From its long legs drifting, close together."

The Imagists' concern with the music of poetry is of course related to the *vers libre* debate which grew out of the popularization of their credo. The conservative critics had their point, too, since for some poets *vers libre* became mere license. But it could also mean freedom within which the poet, in search of authentic rhythms, could exert self-control. Stevens' practice shows his general agreement with Pound and Eliot on this score: Pound said, "The discovery that bad *vers libre* can be quite as bad as any other sort of bad verse is by no means modern"; Eliot stated, "There is no freedom in art. And as the so-called *vers libre* which is good is anything but 'free,' it can better be defended under

10 F. S. Flint, "Imagisme," *Poetry* (March 1913), p. 199, and Pound, "A Few Don'ts," *ibid.*, p. 204.

some other label."[11] Stevens' musical Imagism is a matter
of rhythms which embody feeling and sound with more
precision and variation than are evident in the deliquescent,
vague, impressionistic music discussed earlier.

Stevens' manuscript poem, "The night-wind of August,"
seems an early and awkward attempt through free verse to
achieve a greater freedom and flexibility in his cadences
and line lengths. The speech is more natural and colloquial
than in his twilight-interval poems, the rhythm less metronomic; Stevens intends the variations in line length to accord with the movement of his thought and emotion.

> The night-wind of August
> Is like an old mother to me.
> It comforts me.
> I rest in it,
> As one would rest,
> If one could,
> Once again—
> It moves about, quietly
> And attentively.
> Its old hands touch me.
> But sometimes its breath is a little cold,
> Just a little,
> And I know
> That it is only the night-wind.

Here the rhythm to some extent follows the sense of quiet
meditation, comfort, and security, turning at the end to
the understated awareness of isolation. For all its weakness,
this attempt in free verse looks ahead to those more successful poems in which the curve of emotion is explicitly

[11] Pound quote from "Affirmations," *The New Age*, XVI, 13
(January 28, 1915), 350. Eliot quote from Hughes, p. 73.

and intensely etched out by what might be called rhythmic analogy.

A *Harmonium* poem, "The Wind Shifts" (1917), comes closer to this ideal:

> This is how the wind shifts:
> Like the thoughts of an old human,
> Who still thinks eagerly
> And despairingly.
> The wind shifts like this:
> Like a human without illusions,
> Who still feels irrational things within her.
> The wind shifts like this:
> Like humans approaching proudly,
> Like humans approaching angrily.
> This is how the wind shifts:
> Like a human, heavy and heavy,
> Who does not care.

Part of the effect derives from the repetitions, which maintain the expectancy of "shifting" and underscore the various human feelings associated with the shifts of the wind. Further, the *ly*'s in eagerly-despairingly and proudly-angrily heighten the shift to negation in each case, and "heavy and heavy" in the next-to-last line adds to the effect of leaden monotony. It is this mastery of repetition within free verse which enabled Stevens in the following passage from "Domination of Black" (1916) describing the leaves

> Turning in the wind,
> Turning as the flames
> Turned in the fire,
> Turning as the tails of the peacocks
> Turned in the loud fire, . . .

to involve the reader in the mysterious and frightening sense of turning which leads to the effect of the cosmic simile at the end of the poem:

> I saw how the planets gathered
> Like the leaves themselves
> Turning in the wind. . . .

This is first-rate Imagism—the resources of rhythm and vivid imagery used to render the feeling of isolation in a vast, indifferent universe. "Tattoo," on the other hand, with its repetitions,

> The light is like a spider.
> It crawls over the water.
> It crawls over the edge of the snow.
> It crawls under your eyelids . . .

achieves a slightly eerie beauty.[12]

In "Peter Quince," with its precise emphasis of meaning and emotion supported by variations in rhythm and sound, Stevens created a remarkable example of his musical Imagism. For the musical form of this poem, he had several possible models. Grace Hazard Conkling, for example, who was a trained musician as well as a friend of Amy Lowell, had her "Symphony of a Mexican Garden" published with Amy Lowell's support, in the first number of *Poetry* (1912). The poem is divided into four sections ("The Garden," "The Pool," "The Birds," and "To the Moon") according to technical musical terms—"Poco Sostenuto in A Major," "Presto in F Major," and so on—and the sections have their appropriate rhythms and tonalities. The general quality of the poem is not Imagistic; it is, rather, a mixture of a lush

---

[12] See further discussion of Stevens' free verse technique in the early part of Chapter VIII.

Impressionism and tired echoes of Romantic and Victorian poetry. But nonetheless it is part of the general movement to bring music and poetry closer together, and it contains elements which could have served as hints for Stevens, such as the following:

> An unimagined music exhales
>
> . . . .
>
> Symphonic beauty that some god forgot.
> If form could waken into lyric sound
>
> . . . .
>
> Where the hibiscus flares would cymbals clash,
> And the black cypress like a deep bassoon
> Would hum a clouded amber melody.

John Gould Fletcher's similar but vaguely defined musical arrangements were not measurably tightened by his more Imagistic practice. Fletcher, too, was fond of cymbals in "Irradiations, I":

> A clash of cymbals—then the swift swaying footsteps
> Of the wind that undulated along the languid terraces.

Indeed, his *Preludes and Symphonies* (1914) contained many of the elements which Stevens was experimenting with: the arabesque, pavilions, terraces, pagodas, willows, quiverings and undulations, winds that "came clangering and clattering," clouds, the sea, and, of course, color.

But Stevens, the musical imagist, created in "Peter Quince" his own more succinct "symphony" or "quartet."[13]

---

[13] Newell F. Ford rightly advises that we not " 'freeze' the fluctuant movement of the poem within a single musical formula." See "Peter Quince's Orchestra," *Modern Language Notes*, LXXV, 5 (May 1960), 405. Still, the temptation is strong to do so. In fact, some are tempted to go beyond formulas to specific works by spe-

In contrast to the tenderly reflective music of the beginning of the first section there is at the end the sudden intrusion of the elders' bass music. They felt

> The basses of their beings throb
> In witching chords, and their thin blood
> Pulse pizzicati of Hosanna.

The throbbing and pulsing are made aurally acute as well as comic by the repetitions of the *b* and *p* sounds. The comic grotesqueness of their excitement is augmented by the double meaning of "basses" and by the combination of "witching" and "pizzicati." Similarly, Susanna's poignant and spiritual music in Section II of the poem—in which the few rhymes subtly interlace thought and emotion—is interrupted by the crash of the cymbal and the roaring horns. In Section III, the nervous rhythms and the couplets create a mincing, simpering music appropriate for the Byzantine servant girls. And yet there are modulations in their music

---

cific composers, as Marianne Moore does in drawing a parallel between Handel's Sonata No. 1 and "Peter Quince" (see her statement below in the text and note 14); and Clay Hunt, in a conversation, has said that he detects a marked correlation between the poem and a piece by Couperin. Such parallels are intriguing, but it is perhaps sounder to point to general affinities between Stevens' work and that of individual composers than to those between specific Stevens' poems and specific musical compositions. I would cite, for example, the vigorous high comic spirit shared by Stevens and Mozart or the qualities in his poetry akin to the shimmering brilliancies in Debussy's music. In any event, however subtle the influence of music on his poetry was, the influence was great. It is most apparent, of course, in the wealth of musical imagery and in the direct translation of musical rhythms into verbal notations, the rhythms of strummed instruments for instance ("such tink and tank and tunk-a-tunk-tunk" in "A High-Tone Old Christian Woman").

139

between the "noise" of their arrival and departure and the delicacy of their hushed refrain: "And as they whispered, the refrain / Was like a willow swept by rain." In the latter instance the Imagistic analogy—"whispered" and the "willow swept by rain"—is given emphasis by the repetition of sounds. The music of Section IV is stately and sweeping, and close to the grand manner of "Sunday Morning." This section also evokes a sense of the continuity underlying change, partially by the use of the series of four rhymes ending in *ing* and of the word "interminably," which creates a drawn-out effect like that of "luminously" in "To Madame Alda":

> So evenings die, in their green going,
> A wave, interminably flowing.
> So gardens die, their meek breath scenting
> The cowl of winter, done repenting.

What might have been mere program music, mere effect, as it so often is in Fletcher's symphonies, is turned in "Peter Quince" into a musical architecture which organically serves the whole thematic and emotional conception. With the passage just cited as an example, Marianne Moore says of Stevens,

> But like Handel in the patterned correspondences of the Sonata No. 1, he has not been rivalled. . . . His repercussive harmonies, set off by the small compass of the poem, "prove" mathematically. . . .[14]

One might wonder about the introduction of mathematical proofs into the matter, but not about her sense of the harmonic pattern in "Peter Quince" which gives a compelling order to the theme and emotions in the poem.

[14] *Predilections* (New York, 1955), p. 32.

140

Such success does not mean that Stevens was not often carried away by his musical Imagism, as he was in his use of the "purely imitative sounds" which Rosenfeld referred to. These, like some of the words Stevens fancied, remain, in Rosenfeld's phrase again, "merely . . . morsels rolled upon an epicure's palate."[15] For instance, amid the notations at the bottom of the page of a manuscript poem, "I have lived so long with the rhetoricians," there appears the peculiar phrase, "The nay nay-slack swirl." It is followed by three question marks, and Stevens' doubts were surely justified. In "Primordia," Section 4 (*Opus*), there is the paradox that the trees stand still and drink while

> The water runs away from the horses.
> La, la, la, la, la, la, la, la,
> Dee, dum, diddle, dee, dee, diddle, dee, da.

The playfulness and wit here seem to be ends in themselves.

Stevens, however, was determined to carry his experiments with musical imagism—and the other elements of his style—to extreme limits. And "The Comedian as the Letter C," a virtuoso piece in so many ways, is a tour de force of intricate and witty effects of sound and cadence. In a letter to Renato Poggioli, Stevens pointed to the problem this would cause the translator, and incidentally gave a clue to a meaning in the title which until recently seems to have been overlooked:

> It may be a little difficult to translate *The Comedian as the Letter* C. The sounds of the letter C, both hard and soft, include other letters like K, X, etc. How would it be possible to translate a line like
> > Chequering from piebald fiscs unkeyed,

[15] Rosenfeld, pp. 151, 159.

and preserve anything except the sense of the words? However, it is true that the poem has made its way without reference to the sounds of the letter C.[16]

The intensive Imagistic play of sounds—not simply the C sounds, though they predominate in a great many lines, like "Loquacious columns by the ructive sea" and "Jovial Crispin in calamitous crape"—complements the Elizabethan gusto of Stevens' rhetoric in the poem and his aim, following the example of the Symbolists, to approximate the qualities of music in poetry.

The various C sounds, along with all the other sounds in "The Comedian," would appear to well up from mysterious sources in nature (the "speech belched out of hoary darks / Noway resembling" Crispin's), and these sounds the poet must bring into the musical order of the poem—"syllable / To blessed syllable affined, and sound / Bubbling felicity in cantilene." Thus the sounds which are a part of nature become a part of the nature of the poem; in this case the scoring encompasses both exuberant wit and more exalted harmonies. And the fact that the sounds of C are "both hard and soft" reflects an aspect of Crispin's problem: he must reconcile his fastidiousness with the rawness of his experience, "The florist asking aid from cabbages" (we recall that in the poem from "Primordia, I" the raucous syllables of the gulls and crows join with the beautiful syllables of the bluebird "in the name / of Jalmar Lillygreen"). Further-

[16] R. Poggioli, *Mattino Domenicale Ed Altre Poesie* (Turin, 1954), p. 69. Samuel French Morse in "Wallace Stevens, Bergson, Pater," *ELH*, 31 (March 1964), 24, has alluded to this statement of Stevens', saying "The significance of 'the sounds of the letter C' can be taken with a grain of salt." But even though Stevens would no doubt delight in pulling critics' legs, I must confess to finding at least a grain of truth in the salt.

142

more, Crispin, the comedian whose name combines hard and soft sounds, becomes himself, as the letter C, a part of the texture of the poem, his identity constantly threatened by the flux: "What word split up in clickering syllables / . . . / was name for this short-shanks in all that brunt?" And thus, the articulation of sounds becomes a means by which Crispin can "stem verboseness in the sea"; the "Polyphony" of the sea is not really "beyond his baton's thrust," although Stevens ironically says it is. In the poem, then, the minutiae of his craft support the theme, the wit of conception, the comic point of view, and the modulations of effect. If in some cases the effects derive from excessive ingenuity, the poem nevertheless illustrates Stevens' extraordinary control of sound, which adds so much tautness and exactitude to his style.

THE IMAGES themselves, as well as the sounds, were sometimes excessive or merely ingenious as Stevens sought for radical analogies that would capture the reader's imagination. The problem is that some point of comparison exists between almost any two objects, a fact which Stevens himself eventually recognized—as this statement in "Adagia" (*Opus*) shows: "Not all objects are equal. The vice of Imagism was that it did not recognize this." But early in his career he was still equating "all objects" freely, as may be seen in another section of "Primordia, I":

> The child's hair is of the color of the hay in the haystack,
>   around which the four black horses stand.
> There is the same color in the bellies of frogs, in clays,
>   withered reeds, skins, wood, sunlight.

With a little cleverness, one can carry on the list indefinitely. The comparison in "Bowl" (1916; *Opus*) is grandiose—"For what emperor / Was this bowl of Earth designed?"—but forced. Stevens said in "Adagia," "Some objects are less susceptible to metaphor than others. The whole world is less susceptible to metaphor than a tea-cup is." Such reasoning may explain why "Bowl" remained a fugitive piece. This, however, did not keep Stevens from attempting such farfetched metaphors, most of which were successful, as in the case of the leaves and the planets in "Domination of Black." But in section V of the original "Eight Significant Landscapes" found among the manuscripts the figure collapses:

> Wrestle with morning-glories,
> O, muscles!
> It is useless to contend*
> With falling mountains.

One must agree with William Carlos Williams: "Its alright [sic] to wrestle with morning glories but all mountains are not falling etc. (the usual bunk)."[17] Some of the attempts display refined mental gymnastics or a fine sense of distinctions which become merely tedious, as in section VI

> Crenellations of mountains
> **Cut like strummed zithers;

but as the final lines of this original Section VI of "Eight Significant Landscapes" add,

> Dead trees do not resemble
> Beaten drums.

* "Struggle" erased.

[17] Holograph letter, dated June 2, 1916, kept in an envelope with "Eight Significant Landscapes," among the manuscripts.

** "Are" erased.

It was a sign of discipline against such indulgences that Stevens cut the poem to "Six Significant Landscapes."

He had to call on this discipline to suppress a number of his Imagistic exercises; the inventiveness and the lapidary surfaces often belied a lack of emotional and imaginative depth. "Architecture" (1918; *Opus*), for example, runs riot in architectural metaphors:

> These are the pointings of our edifice,
> Which, like a gorgeous palm,
> Shall tuft the commonplace.
>
> .   .   .   .
>
> How shall we hew the sun,
> Split it and make blocks
> To build a ruddy palace?

And so on. By the 1931 edition of *Harmonium*, Stevens may have decided that "A High-Toned Old Christian Woman" used the imagery of architecture to much better effect, and for this reason left "Architecture" out. The excesses probably derived from Stevens' excitement with the realization of the possibilities of metaphor, but his experiments, however excessive, left an incisiveness, wit, and firmness in his imagery.

His diction also became more precise. The earlier discussions of "Tea" and "Tattoo" have already suggested this addition: "elephant's-ear," for instance, from "Tea," and from "Tattoo," "filaments of your eyes," which is technical, literal, the "exact word." The same can be said for the word "crazy" in "the crazy plough" of "The Silver Plough-Boy," which focuses attention on the eccentric action of the plough, guided by a dancing ploughboy. The aim is to make the impress of the "felt word" inescapable.[18] "Rhom-

18 Among the manuscripts is a group of jottings called "From

145

boids," exact as they are in "Six Significant Landscapes," are unusual enough to cause square-hatted rationalists to adopt sombreros. One wonders in many cases if the word was chosen out of a comic or an Imagistic impulse, and perhaps the answer is both. The result was often words which merely decorate and amuse, words which stick out of the context like cloves on a ham, so that such critics as A. Alvarez can justifiably complain of Stevens' "encrusted style." But more often than not, Stevens could create the indelible phrase—as well as the right metaphor—with diction that was both vivid and integrally part of the context.

Alvarez, in his essay on Stevens, says at one point, "In a way Stevens was the only poet ever to take Imagism seriously." This may be an exaggeration—think of H. D.—but the statement rightly draws our attention to the importance of this element in Stevens' art. Even if Imagism was for many poets at the time no more than "high-minded game played out in the consciously pregnant silences around the images,"[19] it provided him with further techniques for fulfilling the Symbolists' desire to create the experience on the page. But it is the fact that Stevens had a consuming theme of his own that distinguishes him from most of the other Imagists, who in their eagerness to avoid sentimentality and moralizing in poetry all too often ended in the cul-de-sac of art for art's sake. What makes Stevens an Imagist

---

Pieces of Paper," many of which become titles or phrases in Stevens' poems (see Morse, *Opus*, xxxiii). One item among the jottings is "Qualities of a poem," one of which is "felt word." Remainder of the list: "interesting, indigenous to a person, d'un daemon, capable of infuriating with poetry, emotion, to come from an ever-free [?] source, essence, effortless, contagious."

[19] Both quotations from A. Alvarez, "Wallace Stevens: Platonic Poetry," *Stewards of Excellence* (New York, 1958), p. 128.

in the manner of Stevens is that he pursued the several possibilities of Imagism—its economy and objectivity, particularity and sharpness, its innovations in versification, its wit—and followed them to their limits, but always with an eye—and ear—for the ways they would help give poetic life to his sense of the world. Furthermore, no matter how seriously he took Imagism, he refused to be merely an Imagist. Although a number of his poems are predominantly Imagistic, he fused the techniques of this mode with all the other elements of his art.

VI. A Clinging Eye

*S*TRIP Stevens' poems in *Harmonium* of their thematic intensity, their exultation in the power of the imagination to discover the essence of beauty, energy, and change in the physical world, their emotional nuances and their diverse feelings that grow out of Stevens' awareness of the fullness of an earthly life circumscribed by negation and final blankness: strip his poems of these qualities and they remain a collection of empty symbols, Imagistic tricks, witty and humorous contrivances, verbal and rhetorical flourishes, and finally, of surface displays of color and visual detail appropriated from the art of painting. In his debt to painting, Stevens seriously risked the fallacy of imitative form. Indeed, the surface of *Harmonium* nearly persuades the reader that one of his aims was to abolish the distinctions between poetry and painting.

Many of his titles—"Floral Decorations for Bananas," "Of the Surface of Things," "Domination of Black," "Sea Surface Full of Clouds"—declare Stevens' affection for still lifes, landscapes, and seascapes and are obvious signs of his determination to carry over to his poetry the visual impress of painting. "Sea Surface Full of Clouds" (1924) is as close as poetry can be to a series of Impressionistic seascapes; the spiral design of "Domination of Black" (1916) contains the visual dynamics of a painting. And in "Hibiscus on the Sleeping Shores" (1921), Stevens confirms his meaning and effect by a deft shift from a seascape ("the blue / And the colored purple of the lazy sea") to an urban detail that one might observe in a painting by Dufy ("the flaming red / Dabbled with yellow pollen—red as red / As the flag above the old cafe—"). Also, in the manuscript poem "For an Old

Woman in a Wig" (1916), Stevens describes a mood in terms of qualities characteristic of Monet's "Waterlilies":[1]

—There comes a mood that's taken
From water-deeps reflecting opening roses
And rounding, watery leaves, forever shaken,

And floating colors, which the mind supposes
In an imagination cut by sorrow.

With an Impressionist's sensibility, he insisted on the mutations of an object as observed under various shadings of light: in "Hymn from a Watermelon Pavilion" (1922), for example, the "dweller in the dark cabin," in his dream of night, is one "to whom the watermelon is always purple"; he ought to realize the cause for celebration he would have in seeing the melon in the dream of day. To heighten the the sense of light, color, and texture in his poems, Stevens

[1] Michel Benamou has also pointed to the similarity between Stevens and Monet in his essay "Wallace Stevens: Some Relations Between Poetry and Painting," *Comparative Literature*, xi (Winter 1959), 47-60. The essay is reprinted in *The Achievement of Wallace Stevens*, eds. Brown and Haller, pp. 232-248. The reference to Monet is on p. 234 in this volume. This is the key essay on the subject of Stevens and painting, valuable not only because it points out many specific associations between Stevens' techniques and those of modern painting, but also because it illuminates Stevens' metaphysics of art and reality and his understanding of modern painting theory. I concur fully with Benamou's central point in the essay, suggested in the following passages: Stevens' aesthetic "reconciles the Impressionist vision and Cézanne's world within a world" (p. 247); "naturalness and artificiality, delight in appearances and metamorphoses of appearances" (p. 238), "the world of an open-air landscapist; at the other extreme, it has the limits of the painter's studio" (p. 233); "he may very well go on record as a naturalist who thrived on artificiality" (p. 236). N.B. The whole of "For an Old Woman in a Wig" is quoted in note 3, Chapter viii.

on occasion deliberately chose technical terms of painting, like "daubed out" in "The Comedian as the Letter C" (1923); in "Banal Sojourn" (1919) "The sky is a blue gum streaked with rose." And to say in "The Apostrophe to Vincentine" (1918) "Your dress was green" is hardly remarkable, but to add "Was whited green" is to startle the reader, through a verbal approximation of painting technique, into a vivid mental recognition—the object realized in art. With such devices Stevens clarifies our vision; he indirectly evokes the actual by causing us to reflect on the resemblances between it and the visual and tactile qualities of paintings, even though his point of departure often seems to have been graphic art rather than an actual scene or experience.[2] This was just the case in the 1909 manuscript poem "Colors," where he transferred the colors of the Japanese prints to the page.

But Stevens seems to have realized the limitations of relying solely on the names of colors for effect; he even satirized the absurdity of the practice in "Bowl, Cat and Broomstick" (1917). In that unpublished playlet, a light treatise on poetry and aesthetics, the three characters discuss the work of a poetess named Claire Dupray.

BOWL [speaking of "Le Bouquet," one of her poems]:
She tries to stimulate the sense of color and, therefore, her poem consists of nothing more than the names of colors. You read these rapidly and so produce in the mind a visual impression like that produced by the actual sight of dahlias.

[2] And this was evidently his practice, on occasion, throughout his career, for his "Angel Surrounded by Peasants" (1950) was based on a painting by Tal Coat in his possession, now owned by Holly Stevens. Interestingly enough, the "angel" is a large vase in a still life, surrounded by smaller ones.

150

BROOMSTICK: And that is a poem?

CAT: Read just as rapidly as you can.

BOWL: Green, green, green—no doubt, this indicates the stalks—Green, green, green, green, green, yellow, green, yellow, green, green, gray, green, yellow, yellow, white, white, white, green—

BROOMSTICK: We ought to be getting to the flowers soon.

BOWL: We're right in them now. The white, white, white indicates white flowers, white dahlias.

But this is not just parody. However frivolous here, this is the Impressionist's technique, to put us right among the flowers, just as the manuscript poem "Colors" is an attempt to put us right among the colors and emotions of an unstated experience. Earlier in "Bowl, Cat and Broomstick," Bowl, in thumbing through Claire Dupray's volume of poems, comments,

> Banal Sojourn—Old catamaran—an amazing thing in the way it designs the catamaran on the surface of the sea: one of the poems in which by the description of the thing seen, she makes an image of the greatest intensity. Nothing in nature could have revealed what her imagination and sensibility have revealed. . . . Her poems are beautiful. Here are similar poems: Les Dahlias—The Dahlias—what an extraordinary effect one gets from seeing things as they are, that is to say: from looking at ordinary things intensely!

BROOMSTICK: But to look at ordinary things intensely, is not to see things as they are.[3]

[3] "Bowl, Cat and Broomstick" was written for Laura Sherry's Wisconsin Players and produced in the 1917-1918 season; it has

This is an important aesthetic matter, of course, one that Stevens dealt with twenty years later in all of its ramifications in "The Man with the Blue Guitar" (1936): "They said, 'You have a blue guitar, / You do not play things as they are.' / The man replied, 'Things as they are / Are changed upon the blue guitar.' " But what is important here is that in his use of color, Stevens was experimenting with one way of making an extraordinary effect, an intensity. Although "Colors" showed that graphic art is one thing and poetry another, it is clear that Stevens was searching for new ways to give his poetry visual concreteness and subtle emotional suggestion.

INDEED, from his earliest work on, Stevens revealed a visual acuity, a sensitivity to color and light, and an interest in paintings. We recall in the *Advocate* poem "Outside the Hospital" the curiosity of the "princess" regarding the color of the roses: "Red with a reddish light?" she asks. And the *Harmonium* poem "Cy Est Pourtraicte, Madame Ste Ursule, et Les Unze Mille Vierges" (1915) includes not only the Pre-Raphaelite maiden, St. Ursula, but also the color and atmosphere of a medieval painting, certainly appropriate to the situation in the poem: "With flowers, / Blue, gold, pink, green. / She dressed in red and gold brocade." Keats, too, with the clarity of sensuous imagery in his poetry, left his mark on Stevens' work—a lasting one,

---

never been published. See *Opus Posthumous*, p. xxvii. It is obvious that, as S. F. Morse has said in *Opus*, p. xxx, "The seeds of some of the best short poems in *Harmonium* seem to have fallen here" [in "Bowl, Cat and Broomstick"]. From the section quoted, for example, "Banal Sojourn" and "Surface of the Sea" were transformed into titles of *Harmonium* poems.

for Stevens appears to have had a detail from "The Eve of St. Agnes" in mind when he composed his "Credences of Summer," long after *Harmonium*. He says in a letter to Renato Poggioli, explaining the phrase "Half pales of red, / Half pales of green":

> The word pales is used in its heraldic sense [and again we note the medievalism adopted by the Pre-Raphaelites as well as by Keats]. . . . I have forgotten where it is in Keats, but there is a line describing moonlight falling through a stained glass window upon a floor. Keats used words something like this:
>
> and cast warm gules of red.
>
> This immediately led to a remark by some critic that moonlight passing through a window does not take on the color of the glass, as you may remember.[4]

And it was his sensitive eye—perhaps reading into earlier paintings the Impressionists' theory of broken color—that contributed to his statement in "Imagination as Value":

> There is . . . a Giorgione, the portrait of a young man, head and shoulders, in a blue-purple blouse, or if not blue-purple, then a blue of extraordinary enhancings. . . . This portrait is an instance of a real object that is at the same time an imaginative object.[5]

Through his technique, then, the painter was able to bring about such moments of correlation between the real and the imagined. The poet, Stevens realized, could learn from

---

[4] R. Poggioli, *Mattino Domenicale ed Altre Poesie* (Turin, 1954), p. 184, n. x.

[5] In *The Necessary Angel* (New York, 1951 and 1965), p. 152. Hereafter this book will be referred to parenthetically as *N. A.*

the painters, as well as from previous poets who made use of graphic, sensuous, and colorful imagery. He was alert to these qualities wherever he encountered them and in whatever period of art, but the impact of modern painting had a radical effect on his style. The techniques of Impressionism and the movements in painting that followed, along with the complementary and frequently overlapping poetic techniques of Symbolism and Imagism, provided new means for creating "a real object that is at the same time an imaginative object."

It was not until a truly representative selection of the new French painting was exhibited in America that the American poets who had stayed in this country discovered just how much they might learn from the art of painting. Referring back to the time of the 1913 Armory Show, William Carlos Williams was to say, "I think it was the French painters rather than the writers who influenced us, and their influence was great. They created an atmosphere of release, color release, release from stereotyped forms, trite subjects."[6] Stevens, too, reflected in "Effects of Analogy" (N. A., p. 124) that in "recent years, poetry began to change character about the time when painting began to change character." Surely the Armory Show must have meant at least as much to Williams and Stevens as it did to Arensberg. But whereas Arensberg became chiefly an admirer and collector, both Williams and Stevens were far more than connoisseurs in their reaction: they were challenged to transform the idiom of their own work. Before them hung the shocking freshness, color, and immediacy of the new paintings, a variety of new forms, and a new freedom and daring as well as certainty of purpose. No longer

[6] Williams, quoted in John Malcolm Brinnin, *William Carlos Williams* (Minneapolis, 1963), p. 14.

could they tolerate the "stereotyped forms" and "trite subjects" of conventional verse, for in that verse lay a falsifi-
cation of the imagination's encounter with reality.

The chief lesson, then, of the Cézannes, Gauguins, Van
Goghs, Renoirs, Matisses, Picassos, Braques, Picabias, Du-
champs and Villons was that the artist—poet as well as
painter—could cut through the approved academic criteria
for subject matter and technique. The collapse of the old
cultural order had made these criteria less tenable; they
had become a barrier between the artist and the object, the
reality he desired to render. Stevens and Williams, following
the lead of the Impressionists, were to achieve what Monet
desired—a primitive eye. They would recover from blind-
ness and see the world with utmost clarity, without pre-
conceptions. They would be like X in Stevens' "Anecdote
of Canna," who at daybreak "Observes the Canna with a
clinging eye," as though for the first time. In a letter, Stevens advised Williams on the need for visual scrutiny: "One
has to keep looking for poetry as Renoir looked for colors
in old walls, woodwork, and so on,"[7] not that Williams
really required such advice; it was simply part of an interchange of similar aesthetic viewpoints at a time when both
poets had achieved poetic maturity and before their inherent interests carried them along divergent poetic routes.

After the Armory Show, Stevens could no longer be content with such vaporous confections as the 1909 manuscript
poem "Shower"—"Pink and purple / In water mist"—or
"Here the grass grows" (1909, "Concert of Fishes"), with
its more indelible hues—"Blood-red and hue / Of shadowy
blue." But he would continue to use colors Impression-

[7] Stevens, quoted by Williams in Prologue to *Kora in Hell*,
1918; in *Selected Essays of William Carlos Williams* (New York,
1954), p. 13.

istically and symbolically; consider the blue-shadowed silk, which inspires a music of thought and feeling, and the green of earth in "Peter Quince," or this poem from "Carnet de Voyage" (1914) called "One More Sunset," an effort preliminary to "Sunday Morning":

> The green goes from the corn,
> The blue from all the lakes,
> And the shadows of the mountains mingle in the sky.
>
> Far off, the still bamboo
> Grows green; the desert pool
> Turns gaudy turquoise for the chanting caravan.
>
> The changing green and blue
> Flow round the changing earth;
> And all the rest is empty wondering and sleep.

The green of the earth and the reflected blue of the sky, interrelated yet separate, are momentarily united in the "gaudy turquoise for the chanting caravan"; it is a conjunction worthy of celebration, with the chanting caravan anticipating the ring of pagan men toward the end of "Sunday Morning," who "shall chant in orgy on a summer morn." Less fortunate are the arabesque caravan and the gaudy turquoise, exotic in the manner of travel-poster art. Still, despite their weaknesses, experiments like "One More Sunset" and "Colors" prepared Stevens for the accomplished control of color and light in "Sunday Morning," particularly in the first section, where a subtle darkening, "as a calm darkens among water-lights," causes the sunny chair, the green and the orange, to "seem things in some procession of the dead."

But let us look at "Sunday Morning" more closely, since part of its success comes from its fusion of earlier pictorial

styles and techniques and those derived from modern painting. In the design of the poem as a whole, the actual woman,
coffee, oranges, and sunny chair mingle with the artificial
pattern, "the green freedom of a cockatoo / Upon a rug,"
to form a total design in the manner of one of Matisse's
"Odalisque" paintings. Some of these details, as they become central motifs in the poem, undergo further metamorphoses, thus underscoring the theme of change and recurrence. The oranges become, successively, "pungent
fruit" (II), the "new plums and pears / On disregarded
plate" (V), the fruit of paradise that never falls (VI), and
finally the "sweet berries . . . in the wilderness" (VIII).
The cockatoo originates a bird-wing motif, seen in the
bright green wings (II) which recur after the procession of
the dead; in the "wakened birds" with "their sweet questionings" and the "swallow wings" (IV); in the simile "like
serafin," those winged celestial beings (VII); in the quail
whistling "their spontaneous cries" and the pigeons making
their "Ambiguous undulations as they sink, / Downward
to darkness, on extended wings" (VIII). The "wide water"
(I) becomes the static rivers of paradise (VI), the "windy
lake" (VII), and finally the "wide water, inescapable"
again (VIII). Other motifs, chiefly the alternations between earth and sky—reminding us of "One More Sunset"
—and parallels, like the archaic "hinds" associated with the
coming of Christ (III) and the living deer that "walk upon
our mountains" (VIII), also contribute to the design. The
result is an elaborate pattern or tapestry of life and death,
heaven, earth and art, embodied in the order and balance of
the poem. But because the poem is filled with a freshness
inspired by modern painting, it becomes much more than a
tapestry-like piece in the manner of the Pre-Raphaelites or
an arrangement of symbols and colors in the manner of the

157

Symbolists. The poem combines styles drawn from the preceding era and from the contemporary one, including the "savage source" (VII), an element perhaps influenced by the vogue for the primitive in modern painting and sculpture during the period when "Sunday Morning" was composed.[8]

BUT IN Matisse, especially, Stevens found a kindred spirit, whose special genius seems not only to have inspired the opening lines of "Sunday Morning," but also to have left its effect on the poem as a whole and on Stevens' later work. Matisse's ability to transform a pagan joy in life into highly civilized terms, his reverence for life that transcends hedonism, his audacious juxtapositions of colors which ought to clash but instead exhibit new relations and harmonious effects, his combination of the excitement of colors and forms with the stasis and calm achieved in the flattened perspectives of his canvases, his frequent practice of joining the outdoors and indoors into one pattern by framing the light and life of an outside scene in a window of an elegant room, and his conversion of the arabesques of Art Nouveau into his own modern style: all suggest qualities that help to characterize "Sunday Morning," in which the gaudiness of the oranges and the green freedom of the ornate cockatoo pattern in the rug are absorbed into the dreamy, almost static, but profound meditation. In many later *Harmonium* poems the color is less subdued. Crispin, in "The Comedian as the Letter C," finds the colors of a Fauvist's palette in nature: "Into a savage color he went on." He refers to Maya sonneteers who ignore, among other birds, the green toucans, and continue making their pleas

[8] See Benamou's analysis of the pictorial element in "Sunday Morning," *Achievement*, pp. 239-240.

to the night-bird (presumably the nightingale), "As if rasp-
berry tanagers in palms, / High up in orange air were bar-
barous"—and the color combination, at least, is "barbar-
ous," except as Matisse or Stevens would urbanely render it.
But Stevens realized that one could not rest in the immense
satisfaction derived from such combinations. In "Indian
River" (1917), the beauty of "the red-bird breasting the
orange-trees," however pleasing, becomes part of the monotonous "jingle" of existence because "there is no spring in
Florida." Stevens' interest was in the fortuitous recognition
of ideal beauty within change. Matisse was concerned more
with capturing beauty than change, and his method was
only one way of asserting artistic control over nature's force
and vibrance.

Once the Impressionists had conducted their experiments with broken color in order to capture the effects of
light and tone on the subjects under their scrutiny and had
greatly changed the conception of perspective, they opened
the way for more radical experiments in color and form.
These experiments were eagerly pursued not only by Matisse but also by the Pointilists (a hint of whose work seems
to occur in one detail in *Harmonium*: the "cloths be-
sprinkled with colors / As small as fish eggs" in "The Plot
Against the Giant," 1917), and by such individual artists as
Van Gogh and Gaugin, and by the Fauves and Expression-
ists in general. The two latter groups, with their use of color
for nonnaturalistic effects, with their deliberate distortions,
and with their propensity for blocking out their canvases
with large masses of primary, discordant colors, offered Stevens glaring evidence of ways the artist could project his
subjective sense of the beauty and the irrational forces in
life. As a result, at the end of "Disillusionment of Ten
O'Clock" (1915), the drama of the drunken sailor's suc-

cessful nightmare activity is heightened by the visual impact of the colors: he "Catches tigers / In red weather." When, at the beginning of this poem, Stevens contrasts the imaginative poverty of white nightgowns with the bizarre richness of the imagined gowns of green "Or purple with green rings. / Or green with yellow rings, / Or yellow with blue rings," he demonstrates that he could be as brash and playful, and as provocative, with colors as modern painters often were.

Example follows example of his uses of color as a means of projecting his or his speakers' attitudes. In "Peter Quince" the grotesque and humorous deathly "white elders" rudely interrupt the blue and green harmony with their "red-eyed lust." Against the black of negation, Stevens would, as he said in "The Comedian as the Letter C," arrange his "Incredible hues," would "spread chromatics in hilarious dark," as he does in "Domination of Black," the swirling leaves, peacock, and flames playing their parts in evoking a complex emotion of dread and dazzlement at the weird beauty. In "Anecdote of the Prince of Peacocks" (1923), an eerie collocation of colors contributes to the disturbing effect of the invasion of the world of moonlight and dream by Berserk, who personifies the violence of day. "Why," the speaker asks him, "Are you red / In this milky blue?" The first two lines in "The Naked Eye of the Aunt"[9] create an effect as unpleasantly grotesque as nearly anything in Baudelaire's poems and as appalling as the horror-stricken emaciated beings in a lithograph or etching by Edvard Munch: "I peopled the dark park with gowns / In which were yellow, rancid skeletons." Toward the end of

[9] This was the title given to the two stanzas in *Opus* originally meant for "Le Monocle de Mon Oncle," properly excluded because of their brittle dandyism.

the first stanza, the "green bosoms and black legs" convey a febrile, mordant eroticism that one might expect of Toulouse-Lautrec. With green and black again, Stevens in "Thirteen Ways of Looking at a Blackbird" (1917) presents a spooky intimation—"blackbirds / Flying in a green light"—that would seem to owe as much to theatrical lighting as to a painting, though the effect is Expressionistic either way. Whether defined as Expressionistic or Symbolic, however, these examples constitute only a partial catalogue of the variety of effects Stevens achieved with his incredible hues and with black and white.

The atmosphere of dream and nightmare evident in a number of the examples above is as significant as the colors which accentuate it. By drawing on the distortions of dream experience in the manner of some of the modern painters, Stevens found further means of projecting the subjective sense on the object, giving it the strange lucidity that we encounter in our own dream states. By the metamorphic imagery of dream, the fourth landscape in "Six Significant Landscapes" (1916), brings a romantic vastness and beauty within the range of human assimilation. The landscape includes some of the bejeweled atmosphere characteristic of Mallarmé and Baudelaire but also qualities similar to those in a painting by Klee or Chagall.

> When my dream was near the moon,
> The white folds of its gown
> Filled with yellow light.
> The soles of its feet
> Grew red.
> Its hair filled
> With certain blue crystallizations
> From stars,
> Not far off.

161

Because of the hallucinatory effect, space shrinks, the imagination expands, and the illogical perspective surprises the reader into a recognition of heavenly grandeur. Compare this with the attempt to achieve a similar effect in the final stanza of the manuscript poem "April" (1908):

> Sweeping green Mars, beyond
> Antique Orion,
> Beyond the Pleiades,
> To vivid Zion.

It speaks of vividness; the later poem projects it pictorially. Chagall comes to mind again when the woman who speaks in Stevens' "Explanation" (1917) regrets that she had not imagined herself "In an orange gown, / Drifting through space, / Like a figure on the church-wall." The image has a Chagall-like otherworldly charm. And when the sea in "The Doctor of Geneva" (1921) sets the rationalist's mind "Spinning and hissing with oracular / Notations of the wild, the ruinous waste," the effect is reinforced with an image that might well have been inspired by the paintings of Kandinsky: "the steeples of his city clanked and sprang / In an unburgherly apocalypse."

Such imagery often brought Stevens to the edge of Surrealism, which has much in common with Expressionism; but he skirted it because he desired to accomplish more than presenting the unconscious as a manipulated flight from reality or as a witty exercise indulged in for its superficial surprises. "The essential fault of surrealism," he was to say in "Adagia" (*Opus*), "is that it invents without discovering. To make a clam play an accordion is to invent not to discover. The observation of the unconscious, so far as it can be observed, should reveal things of which we have previously been unconscious, not the familiar things of which we have been conscious plus imagination." What Stevens desired and could observe in modern painting were those pictorial formulations of the strange and unpredictable, those dream- and nightmare-like scenes which nonetheless depict parts of our real, perhaps most profound (if unconscious) experience.

In the manuscript poem "For an Old Woman in a Wig" (1916) one phrase, "the green-planed hills," would seem pertinent to the flat prismatic ordering in a Cézanne landscape. Cézanne worked out those techniques which enabled him to impose aesthetic logic on nature and at the same time adhere to the essential spirit of his subject; his landscapes are marked by pronounced abstract patterns within the shimmering, luminous scenes they depict, and his still lifes—which in their rich, clean color and form seem detached from the physical world—convey nevertheless a sense of physical substance, vivid as life itself. The attraction Cézanne's work held for Stevens, however, is at best elusively reflected in *Harmonium*. Even the phrase "the green-planed hills" is a tenuous example of Stevens' interest; indirectly the influence of Cézanne may have been great, but the effect of the lessons Stevens learned from him seems more evident in the later poetry. *Harmonium* shows much more clearly Stevens' interest in the techniques of Cézanne's artistic descendants, the Cubists.

These painters, in refusing to submit to natural or cultural confusion, imposed by sheer will an abstract, faceted order upon the multiplicity of experience—reducing the object to fragments and then restructuring it. Stevens' "The Public Square" (1923) begins with a stanza that strongly suggests the Cubist mode:

163

> A slash of angular blacks
> Like a fractured edifice
> That was buttressed by blue slants
> In a coma of the moon.

Then, with something of a surrealistic quality, "the edifice fell";

> A mountain-blue cloud arose
> Like a thing in which they fell,

> Fell slowly as when at night
> A languid janitor bears
> His lantern through the colonnades
> And the architecture swoons.

In "Anecdote of the Prince of Peacocks" (1923) the prince encounters the sharply defined traps set for him by Berserk; they have a Cubistic angularity: "the blue ground / Was full of blocks / And blocking steel." In the fifth landscape of "Six Significant Landscapes" such angularity is combined with the Imagistic comparisons which chiefly define the scene: "the knives of the lamp-posts," "the chisels of the long streets," "the mallets of the domes / And high towers." The women in "Floral Decorations for Bananas" (1923) who "will be all shanks / And bangles and slatted eyes" would appear to bear a family resemblance to Duchamp's "Nude Descending A Staircase," which reminded one critic at the time of the Armory Show of an explosion in a shingle factory. In a more serious vein in "Metaphors of a Magnifico" (1918), Stevens seems to have the Cubists' ability to see different perspectives of an object simultaneously; the soldiers are twenty men crossing a bridge, or twenty men crossing twenty bridges, or one man crossing one bridge. One must assimilate the multiplicity here just as the viewer of Duchamp's painting must assimilate the fragmentation and multiplicity of the nude descending the staircase. It is the problem posed for the reader of Stevens' earlier poem "Thirteen Ways of Looking at a Blackbird" (1917), the title of which alludes humorously to the Cubists' practice of incorporating into unity and stasis a number of possible views of the subject observed over a span of time; thus the poem combines at least a recognition of Cubism along with what it owes to Imagism and the art of the haiku.

Stevens made no wholesale borrowings from the Cubists, no matter how much he admired Picasso and Braque, but he could sympathize strongly with their anti-academicism and with their ordering the raw material of experience into tense symmetry. The Cubists no doubt encouraged his own aesthetic daring, and at the same time their stringent subjection of matter to form must have acted as a check on his luxuriance of imagination, so that even his most extravagant poems are tightly controlled.[10] Nevertheless, the geometry in the approach of the Cubists was too rigid for Stevens. For him, the mind must constantly reach its new accords with nature, capturing its fluidity in poetic form that does not because of its abstraction exclude life. For him, Cubism, like Imagism, was a maneuver in the direction of art for art's sake; modernists could arrive there as readily as the late nineteenth-century aesthetes. Stevens had a more inclusive aim in mind.

EVEN SO, with his great interest in painting of all schools, Stevens almost constantly took this risk. The saving grace

[10] One cannot help thinking here, incidentally, that Brancusi's sculpture must have had a similar salutary effect, with its absolute purity of form—form in nature abstracted.

for him, however, was that he so clearly recognized the danger. "A perfect fruit in perfect atmosphere," he says with derisive tone in the final section of "New England Verses" (1923); "Nature as Pinakothek. Whist!" and he calls for Chanticleer to herald actual day, regardless of his profound desire for the perfect fruit. And yet without art, without the Pinakothek, the interdependence between the ideal and the actual collapses; Stevens avoided this other danger partly by his habit of seeing nature through the painter's eye. The problem is dramatized in "Anecdote of the Jar" (1919); there the speaker would arrange, if he could, the wild landscape into the order of a still life. His success is qualified, but art and the imagination do at least impose an idea of order that creates a bond between the speaker and sprawling reality.

To extend the point about seeing nature through the painter's eye: just as the painter transforms reality into a reality on canvas, that new reality prepares the observer, in the constant interplay between art and nature, to return to the actual, and discover there what he had not realized before. So it was with Stevens, who, with his eye educated by modern art, reacted to those qualities in nature which had their counterparts in the paintings, discovering not only new sources of beauty and color and light but also the essential energy, even violence, in nature itself. Perhaps it was the new paintings which to a great extent lay behind his enthusiastic response to the actual Florida landscape and led to the eruption in the later *Harmonium* poems of the florid, sensuous, and often wild imagery of the subtropics. It is often a jungle world that is presented, as in "Nomad Exquisite" (1923): "the immense dew of Florida / Brings forth / The big-finned palm / And green vine angering for life." In "Floral Decorations for Bananas" (1923) it is this violent beauty and sexual energy that must be brought into a new decorum, controlled by the art of floral arrangement or of the still life, though here the details threaten to ooze and dart from the "canvas":

> And deck the bananas in leaves
> Plucked from the Carib trees,
> Fibrous and dangling down,
> Oozing cantankerous gum
> Out of their purple maws,
> Darting out of their purple craws
> Their musky and tingling tongues.

If this imagery seems extravagant, it is extravagant in the manner of modern painting—or of tropical life; Stevens had found the poetic means to present those qualities in nature which flourish in Florida, Central America, and the Caribbean, as well as a flamboyant means of conveying one of his central themes. The modern painters suggested several ways of admitting violence into their works while controlling it aesthetically. Wordsworth never faced the problem, posed by Aldous Huxley in our time, of adjusting his view of nature to the tropics' "angering for life," but Stevens, with Wordsworthian outlook, did face it, if only in the semitropics. And in the matter of style this meant a striking addition to what he had derived from *fêtes galantes* paintings and poetry, from the Pre-Raphaelites, from orientalism—and even from the Impressionists.

Painting in many ways, then, dramatized for Stevens the function of the artist—to reconcile or balance his rage for order with the inconstancy and force of life that impinge upon him and threaten to overthrow the control his imagination asserts. And as he became increasingly aware that "poetry and reality are one," modern painting suggested to him further means of rendering that fusion, for establishing the "blissful liaison" he sought. The price he paid is the art-gallery or hothouse atmosphere that is a part of the total effect of *Harmonium*. What he gained is the freshness and brilliance, the dense palpability and visual clarity, the essence of the object observed. A follower of all the movements in modern painting, he learned most perhaps from the Impressionists. Henry James defined Impressionism in literature as a "hovering flight of the subjective over the outstretched ground of the case exposed."[11] For the Impressionist and for Stevens, technique must render the "case exposed" with the utmost lucidity and immediacy. This aim parallels and complements the Symbolists' aim to divine the correspondences between the subjective and objective and to present them in ineffable correlations of word, music, and symbol, and the Imagists' aim to capture unique resemblances, presenting them with an objective exactness of image, diction, and rhythm. For Stevens, "The world about us would be desolate except for the world within us,"[12] and his desire to bring these two worlds together on the page, in the poem, was fulfilled to a great extent by the overlapping techniques of these three movements.

[11] James, *The Future of the Novel*, ed. Leon Edel (New York, 1956), p. 281.
[12] "The Relations Between Poetry and Painting," *N. A.*, p. 169.

VII. Dandy, Eccentric, Clown

WHEN Pound, Williams, Eliot, Stevens, and others rebelled against the verse written by prominent American poets during the Nineties and early years of the new century, one of the main strategies for subverting the respectable, almost unfailing solemnity of this verse, with its poetical pieties and pallid idealism, was to turn deliberately to the irony, wit, satire, and humor that these earlier poets had largely excluded. This strategy not only broke through the narrowly circumscribed view of what was suitable poetic language and tone; it also enabled the poet to explore a wider spectrum of human experience. And since the rebels were themselves poets with vulnerable sensibilities in an age that held no respect for poetry, they could use such rhetorical devices as irony for a protective covering.

The poet's misuse of irony, of course, can undermine his intentions as effectively as sentimentality can. In avoiding unguarded emotional expression, the poet can create too much detachment and distance and thus obscure meaning and emotion altogether. Or the ironic can be too firmly allied to an underlying cynicism or futility, as it was with Donald Evans. Also, it can be merely flippant, containing too much that is merely antibourgeois and depending too much on shock effect for its own sake. It could in the period under discussion be simply a repudiation of the nineteenth-century moral stance, without containing anything positive in itself. Stevens did not fully escape these dangers, but irony, wit, and the bizarre enabled him to present the romantic in new guises, just as they enabled him to become bolder, less fragilely aesthetic. The Elizabethans and Jacobeans had found that wit, irony, the comic, and the grotesque were not incompatible with a serious analysis of man's condition. And if Laforgue's transformation of Hamlet through bizarre irony does not achieve the tragedy and depth in Shakespeare's play so much as it conveys the pathetic plight of princely aspirations in the modern world, it reveals one of the recourses for a poet in our era.

Stevens' innate sense of the ironic and comic incongruities in life, combined with his abiding interest in the interactions between reality and imagination, accounts for the great variety of witty, humorous, grotesque, and satirical effects in his verse, effects apparent as early as his Harvard stories and the "Ballade of the Pink Parasol." In this poem and in the early manuscript poems, he used the delicate, nostalgic irony and wit of the rococo and *fêtes galantes* traditions, as exemplified by Austin Dobson and Verlaine. But Dobson was no Alexander Pope, and one feels Pope's presence in *Harmonium* much more strongly than Dobson's, whose best work appears exceedingly shallow and dainty when placed beside a poem like "The Rape of the Lock." This poem of Pope's especially, with its civilizing mockery of social imbalance, its delight in the very world it gaily punctures, its brilliance of conception, its grace of wit, humor, and phrasing, and its underlying serious affirmation of an appropriate decorum that makes human intercourse possible, has many affinities with Stevens' own outlook and style, even though specific parallels are not evident. Similarly, as he absorbed other influences, he refined the antiphilistinism and macabre irony which delighted him in such Decadents as Wilde and Beardsley. Then, seeking more forceful ways to present the inner violence of the imagination, he found further models in the French Symbolists and ironists, in stage comedy, especially the Elizabethan, and in native American humor. In fact, as he converted all of these approaches to his own use, they became interfused, modifying and reinforcing one another.[1]

In his dandyism, for example, Stevens seems to have proceeded simultaneously in two directions from his starting point, the gentle and despairing irony of Pierrot. On the one hand, he moved toward the citified dandyism suggested by Baudelaire and Laforgue; here it was natural for him to appropriate some of the innovations of the whole nineteenth-century French ironist tradition, with its antibourgeois, antirationalist tendencies—and thus he was carried beyond mere dandyism. On the other hand, he moved toward the clowns and fops of stage comedy, toward Peter Quince and Crispin;[2] again, the movement is beyond mere dandyism. And in both cases, this movement was also toward more vigorous disguises.

[1] See Daniel Fuchs, *The Comic Spirit of Wallace Stevens* (Durham, N.C., 1963), for an extensive study of Stevens' irony and humor. His first chapter, "Stevens' Comic Milieu," defines the nature of Stevens' comic spirit by comparing his qualities with those of precursors and contemporaries.

[2] See Michel Benamou, "Jules Laforgue and Wallace Stevens," *The Romanic Review*, L, 2 (April 1959); he says "Stevens' Pierrot became metamorphosed into a heroic, if comic figure of celebration—from Pierrot to Hoon" (p. 109). I am much indebted to this essay in my own discussion of Stevens and Laforgue later in this chapter and agree with his observation that "it was the artist in Laforgue, and not the Pierrot, who attracted Stevens most" (p. 107)—yet this is not for a moment to diminish the importance of the Pierrot, who after all was essential to the art. See also H. R. Hays, "Laforgue and Wallace Stevens," *The Romanic Review*, xxv, 3 (July-September 1934); he suggests that Stevens is more of a realist than Laforgue (p. 245). Also, Hugh Kenner's discussion of Eliot's derivations from Laforgue, in his chapter "Laforgue and Others" in *The Invisible Poet: T. S. Eliot* (New York, 1959), throws light on Stevens' own derivations.

171

Carlos, in "Carlos Among the Candles" (1917; *Opus*), and Bowl, in the manuscript play "Bowl, Cat and Broomstick" (1917) are cousins of Pierrot and equally ineffectual. They are rococo eccentrics, evidently drawn from French stage comedy. Carlos is described as "an eccentric pedant of about forty. He is dressed in black. He wears close-fitting breeches and a close-fitting, tightly-buttoned, short coat with long tails. His hair is rumpled. . . . He speaks in a lively manner, but is overnice in sounding his words." Stevens describes Bowl as wearing "a gown falling below his knees. It is black covered with a faded silver pattern. Flat Hat. Jewel in the hat. Black stockings. Small silver buckles on his shoes." He speaks with "finical importance." Stevens, with his versions of Pierrot and foppish pedants, was parodying his own position, exaggerating the poet's absurdity in the light of ordinary experience, so that he could present his serious themes without seeming ponderous. But these figures are too quaint and precious, like the name Peter Parasol, which Stevens used as a title for a fugitive poem (1919; *Opus*) and as a pseudonym when he sent his serious war poem "Phases" to *Poetry* in 1914. His themes and his muse demanded more effective means of countering the tedium and discord in life.

ONE WAY was to include more directly the negations of existence, particularly those of the modern world, as Baudelaire and Laforgue had done—with the influence of Laforgue on Stevens being the stronger in this regard. Stevens was aware of the profound negations of earthly life, but he did not seem to be burdened by the extreme sense of evil and diabolism which underlay Baudelaire's dandyism. Thus his work contains few specific borrowings from Baudelaire's hell, though Baudelaire's ironic "A Une Madone," with its

Madonna, daggers, mockery, and desire, may have supplied a few hints for the first section of Stevens' more gay "Le Monocle de Mon Oncle" (1918). But however grim and ironic Stevens might be at times, it was not often in Baudelaire's manner; Stevens' point of view was more comic, and his dandyism was more in the manner of Laforgue.

It is true that after the formative stage of his career Stevens had fewer and fewer elements in his style that can be attributed to Laforgue, but Laforgue seems to have been a very important influence behind Stevens' bringing into his poetry more naturalistic detail and the modern city with its meaninglessness, and his acquiring a surer hand in the ironic manipulation of the actual and the romantic. Laforgue's irony is not, however, merely that of the nonchalant dandy of "Solo de Lune" ("Je fume, étalé face au ceil / Sur l'imperiale de la diligence"); it is also a cosmic irony based on the sense of being isolated in a vast, alien universe. The irony hardly covers the despair, the uncertainty. As he said in "Complainte de Lord Pierrot," "Où commence, où finit l'humaine / Ou la divine dignité? / Jonglons avec les entités. . . ." In "Le Concile Féerique" the earth "C'est un bien pauv'monde / Dans l'infini bleu"; his uncertainty is similar to Stevens' in "Domination of Black" (1916): "I saw how the planets gathered / Like the leaves themselves / Turning in the wind. / I saw how night came, / . . . / I felt afraid." Laforgue's poetry is full of an autumnal mood, of cold winds and grey skies, of rain. Stevens' "Domination of Black," in which he expressed fear in the midst of a naturalistic universe, seems to have several antecedents in Laforgue's poetry: not only is there the autumnal setting, but we also find the blackness, the wind, and the fire. In Laforgue's "Noire Bise," there is also a "domination of black":

> La nuit est à jamais noire,
> Le vent est grandement triste,
> Tout dit la vieille histoire
> Qu'il faut être deux au coin feu,
> Tout bâcle un hymne fataliste. . . .

And perhaps in writing his "hymne fataliste" Stevens recalled "the cry of the peacocks" from Laforgue's "Le Concile Féerique": ". . . le triste / Cor des paons réveille fait que plus rien n'existe!"

It seems clear that "Domination of Black" was to an important extent made possible by examples from Laforgue, which suggested ways of including a sense of fear and isolation in a naturalistic universe while at the same time transcending the negation by a highly charged, moving tour de force of art:

> The colors of their tails
> Were like the leaves themselves
> Turning in the wind,
> In the twilight wind.
>
> .   .   .   .
>
> I heard them cry—the peacocks.
> Was it a cry against the twilight
> Or against the leaves themselves
> Turning in the wind . . .

Such an accomplishment stands out all the more clearly when compared with the *fin de siècle* negation and futility in these lines from the fifth poem of "Carnet de Voyage" (*Trend,* 1914):

> . . . The new born swallows fare
> Through the spring twilight on dead September wing.
> The dust of Babylon is in the air
> And settles on my lips the while I sing.

174

From this mere competence in the manner of the Nineties to the control of color, cadence, and design for the forceful effect of "Domination of Black" is a major advance in Stevens' art.

Laforgue's pessimism sprang not only from the negation of the universe but also from contemporary cultural emptiness. He dealt ironically with this emptiness by bringing Pierrot into the bleakness of the modern city. Although the speakers in the *Harmonium* poems do not seem as neurotically paralyzed by the world as Laforgue's do, they are often individuals of refined sensibility, connoisseurs, who are out of tune with materialistic ugliness. "Faudra-t-il vivre monotone?" asks Laforgue in "Complainte D'un Certain Dimanche." Stevens would often ask essentially the same question, but his despair is modified by his exuberance. Such qualifications aside, it would seem that under Laforgue's influence Stevens brought the modern city into his poetry, "toute la misère des grands centres."

It is the monotony, the emptiness, the meaninglessness of city life which distresses the two poets more than the misery, however. Notice, for example, the similarity between Laforgue and Stevens in their choice of details representative of the domestic bourgeois culture of the city. Several details have to do with that dull task, sewing: "Soeur faisait du crochet"; "Et les voilà qui rebrodent / Le canevas ingrat de leur âme à la mode"; "Avec ces anonymes en robes grises, / Dans la prière, le ménage, les travaux de couture"; and " 'Tu nous laiss's et tu t'en vas, / . . . / Broder d'éternels canevas.' / . . . . / . . . peut-être brodent-elles / Pour un oncle à dot, des bretelles?"[3] Sew-

---

[3] Beginning with "tout la misère," the Laforgue quotations are from the following poems: "L'Hiver Qui Vient"; "Complainte de L'Oubli des Morts"; "Complainte d'une Convalescence en Mai";

ing becomes a motif in several of Stevens' poems: "That sheet / On which she embroidered fantails once . . . ," "Ach, Mutter, / This old, black dress, / I have been embroidering / French flowers on it," and "What breech-cloth might you wear— / Except linen, embroidered / By elderly women?" (contrasted to a breech-cloth "Netted of topaz and ruby / And savage blooms").[4] But even these examples of Stevens' contain a buoyancy characteristic of his difference from Laforgue.

Stevens also used other Laforguian details to evoke urban emptiness, such as, "The wind attendant on the solstices / Blows on the shutters of the metropoles," in "The Man Whose Pharynx Was Bad" (1921). "Chiaroscuro," an early manuscript poem (composed around 1907 or 1908, according to information in letters, Stevens' daughter reports) uses such an atmosphere:

> The house-fronts flare
> In blown rain.
> The ghostly street lamps
> Have a pallid glare.
>
> A wanderer beats
> With bitter droop,
> Along the waste
> Of vacant streets.

"Noire Bise"; and "Complainte des Pianos Qu'on Entend Dans Les Quartiers Aises."

[4] Beginning with "That sheet / On which . . . ," the Stevens quotations are from the following poems: "The Emperor of Ice-Cream"; "Explanation"; and "Exposition of the Contents of a Cab." "Exposition . . ." was in the first edition of *Harmonium* (1923); now in *Opus*.

Suppose some glimmer
Recalled for him
An odorous room,
A fan's fleet shimmer

Of silvery spangle,
Two startled eyes,
A still-trembling hand
And its only bangle.

The rain, ghostly street lamps, and the waste of vacant streets are elements in a typical Laforgue urban landscape: "Jette sur le pavé de chaque boulevard / . . . sous le gaz blafard," from "La Première Nuit," and "Grelottants et voûtés sous le poids des foulards / Au gaz jaune et mourant des brumeaux boulevards," from "Couchant D'Hiver," are very similar in detail and tone to what one finds in Stevens' poem, although "bitter droop" is lamentable, especially compared with "voûtés sous le poids des foulards." The poem, in its contrast of vacant streets and the "still-trembling hand / And its only bangle," seems a poor attempt in the manner of Eliot's "Love Song of J. Alfred Prufrock"—not that Stevens was imitating Eliot, whose poem appeared in *Poetry* in June 1915. But both poets used the method of contrast between Laforguian streets and elegant feminine beauty for their own quite different purposes. Eliot used bored women with braceleted arms not only to suggest the spiritual emptiness of contemporary upper classes but also as a focal point for Prufrock's sexual inhibitions and his paralysis of will; Eliot is more psychological than Stevens, whose woman, in an atmosphere of Mallarméan odorous richness evokes a sense of imaginative beauty in contrast to the naturalistic emptiness outside. This method of ironic juxtaposition, which grew naturally out of his thematic concern with imagination and reality, became sharpened, after its first uses in the undergraduate work, by the influence of Symbolism and Laforguian elements. In "Chiaroscuro" the device is too arbitrary, too obvious, the result too much a pastiche, but Stevens learned to play many more subtle variations on this method, as in "Tea" (1915), which seems to be a maturer version of the manuscript poem.

Laforgue discovered a number of ways to ridicule the *bourgeoisie*. He does so with considerable humor and wit in "Complainte des Pianos Qu'on Entend Dans les Quartiers Aises," as is evident in these passages:

> Ces enfants, à quoi rêvent-elles,
> Dans les ennuis des ritournelles?
>
> —"Préaux des soirs,
> Christs des dortoirs! . . ."

. . . .

> Mon Dieu, à quoi donc rêvent-elles?
> À des Roland, à des dentelles?
>
> —"Cœurs en prison,
> Lentes saisons! . . ."

And what Stevens assimilated from such poems contributed to his treatment of bourgeois dullness in his lightly satirical "Disillusionment of Ten O'Clock (1915); here the empty monotony of white nightgowns (one thinks here of Laforgue's "Anonymes en robes grises" referred to earlier) and of people going to bed punctually at ten is contrasted with the bizarrely colored gowns, "purple with green rings," and the "socks of lace / And beaded ceintures."

178

But also in contrast to the regularity of ten o'clock bed-times is the irrational world of "an old sailor" who "dreams of baboons and periwinkles" and of catching tigers "In red weather." Stevens in "Disillusionment" presents an imaginative violence against the meaningless regularity and order of the literal-minded, and it is quite possible that a reading of Corbière had some influence here. In "La Fin," Corbière with his customary swaggering irony contrasts the life in death of the ordinary sailor with the death in life of those on land:

> . . . L'âme d'un matelot
> Au lieu de suinter dans vos pommes de terre,
> Respire à chaque flot.

Earlier in the poem an association of sailors, boots, and drink parallels Stevens' "old sailor, / Drunk and asleep in his boots": ". . . ils sont morts dans leurs bottes! / Leur *boujaron* au cœur, tout vifs dans leurs capotes. . . ."[5]

Corbière's influence is perhaps evident also in two images in "Peter Quince," which could possibly be transformations from a stanza in Corbière's "Insomnie":

> Insomnie, es-tu l'Hystérie . . .
> Es-tu l'orgue de barbarie,
> Qui moud l'*Hosannah* des Élus?
> —Ou n'es-tu pas l'éternel plectre,
> Sur les nerfs des damnés-de-lettre,
> Raclant leurs vers—qu'eux seuls ont lus?

[5] Benamou in "Wallace Stevens and the Symbolist Imagination," *ELH*, 31 (March 1964), p. 43, n. 20, cites lines in Baudelaire's "Le Voyage" as a possible source of Stevens' conception here. Both are relevant, and it is also possible that Corbière may have played on the themes of Baudelaire in his own way.

The witty, ironic treatment of the disagreeable, the odd juxtaposition of Hosannah with the ordinary barrel organ, the playing of music on the nerves, all have much in common with Stevens' passage concerning the "red-eyed elders," who felt

> The basses of their beings throb
> In witching chords, and their thin blood
> Pulse pizzicati of Hosanna.

And perhaps the final three lines of Corbière's stanza lie behind Stevens' lines:

> Susanna's music touched the bawdy strings
> Of those white elders; but escaping
> Left only Death's ironic scraping.

Michel Benamou suggests a line in Laforgue's "Sieste Éternelle," "L'Archet qui sur nos nerfs pince ces tristes gammes," as a source for the above lines, which indicates how difficult it is to pin down specific sources for lines in Stevens' poems, so thoroughly had he assimilated his wide reading.[6] But at least the discussion of Corbière suggests that Laforgue was not the only inspiration behind Stevens' ironic treatment of the conflict between the romantic and the bourgeois. In "Petit Mort Pour Rire" Corbière advises the poet "—Les bourgeois sont bêtes— / Va vite, léger peigneur de comètes!"

THE REFERENCES to Baudelaire, Laforgue, and Corbière can only begin to suggest how much Stevens owed to the French for the nature of his own irony. One cannot demonstrate any specific parallels between his poetry and that of Valéry Larbaud, for example, but William Jay Smith has

---

[6] See *Romanic Review* (April 1959), p. 113.

alluded to their general similarity in some respects.[7] In both a suave dandyism flourishes in a setting of luxurious sea travel to exotic places. Mallarmé's poetry could be ironic and satirical as well as rarefied and musical, and a distinct parallel exists between Mallarmé's wicked "Une Negresse . . ." and Stevens' lighter "The Virgin Carrying a Lantern" (1923) for both concern an unusual infatuation of a Negress for a young girl. Also Samuel French Morse suggests that Stevens' "Peter Parasol" imitates Apollinaire's irony.[8] Pertinent, too, is the general example of Rimbaud's fantastic, discordant irony; might not some of the extravagant tropical and storm imagery in Stevens' "The Comedian as the Letter C"—the "savagery of palms, / . . . the thick cadaverous bloom / That yuccas breed, and of the panther's tread," as well as "the valet in the tempest was annulled"— owe something to the extraordinary odyssey of Rimbaud's "Le Bateau Ivre" with its "incroyables Florides / Mêlant aux fleurs des yeux de panthères à peaus / D'hommes!" and "La têmpete a béni mes éveils maritimes"?

Whether or not "Le Bateau Ivre" was partial inspiration for "The Comedian," the glorification of the irrational, which appeared as early as 1915 in Stevens' "Disillusionment of Ten O'Clock," played an increasingly important part in the *Harmonium* poems. Insofar as irony often pre-

[7] See Smith's Introduction to his translation of Larbaud's *Poems of a Multi-Millionaire* (New York, 1955).

[8] W. Y. Tindall mentioned the association of Mallarmé's "Negresse" and Stevens' "Virgin" in *Wallace Stevens* (Minneapolis, 1961), p. 18. Morse says of "Peter Parasol": "Stevens intended the poem to be an imitation of the ironic sentimentalities that Apollinaire handles with such skill in *Le Bestaire* . . . and *Alcools,* but it does not quite come off." See "Wallace Stevens, Bergson, Pater," *ELH*, 31 (March 1964), p. 2, n. 2.

sents the fantastic in opposition to what is commonly considered as valid knowledge of reality through reason, it is, like Symbolism, a function of the irrational approach to experience. This approach had a profound effect on Stevens' imagery and technique. He filled his poems not only with wit, but with a surprising and often disconcerting sense of the layers of awareness ignored by the rationalist. Stevens, in his essay "The Irrational Element in Poetry," cited Rimbaud along with Mallarmé and Freud as major sources of this element in modern poetry.[9] In part, this essay may be taken as explanation of his own practice, for the poems of *Harmonium* were written during a time of growing interest in the workings of the unconscious—with the amount of imagery in *Harmonium* based on dreams seeming to reflect this interest. And what he found in the French poets from Baudelaire on paralleled the irrational element he observed in modern painting. Stevens was ready for such inspiration, from whatever sources, having even at Harvard shown an interest in the fantastic and irrational, particularly in the farcical and nightmarish confusion of the prose sketch "In the Middle of the Night."

A group of four manuscript poems exemplifies Stevens' interest in the irrational; three of them attempt, with wittiness of diction and conception, a sportive satire at the expense of rationalists; the fourth is an experiment in the macabre and grotesque. The first of these (untitled) seems by its unfinished state (the lack of punctuation) to be an early abortive effort to convey with immediacy and wit the

---

[9] *Opus*, pp. 218-219 (written about 1937; see *Opus*, p. 301). See also Marcel Raymond, *From Baudelaire to Surrealism* (New York, 1950), and Wallace Fowlie, *The Age of Surrealism* (New York, 1950, and Bloomington, 1960), both of which trace the course of irrationalism in modern French poetry.

contrast between the beauty in nature and the negation of rationalists who are treated with contemptuous comic irony:

> I have lived so long with the rhetoricians
> That when I see a pine tree
> Broken by lightning
> Or hear a crapulous crow
> In dead boughs,
> In April
> These are too ready
> To despise me
> It is for this the good lord
> Gave the rooster his lustre
> And made sprats pink
> Who can doubt that Confucius
> Thought well of streets
> In the spring-time
> It is for this the rhetoricians
> Wear long black equali
> When they are abroad.

The prosaic flatness of "These are too ready / To despise me" also suggests that the poem was an early attempt; but there is a certain flourish to the first line, and by the end of the poem the rhetoricians, whose black garb shields them from the beauty of nature, are firmly and humorously associated with the negative—the crow, for instance. Confucius' awareness of this beauty is a comment on the unfortunate difference between the ancient oriental philosophy and rationalistic Western thought. The black cloaks of the rhetoricians suggest their alliance with death and their lack of emotional response to "streets / In the spring-time." They do not organize life in terms of nature's beauty. And along with the playful but serious ridicule of the rhetori-

183

cians is the comic effect of the diction: "crapulous crow,"
"made sprats pink," and "long black equali" (presumably
academic robes, with the coined word "equali" intended to
stress the reduction of the rhetorician's life to uniformity).
In these phrases, as well as in "rooster . . . lustre," witty
repetitions of sound accentuate both the ridicule and the
delight.

Another, perhaps later, manuscript poem, "An Exercise
for Professor X," seems more finished, more balanced:

> I see a camel in my mind.
> I do not say to myself in English,
> "There is a camel."
> I do not talk to myself.
> On the contrary, I watch
> And a camel passes in my mind.
> This might happen to a Persian.
> My mind and a Persian's
> Are as much alike, then,
> As moonlight on the Atlantic
> Is like moonlight on the Pacific.

The speaker presents Professor X with strange and humorous food for thought. The very framework of the poem—
a unique exercise in logic—mocks the rationalist professor,
who as X is devoid of personality. Reducing experience to
matter of fact, he is unaware of the nuances of reality and
is divorced from nature; a camel would not pass through
his mind. One must have the imagination of a Persian to
perceive the reality of a camel, or the effect of moonlight
on the oceans. Finally, the professor is left to ponder the
differences between the speaker and a Persian, between
Atlantic and Pacific; he is left to ponder the relationships
of language, perception, and reality. A similar ridicule of

rationalists is presented with more verve in the sixth poem of "Six Significant Landscapes" (1916):

> Rationalists wearing square hats,
> Think, in square rooms,
>
> . . . .
>
> They confine themselves
> To right-angled triangles.
> If they tried rhomboids,
> Cones, waving lines, ellipses—
> As for example, the ellipse of the half-moon—
> Rationalists would wear sombreros.

By the gay wit of conception and diction—the contrast of square hats and sombreros and the "ellipse of the half-moon"—Stevens renews the Romantic point of view; he makes it contemporaneous, not a "relic of the imagination," to use his own phrase.[10] Incidentally, Laforgue also made witty use of geometry in "Autre Complainte de Lord Pierrot": "La somme des angles d'un triangle, chère âme, / Est égale à deux droits."

In the third manuscript poem, "Dolls," the "greybeards" referred to are also members of Stevens' collection of philosophers, rationalists, logical positivists, and theologians. They anticipate the "dark rabbi" and "rose rabbi" in "Le Monocle de Mon Oncle" (1918), for which this poem seems, in theme and method, to be a model,[11] although it

[10] From "A Poet that Matters," a review of Marianne Moore's *Selected Poems*, in *Opus*, pp. 250-251.

[11] Carl Van Vechten in "Rogue Elephant in Porcelain," *Yale University Library Gazette*, XXXVIII (1963), 49, mentions that in the winter of 1914-1915 Stevens wrote a poem called "Dolls." This would place the beginnings of "Le Monocle de Mon Oncle" about four years before publication. See also "Stanzas for 'Le Monocle

deals less successfully with the interdependence of the sexual and the spiritual than does the later poem. By a paradoxical equilibrium, one is involved in the other: think of Eve and one is perplexed with apple-buds; pray and one is confronted by the "seduction of a scented veil"; think of angels and one presumably makes them creatures of earth.

> The thought of Eve, within me, is a doll
> That does what I desire, as, to perplex,
> With apple-buds, the husband in her sire.
>
> There's a pious caliph, now, who prays and sees
> A vermeil cheek. He is half-conscious of
> The quaint seduction of a scented veil.
>
> Playing with dolls? A solid game, greybeards.
> Think of cherubim and seraphim,
> And of Another, whom I must not name.

The wit is forced in this poem, especially in the Eve-doll equation. Stevens' use of dolls is more satisfactory in "Le Monocle de Mon Oncle," XI: "If sex were all, then every trembling hand / Could make us squeak, like dolls, the wished-for words." The final line of "Dolls" is altogether too arch—is "Another" supposed to suggest Mary or an actual woman, or both? In the middle stanza, however, the light mockery of the arabesque details makes it possible for Stevens to include the "scented veil" without a humorless indulgence in quaintness. Notice, too, the growing fluency and wit in the use of assonance and alliteration.

Stevens, following in a tradition extending from Poe and Baudelaire through the English Decadents to the Arens-

---

de Mon Oncle,'" *Opus*, p. 19, so named by S. F. Morse, as explained in *Opus*, p. xix.

berg group, also explored the more grotesque and macabre elements of experience. Some time in late 1914 or early 1915 he must have sent Harriet Monroe some poems containing the macabre or weird, for on January 27, 1915, she wrote him a post card saying, "I don't know when any poems have 'intrigued' me so much as these. They are recondite, erudite, provocatively obscure, with a kind of modern-gargoyle grin in them—Aubrey Beardsleyish in the making. They are weirder than your war series, and I don't like them, and I'll be blamed if I'll print them; but their author will surely catch me next time if he will only uncurl and uncoil a little—condescend to chase his mystically mirthful and mournful muse out of the nether darkness. . . ." Which poems these were is not known, but the fourth manuscript poem in the group mentioned is clearly an experiment in the macabre, and perhaps it comes from this period. "Headache" is certainly "provocatively obscure," as Stevens in this poem pushed toward the outer limits of the weird and the use of grim humor.

> The letters of the alphabet
> Are representative of parts[a] of the head.
> Ears are *q*s
> *L*s are the edges of the teeth
> *M*s are the wrinkled skin between the eyes
> In frowns.
> The nostrils and the bridge of the nose
> Are *p*s or *b*s.
> The mouth is *o*.
> There are letters in the hair.[b]
> The alphabet is a collection

[a] "parts of" added.
[b] Written in above line 11.

Of satirical design.
Worms frown. . [They]° are full of mouths.
[They]ᵈ bite, twitch their ears . . .
They lure.ᵉ
The maker of the alphabet
Had a headache.

This Imagistic and macabre piece produces a sense of disagreeable, sly wit. Perhaps it is meant in part to be a spoof of the peculiar imaginative vowel associations in Rimbaud's "Voyelles," in which the letter "u" signifies "des rides / Que l'alchimie imprime aux grands fronts studieux." Does the poem mock us because, however much we strain to rise above nature by abstracting a system of verbal signs from it, we do no better than the gruesome worms whose food we ultimately become? Or is the poem a grotesque means of suggesting the destructive power of language, with the worms figurative words which bite and lure? Whatever the meaning, the grotesquerie is clear. One cannot be sorry this poem was never published. Stevens had better use for the worms in "The Worms at Heaven's Gate" (1916).

This poem seems to be the most mentioned product of Stevens' grotesque strain, and surely it would be difficult to find a more unique funeral procession in literature. Stevens' use of a dead body and worms may have been a reaction to his reading of Baudelaire's "Une Charogne," but Baudelaire's emphasis is on decay and putrescence. However, in Stevens' poem death is the mother of beauty, as in "Sunday Morning," where death brings renewal and

° Second dot added; "they" canceled.
ᵈ "They" canceled.
ᵉ This line canceled, and "They are full of the devil" erased—second word illegible.

an awareness of beauty on this earth. Despite the gruesomeness provided by the title, "The Worms at Heaven's
Gate" is seriously affirmative and comically joyous. Every
thing works to accentuate meaning and emotional effect.
The procession takes on a vivid imaginative life: "Out of
the tomb, we bring Badroulbadour, / Within our bellies,
we her chariot." The reality of physical death and decay
is presented by what is both comic exaggeration and literal
truth: the terribly explicit naming of parts—how graphic
is "one by one, / The lashes of that eye"—and the effect of
"bundle," which so clearly draws attention to the condition of the body without life while it prevents even a hint
of necrophilia, which would destroy the desired effect. The
name Badroulbadour is in itself comic, and at the same time
the syllabication comically enhances the rhythm of the
procession. But lest the reader forget that Badroulbadour
was a princess, Stevens defines her beauty by delicate, evocative phrasing: "its white lid. / . . . the cheek on which that
lid declined, / . . . the hand, / The genius of that cheek."
The word "genius" particularly emphasizes that the princess's beauty was more than skin deep, that her gestures
emanated a spiritual afflatus. One must recall, too, her associations with fable and thus the imagination: she was the
princess in the *Arabian Nights* who married Aladdin. Death
is the mother of beauty, and Stevens, a literalist of the
imagination, brings her to life through the agency of those
paradoxical worms, which perform a role in the life cycle
of decay and regeneration. The worms do bring Badroulbadour *out* of the tomb, as the repetition of the first line
at the end emphasizes.

William Carlos Williams deserves much credit for his
hand in this poem. Among the manuscripts is a letter of his

to Stevens, written a month before the poem came out, in which Williams seems dictatorial, but his advice was good:

June 8, 1916

Dear Stevens :—

. . . I am keeping a copy of "The Worms at Heaven's Gate" which is to my mind a splendid poem. An exchange of letters may be necessary before we agree on the final version of the thing as I am thoroughly convinced that a change or two will strengthen the poem materially. . . .

Yours

Williams   [signed in pencil]

P.S. [separate sheet]

I have changed line two from:
"Within our bellies, as a chariot,"
to the following:
"Within our bellies, we her chariot,"

I think the second version is much the better for the reason that THE WORMS ARE HER CHARIOT and not only seem her chariot. Then again: "bellies" "as a chariot" (plural and singular) sounds badly while "we her chariot" has more of a collective sense and feels more solid. What do you say?

I have left off the last two lines for the obvious reason that they are fully implied in the poem: the lowness of the worms, the highness of Badroulbadour. This is a weakening of the truth by a sentimental catch at the end.

For Christ's sake yield to me
become great and famous.

Williams

Stevens obviously took Williams' advice. But he did not yield slavishly; Williams would compose a set of funeral directions his way in "Tract," and Stevens his way in "The Emperor of Ice-Cream."

Stevens' predilection for the bizarre, the irrational, and the grotesque, as seen in the four preceding manuscript poems as well as in "The Worms at Heaven's Gate," is certainly exploited fully in *Harmonium*. That volume is rich in imagery that strikes directly at the reader's own fund of unconscious experience, evoking a vivid sense of the fantastic or of reality perceived from odd perspectives. Distorted, perplexing landscapes and figures loom up, projecting the inner violence of the imagination, giving the object and the emotion a presence, an authenticity. The boundaries of reality are extended to include the unconscious, and the interplay between the imagination and the actual is dramatized and made more complex, with attendant effects of wit, humor, and grotesquerie, often combined as they are in the unconscious. One example of this is Section XI of "Thirteen Ways of Looking at a Blackbird," which with wit and a nightmarish eeriness creates a sharply delineated impression—a premonition—of death:

> He rode over Connecticut
> In a glass coach.
> Once, a fear pierced him,
> In that he mistook
> The shadow of his equipage
> For blackbirds.

The speaker in "The Cuban Doctor" (1921) "went to Egypt to escape / The Indian, but the Indian struck / Out of his cloud and from his sky." The Indian is possibly a personification of death or of the inscrutable powers in the

191

universe, made awesome by the savage, nightmarish associations established in the poem. The rest of the poem
creates a forceful counterpoint between nightmare and
actual experience:

> This was no worm bred in the moon,
> Wriggling far down the phantom air,
> And on a comfortable sofa dreamed.
>
> The Indian struck and disappeared.
> I knew my enemy was near—I,
> Drowsing in summer's sleepiest horn.

The horror produced in the speaker by the lightning—"The
Indian struck / Out of his cloud"—is intensified by the
negative statement in the stanza beginning "This was no
worm. . . ." The security of summer, when the peaceful
richness of life is most evident, is deceptive indeed; the
Indian can strike even then, and anywhere.[12]

To place side by side a manuscript poem, called "The
Anecdote of the Prince of Peacocks" and the poem in its
final form (1923) is to recognize how Stevens deepened his
awareness of the irrational forces in experience and how
he became surer, technically, in presenting his response to
these forces:

> Manuscript
>
> In the land of the peacocks, the prince thereof,
> Grown weary of romantics, walked alone,
> In the first of evening, pondering.

[12] It is just possible that Stevens in writing this poem had Poe's
"The Conqueror Worm" in mind: "But see . . . / A crawling shape
intrude! / A blood-red thing that writhes from out / The scenic
solitude!" Both poems achieve a macabre sense of the inevitable
terror of death, if in very different ways.

"The deuce!" he cried.

And by him, in the bushes, he espied
A white philosopher.
The white one sighed—

He seemed to seek replies,
From nothingness, to all his sighs.

"My sighs are pulses in a dreamer's death!"
Exclaimed the white one, smothering his lips.

The prince's *frisson* reached his fingers' tips.

Harmonium
In the moonlight
I met Berserk,
In the moonlight
On the bushy plain.
Oh, sharp he was
As the sleepless!

And, "Why are you red
In this milky blue?"
I said.
"Why sun-colored,
As if awake
In the midst of sleep?"

"You that wander,"
So he said,
"On the bushy plain,
Forgot so soon.
But I set my traps
In the midst of dreams."

I knew from this
That the blue ground

193

Was full of blocks
And blocking steel.
I knew the dread
Of the bushy plain,
And the beauty
Of the moonlight
Falling there,
Falling
As sleep falls
In the innocent air.

The early version, with mannered, arch, and febrile irony, thinly sketches out the situation and theme; it states the prince's reaction, but elicits no concern for his exquisite shudder. But Berserk is no mere white philosopher, smothering his lips. The vague but uncontrollable terror evoked by his name, his redness, and the traps of "blocking steel," along with the poem's more effective rhythms, make his invasion of the prince's blue, moonlit realm truly nightmarish. And yet the poem creates a strange, disquieting beauty out of the prince's predicament, caught as he is between his romantic peacocks and the undeniable red violence of reality which nevertheless enhances the effect of moonlight. Here is one fulfillment of such manuscript experiments as "I have lived so long with the rhetoricians" and "An Exercise for Professor X" and Stevens' general interest in the bizarre.

The protean elements of dream and nightmare—the fantastic characters that haunt the unconscious world, threatening and comic, abnormally large and small ("You ten-foot poet among inchlings" in "Bantams in Pine-Woods," 1922), the inhabitants of the ordinary world who are presented in all their strangeness (like the "roller of big cigars"

in "The Emperor of Ice-Cream," 1922), the unusual lo-
cales and events that undergo surprising metamorphoses—
enabled him to present with intensity those discoveries of a
deeper reality through the imagination.

"DISILLUSIONMENT of Ten O'Clock" combines some of the
main qualities referred to thus far: the rococo dandyism in
the "socks of lace"; the Laforguian dandyism in the nonchalant though despairing recognition of banality in the
title; and some of Corbière's satirical edge and glorification
of the bizarre and irrational. But the poem also has a general farcical or comical spirit that unites all of these elements without dominating them. This spirit, already notice-
able in some of the Harvard work, became increasingly evident in the *Harmonium* poems, culminating in "The Comedian as the Letter C." It is his large, buoyant sense of the
comic that greatly qualifies Stevens' debt to the modern
French ironists.

Stevens' Crispin derives in large part from other, earlier
sources that caught his interest as he tired of the gentle and
despairing Pierrot: Crispin is not merely a dandy and ironist of modern lineage; he is also Beaumarchais' Figaro, barber and valet, as well as Voltaire's Candide of the French
tradition, and the clown or fop of the English tradition of
stage comedy. No doubt, English stage comedy inspired
much of Stevens' comic zest. One obvious example of this
inspiration is "Peter Quince at the Clavier"; a full appreciation of the Susanna legend retold there depends on one's
recollection of the farcical struggle of Shakespeare's Quince
in A *Midsummer Night's Dream* with his production of
Pyramus and Thisby, and his desire to reconcile imagination and reality. The terms "The ribboned stick, the bel-

lowing breeches" in "The Comedian" have an Elizabethan ring to them if not the precise comic rhetoric of the insults Prince Hal and Falstaff fling at one another. Ben Jonson, too, seems an important source of Stevens' comic irony.

In several ways, Crispinus in Jonson's *Poetaster* seems a partial model for Stevens' Crispin. Crispinus, a fop, very carefully observes the manners of polite society—observes and only observes—and thus, like Crispin before he goes to sea, he knows no more than the surface civilities in human experience. Chiefly, however, Crispinus, who refers to himself as a scholar, is a pretentious would-be poet who is finally brought to law and purged of outlandish and windy words when Horace administers some special pills. In a farcical trial scene he vomits up such monstrosities as "ventositous," "prorumped," and "obstupefact." Stevens, through Crispin, revels in his own extravagant and comic diction—"nincompated pedagogue" for example.[13]

Another likely model for Stevens' Crispin is Jonson's Sir Politic Would-Be in *Volpone*. Like Crispinus, Would-Be makes much of being an observer of life, but he completely misses reality because he is so concerned with superficial minutiae. "I so love to note and observe," he says. He keeps a diary and jots down notes regarding his every experience: *"Notandum . . . ," "Item. . . ."* Would-Be had traveled by sea to Venice and is very proud of the way he has adapted to the new environment, though he succeeds only in aping outer manners and is taken in by Volpone.

[13] See S. F. Morse's discussion of "The Comedian as the Letter C" in "Wallace Stevens, Bergson, Pater," *ELH*, 31 (March 1964), especially n. 16, p. 17, in which he compares it with *Poetaster*. The fact that we have both seen associations between Stevens' Crispin and Jonson's Crispinus confirms my conviction that Stevens not only knew Jonson's works but was most enthusiastic about them.

He can spy out plots where they do not exist and claims knowledge of information being sent in cabbages, oranges, muskmelons, apricots, lemons, and pome-citrons. He is avid for news of porpoises recently seen in the Thames. Surely some of this nonsense prompted Stevens' statement, "the eye of Crispin, hung / On porpoises, instead of apricots." Further, Would-Be's first words in the play, at the beginning of Act II, are "Sir, to a wise man, all the world's his soil," which can be compared with Stevens' "Nota: man is the intelligence of his soil."

Finally, in Jonson's *The New Inn* one of the characters is an entomologist who examines fleas and other insects through a "multiplying glasse" and who may have suggested to Stevens the notion of making Crispin a "lutanist of fleas," and "inquisitorial botanist." Later in Jonson's play, in a discussion of costume and fashion, Sir Glorious Tipto mentions in a list of wearing apparel a "*Naples* hat" and a "cloake of *Genoa*"; these may have led to Stevens' "cloak / Of China, cap of Spain" in "The Comedian."

Such parallels not only suggest that Stevens may very well have put objects of Jonsonian satire and farce to use in creating his own protagonist, Crispin, but also indicate an important source of inspiration for Stevens' often boisterous comic diction, rhetoric, and tone. Jonson's plays abound with words like "mincing," "quirky," "mustachio," "magnifico," "concupiscence," "sprats," "puissant," "fubb'd," "catarrhs"—all used by Stevens for comic or ironic effect. Such words of course occur quite generally in Elizabethan comedy; the important thing is the comic energy and wit they add to Stevens' style. One sees further examples of this Elizabethan comic vitality in Stevens' phrases "ward of Cupido," "lustiest conceit," "a gobbet in my mincing world," and "arrant stinks," and in his use of "cozener," "pronunciamento," "blackamoor," "knave," "thane," and "quotha." Elizabethan antecedents seem apparent in the witty word play, the delight in sound, the comic thrust of Stevens' verse, as in these lines from "The Emperor of Ice-Cream": "Call the roller of big cigars, / The muscular one, and bid him whip / In kitchen cups concupiscent curds." This is similar to the exuberant alliteration in a question by Captain Tucca in *Poetaster*: "What! will the royal Augustus cast away a gentleman of worship, a captain and a commander, for a couple of condemned caitiff calumnious cargos?"

IN MAKING use of the effects of Elizabethan stage comedy, Stevens did not always overcome the danger of a blatant archaism; at times the practice leads to mannerism, to mere display, but on the whole the practice is controlled and the effects successfully merged with the other elements of his style, adding delight and richness. Furthermore, the risk of archaism was countered by the use of comic and humorous elements in the native American tradition, elements which tend to naturalize and update his comic vigor. Take, for example, the following stanza from "Ploughing on Sunday" (1919):

> Remus, blow your horn!
> I'm ploughing on Sunday,
> Ploughing North America.
> Blow your Horn!

With its exaggeration, its expansive wit, and its slap at blue laws, it is one of a number of indications in *Harmonium* of Stevens' debt to Whitman.[14] This stanza also points to Ste-

[14] S. F. Morse, "The Native Element," *Kenyon Review*, xx (1958), 465, was the first article to draw due attention to Whitman's importance to Stevens. Joseph N. Riddel has further explored

vens' awareness of rural and frontier America, and, in Remus, to the Negroes and other reminders of the native folk tradition. In "The Jack-Rabbit" (1923), the rabbit "sang to Arkansas" and "The black man said, / Now, grandmother, / Crochet me this buzzard / On your winding-sheet" (perhaps a fusion of the native elements with the motif of sewing and embroidering from Laforgue). Here death is leavened by the colloquial idiom and the buzzard—a bird which appears frequently in native folk and humorous literature. Stevens uses it several times in his poems, along with bantams, grackles, and turkey-cocks. For example, we find buzzards in "Two Figures in Dense Violet Night": "Say, puerile, that the buzzards crouch on the ridge-pole"; and again in "The Jack-Rabbit": "The entrails of the buzzard / Are rattling." The exaggeration evident in this last example is one of the chief attributes of native American humor, others being its fantasy, nonsense, and irreverence, its use of the vernacular, and its anecdotal quality. "The Jack-Rabbit" includes several of these attributes, as do many of the poems in *Harmonium*.

Michael Lafferty traces some of Stevens' colloquial idiom and use of exclamatory sounds—"ai-yi-yi" for example—and unusual employment of prefixes and suffixes—such as guzzly, funest, bazzling, and oozer—to his origins in Pennsylvania Dutch country.[15] But in "Life Is Motion," Stevens suggested the open joy of the frontier with "Ohoyaho, / Ohoo";

---

points of comparison between Whitman and Stevens in his essay "Walt Whitman and Wallace Stevens: Functions of a 'Literatus,' " *The South Atlantic Quarterly*, LXI, No. 4 (Autumn, 1962), reprinted in *Wallace Stevens, A Collection of Critical Essays*, ed. Marie Boroff (Englewood Cliffs, N.J., 1963).

[15] Lafferty, "Wallace Stevens: A Man of Two Worlds," *Historical Review of Berks County*, XXXIV, IV (Fall 1959), 111, 112.

and such imitative sounds and musical syllables as "rou-cou-cou" may have derived from the general folk tradition (as well as from his own observation). Of greater significance are the colloquial quality and the vernacular terms: "When this yokel comes . . . / Whetting his hacker . . . ," "Exit the whole shebang," "cares a tick," "blubber of tom-toms," "hankering," "cantankerous," and "hullabaloo." In this practice he is at least indirectly in the tradition of Whitman and Twain. More important, he mastered the art of combining the vernacular with other levels of speech.

His fondness for the anecdote (the term appears in a number of his titles) and his mockery of the pompous, as of the high-toned old Christian woman, are also elements that tend to relate his wit and vitality to his American background. But perhaps above all, his exaggeration and his originality of word and image, both so evident in his poems, are what cause the English to see Stevens as distinctly American.[16] The qualities referred to here contribute freshness, earthiness, gaiety, and humor as well as a native quality. In the early *Harmonium* poem "The Silver Plough-Boy" (1915; *Opus*) Stevens saw the advantage of modifying his aestheticism with such details, and it is important to recall that Crispin is brought by Stevens to the American environment where he can play on the "categorical gut" of the banjo.

Stevens' parodying of what is revered or classic, so that it is renewed and can flourish in the contemporary world, might be attributed to the element of mockery mentioned above. By stripping away automatic attitudes of respect, and thus indifference, he makes possible a fresh reaction and gives a bonus of amusement. With a gentle sense of

[16] See Frank Kermode, *Wallace Stevens* (Edinburgh and London, 1960), p. 13.

the speaker's absurdity, Stevens in "Peter Quince" renews
the Apocryphal story of Susanna and the Elders. Similarly,
in "Cy Est Pourtraicte" (1915) he gives a roguish turn to
the *Legenda Aurea* story of Ursula:

> [The Lord] felt a subtle quiver,
> That was not heavenly love,
> Or pity.
>
> This is not writ
> In any book.

The exquisite and vital Ursula evokes a very human response in the Lord, and the poem makes its serious point
concerning the unity of earth and heaven, of flesh and
spirit. It appears that the two poems "Lulu Gay" and "Lulu
Morose" (1921; *Opus*) are Stevens' parody of "L'Allegro"
and "Il Penseroso," even to the parallel sounds in the
titles. And perhaps Stevens' "Banal Sojourn" (1919), with
its "slum of bloom," in which "one damns that green shade
at the bottom of the land," is in part a humorous and
ironic commentary on Marvell's "The Garden" with its
famous lines, "Annihilating all that's made / To a green
thought in a green shade." Stevens' "On the Manner of
Addressing Clouds" (1921) seems very much like his variation on a theme by Browning, done with a touch of parody.
More specifically, it would seem that Stevens is addressing
the members of the funeral procession in Browning's "A
Grammarian's Funeral" as "Gloomy grammarians." Aside
from their ascending funeral processions involving grammarians, both poems give lofty consideration to the dignity
of speech and thought (Browning: "Did he not magnify
the mind . . . ?" Stevens: "The . . . still sustaining pomps
for you / To magnify"); both have to do with music, seasons, and especially clouds. Not only is the lofty style of

201

Stevens' poem protected by the playful mockery of "Gloomy grammarians" (also addressed as "Funest philosophers"), but also an interesting dialectic of meaning is established between the two poems.

"AND what descants, he sent to banishment!" exclaims Stevens concerning the lesser poems Crispin now rejected. Certainly after making the innovations which have been discussed in this chapter, Stevens must have found many of his earlier songs tame indeed. He had broken through the limitations of "twilight-interval" Romanticism; he could no longer remain content with the more attenuated qualities of the *fêtes galantes* mode or with the soft lushness of scented veils, shimmering surfaces, and deliquescent music—though he did retain the delicacy and sumptuousness acquired through his early experiments. When successful with irony, Stevens brought the actual and the imagined into a counterpoise that gave his poetry a new intensity. At the same time he moved rapidly toward his characteristic gaiety, his comic vitality and *brio*. Also, by an increasing use of the irrational element—of bizarre situations and points of view, of fantastic personae—he more pointedly revealed the beauty or grotesqueness of the actual world and the power of the imagination. His voice became freer and bolder, as he developed his rhetorical exuberance and discovered more startling and diverse diction and imagery. He created, nevertheless, a poetic ambience within which Tennysonian refinement and the noble voices of tradition found renewed life: Stevens, like Crispin, wanted a poetry that was "Prickly and obdurate, dense, harmonious, / Yet with a harmony not rarefied / Nor fined for the inhibited instruments / Of over-civil stops."

VIII. Noble Accents and Inescapable Rhythms

ON THIS period of second thoughts about the innovations wrought by Imagism and Symbolism in twentieth-century poetry, there are those who feel that these innovations caused an unfortunate deviation from the central tradition of English and American poetry.[1] It is true that much in the work of such poets as Eliot, Pound, and Stevens suffers from convolutions of style and meaning that will wither in the trials of time; no doubt a number of Stevens' most mannered efforts will meet this fate. And yet for him the modernist innovations were essential to his becoming a major modern poet, one who, inspired by the contemporary resurgence of faith in the validity of poetry, included the traditional as a vital component of his art. His lyricism, his stately eloquence, his "noble accents" all derive from the tradition, but they are made current by the spirit of innovation. Stevens' discovery of more congenial rhythms in his free verse practice, which enabled him to achieve more explicitly his desired meanings and emotions, was concurrent with his achievement of greater fluency in his more regular metrical patterns, as he became both an avant-garde poet and a traditionalist.

In "Effects of Analogy" (N. A., pp. 124-125) he cites a free verse passage from Eliot as an example of music in modern poetry. What he says is worth quoting at some length for its bearing on his own practice:

> But, after all, the music of poetry has not come to an end. Is not Eliot a musical poet? Listen to part of what

[1] Graham Hough, for one, takes this view in *Image and Experience* (London, 1960), p. 56.

the lamp hummed of the moon in "Rhapsody on a
Windy Night":

> A washed-out smallpox cracks her face,
> Her hand twists a paper rose,
> That smells of dust and old Cologne,
> She is alone
> With all the old nocturnal smells
> That cross and cross across her brain.
> The reminiscence comes
> Of sunless dry geraniums
> And dust in crevices,
> Smells of chestnuts in the streets
> And female smells in shuttered rooms
> And cigarettes in corridors
> And cocktail smells in bars.

This is a specimen of what is meant by music today.
It contains rhymes at irregular intervals and it is intensely cadenced. But yesterday . . . music meant
something else. It meant metrical poetry with regular
rhyme schemes repeated stanza after stanza. All of the
stanzas were alike in form. As a result of this, what
with the repetitions of the beats of the lines, and the
constant and recurring harmonious sounds, there actually was a music. But with the disappearance of all
this, the use of the word "music" in relation to poetry
is . . . a bit old hat: anachronistic. Yet the passage
from Eliot was musical. It is simply that there has been
a change in the nature of what we mean by music.

By 1915, the year when "Cy Est Pourtraicte," "Tea," "Peter
Quince at the Clavier," "The Silver Plough-Boy," "Disillusionment of Ten O'Clock," and "Sunday Morning" were

204

published, Stevens was fully aware of the change in the nature of music; in fact, he had become a writer of his own "intensely cadenced" verse with "rhymes at irregular intervals." "Cy Est Pourtraicte," for example, for all its difference in subject and tone from the Eliot passage, is remarkably like it in the nature of its music.

> "But here," she said,
> "Where none can see,
> I make an offering, in the grass,
> Of radishes and flowers."
> And then she wept
> For fear the Lord would not accept.
> The good Lord in His garden sought
> New leaf and shadowy tinct,
> And they were all His thought.
> He heard her low accord,
> Half prayer and half ditty,
> And he felt a subtle quiver,
> That was not heavenly love,
> Or pity.

Both Stevens and Eliot, taking advantage of the new liberties and in their separate ways following the example of Laforgue, for one, refused to subject their aims to the constrictions of the prevailing verse forms, refused to let their voices drown in the anonymity of popular poetic idiom. Yeats, with the advantage of a viable native oral tradition, was in a better position to charge conventional forms with his individual style, but for these two a different freedom was essential.

Stevens' exploitation of the new approaches opened to him is reflected in the large number of free verse poems in *Harmonium*. In these, he not only cultivated the minutiae of his craft—the intricate interplay of sounds and syllables and the variation of rhythms for sharply defined effects; he also found that he could control the movement and form of a poem by a rhetoric of the occasion, one not restricted by a predetermined metrical pattern but one in which a control of the rhetoric has to take the place of metrical regularity as the framework of the poem, persuading the reader that a structure does, after all, exist. The reader must respond not to a series of regularly scanned lines, but to the rhetorical emphasis. Thus, in "Thirteen Ways of Looking at a Blackbird," he is lost unless he reads this section with an ear for the natural accents of speech:

> I know no ble ac cents
> And lu cid, in es cap ab le rhyth ms;
> But I know, too,
> That the black bird is in volved
> In what I know.

Here the repetitions of "I know," the sustained stresses on "I know noble" and "I know, too," the spondee on "blackbird" in the center of the unstressed syllables, the reverberant emphasis of "inescapable," the resolution of the statement in the two iambic feet at the end, along with the several repetitions of sound, all produce the total effect of confidence in the power of language to create order that includes the knowledge of death—and without any concern for the old distinctions between prose and poetry.

Frequently, Stevens approached the rhythms of prose even more closely. This was in part the strategy of ironic understatement, or of moving into a poem in an offhand, "anti-poetic" way: "I am what is around me. / Women understand this," he begins in "Theory" (1917), and he

206

goes on to present theory without pompousness: "These are merely instances." In such a "prose" context, the illustrations must then carry the strength of the theory, and they do:

> One is not a duchess
> A hundred yards from a carriage.

> These, then are portraits:
> A black vestibule;
> A high bed sheltered by curtains.

In "Of the Surface of Things" (1919) the unemphatic prose rhythms of "In my room, the world is beyond my understanding; / But when I walk I see that it consists of three or four hills and a cloud" contrast strikingly with the metrical regularity of the line the speaker has written: " 'The spring is like a belle undressing.' " And in "Banal Sojourn" (1919), Stevens begins with the flat prose of stage directions: "Two wooden tubs of blue hydrangeas stand at the foot of the stone steps. / The sky is blue gum streaked with rose. The trees are black." The flatness here, in perfect accord with the expression of bored discontentment in the poem, also prepares appropriately for the rest of the poem, where the stresses, if they do not follow a regular metrical pattern, do support the rhetoric of a comic character, as in a play:

> Par die! Sum mer is like a fat beast, slee py
> in mil dew,
> Our old bane, green and bloat ed , se rene
> who cries. . . .

Note, too, incidentally, that the stresses reinforce the effects of alliteration and internal rhyme.

More often than not, within his seemingly prosaic free
verse Stevens created the "intensely cadenced" effects that
are an identifying characteristic of his style, one which
succeeds and surprises in a multiplicity of ways. In "Earthy
Anecdote" (1918), Stevens underscores the shift from the
aimless clattering of the bucks to their unified movement
in a swift curving line:

> Wher ev́ er they wént,
> They wént clát ter ing,
> Un tíl they swérved
> In a swíft, cír cu lar líne
> To the ríght,
> Be caúse of the fíre cát.

He does this partly by tightening the rhythm in the third
line, with its two iambic feet, and then increasing the
tempo in the next two, basically anapestic, lines. But these
do not trip along: the adjacent accents on "swíft" and "cír-
cular" contribute a firm continuity to the movement. Then
the power of the firecat is emphasized by the spondee at
the end. The next section of the poem repeats the movement, this time to the left. Thus, with efficient variations
in rhythm, with varying line lengths and repetition, Stevens transforms the actions of the animals on the plains to
something very like the sweeping dance movements of a
ballet corps, and he creates a mounting interest in the fate
of the bucks and the significance of the firecat. The range
of rhythmic effects in his free verse extends from the heavy
beats in "Cortege for Rosenbloom" (1921), which accentuate the slow march of a funeral procession

the tréad / Of the deád. / Rós en bloóm is deád

to the delicacy in "Infanta Marina" (1921), which is enhanced by the number of unstressed syllables between the stressed ones:

> She máde of the mótions of her wríst
> The grán di ose gés tures
> Of her thought.

> The rúmp ling of the plúmes
> Of this créa ture of the éve ning
> Cáme to be sléights of sáils
> Ó ver the séa.

The delicacy is supported by a firmness, evident in the junctures of stresses and repeated sounds in "made" and "motions" and in "rumpling" and "plumes."

The same spirit of freedom that inspired the carefully controlled effects in his free verse also inspired his accomplishments in more regular forms. Stevens did not reject these forms as long as he could reconcile his own rhetoric with them. "The Worms at Heaven's Gate" (1916), earlier than "Cortege" and Infanta," succeeds to a great extent because within the blank verse form Stevens harmonized the insistent rhythms of a funeral procession with a delicacy of rhythm akin to that in "Infanta":

> Óut of the tómb, we bríng Badróulbadóur;

then in lines three and four,

> Hére is an éye. And hére are, óne by óne,
> The lásh es of that éye and its white líd

the reversed initial foot and the following caesura help draw specific attention to the eye; the following three iambic feet maintain the pace of the procession; and the spondees on "that eye" and "white lid" substantiate the reflective consideration of Badroulbadour's exquisite beauty. In the next-to-last line of the poem, Stevens did not hesitate to give full stress to the three main words and let very light accents fall on the preposition and conjunction:

The bún dle óf the bó dy and the féet.

It was important to hasten over the merely physical attributes of the queen, and the metrical telescoping of the line fits that intention without disturbing the processional rhythm.

In "Sunday Morning" Stevens first successfully brought traditional elements into a harmonious counterpoise with the new in order to write a poem of lofty purpose. And it appears that he carried into its stately blank verse some of the rhetorical flexibility and meticulous control of poetic effects evident in the free verse poems of the same period.[2] The poem begins with seeming casualness,

[2] See Harvey Gross's analysis of the opening lines of "Sunday Morning" in his study of Stevens' prosody in his recent book, *Sound and Form in Modern Poetry* (Ann Arbor, 1964), p. 237; he and I are very close here. I am very much in sympathy with his conclusions about Stevens' prosody, chiefly that Stevens combined rhetorical freedom—and certainty—with a command of formal structures. His study of Stevens in his chapter "Hart Crane and Wallace Stevens" (pp. 215-246) is valuable for its prosodic analysis and should be read in conjunction with J. V. Cunningham's discussion of Stevens' uses of the traditional in his essay "The Poetry of Wallace Stevens," *Poetry*, LXXV (December 1949), 149-165, reprinted many times, most recently under the title "Tradition and Modernity: Wallace Stevens" in *The Achievement of Wallace Stevens*, eds. Ashley Brown and Robert S. Haller (Philadelphia, 1962), pp. 123-140.

Com plá cen cies òf the péig noir, and láte
Cóf fee and o ran ges in a sun ny chair,

with just three real stresses in the opening line; only in the final three feet of the second line does the basic iambic pattern of the poem begin to emerge clearly. But the first line ingrains itself upon our aural consciousness, partly because the repetitions of sound in *pla, peig,* and *late* are enhanced by being the only stressed syllables in the line. Then several of the sounds in the second line—the initial *c,* the vowel in "chair," the *or* in "oranges," the *s's* and *n's*— echo sounds in the first. Here are just two more instances of the rhythmic variations in this section which combine with the adroitly chosen words and images and interlacing repetitions of sound to intensify the meaning and the modulations of tone: in the fifth line—"The holy hush of ancient sacrifice"—the sound effects give aural definition to the silence, and the regular iambic feet are appropriate to the dimly recalled ritual; in these two lines,

Wínd ing a cróss wíde wá ter, with óut sóund.

The dáy is líke wíde wá ter, with óut sóund,

the slow pace, the lengthening through the spondees, the additional accent in each line, the alliteration, the series of long vowels, and the repetition of the phrases all give maximum support to the unearthly quietude.

SUCH FINESSE within regular metrical forms—whether blank verse, verse in consistent dimeter, trimeter, or tetrameter lines, stanzas of equal line lengths or repeated patterns of longer and shorter lines, with or without rhymes—did not come magically to Stevens, even though he was blessed

211

with an ear for creating effects with an uncanny rightness: he had to train and refine his ear, and it sometimes failed him. He had to discover those fine balances where conversational ease and natural rhetoric move within the external form, where feeling, thought, and art become one, where poetry is, as he said in his introduction to *The Necessary Angel*, "the movement of a self in the rock." Only about a year earlier than "Sunday Morning," according to publication dates, he made an effort to achieve a forceful effect in the first stanza of the sixth poem in "Carnet de Voyage" (*Trend*, 1914):

> Man from the waste e volved
> The Cy ther e an glade,
> Im posed on bat ter ing seas
> His keel's di vi ding blade,
> And sailed there un a fraid.

Despite the variations, the stanza, in concept and diction as well as in metrics, produces a rigid and declamatory effect. Also, in the following lines from an unpublished section of "Phases" (1914), the combination of theme, stress, alliteration, and other sounds is melodramatically insistent:

> No more, the shape of false con fu sion.
> Bare his breast and draw the flood
> Of all his Ba by lo ni an blood.

Compare these passages with this stanza in "Homunculus et La Belle Étoile" (1919), in which the rhetoric of heightened speech governs the stresses within the basically four-foot lines:

212

It might well be that their mis tress
Is no gaunt fug i tive phan tom.
She might, af ter all, be a wan ton,
A bun dant ly beau ti ful, ea ger. . . .

And compare them, too, with this basically pentameter stanza from "The Cuban Doctor" (1921), wherein the accents and sounds reinforce each other without doing so blatantly; this unerring control is one sign of Stevens' particular genius:

This was no worm bred in the moon,
Wrig gling far down the phan tom air,
And on a com for ta ble so fa dreamed.

One further example to illustrate the nature of Stevens' development in his command of prosody: behind the iambic pentameter, three-line stanzas of "Sea Surface Full of Clouds" (1924), marked by their eccentric but deft rhyming and subtle metrical variations, lay the manuscript experiment "For An Old Woman in a Wig" (ca. 1916). This was an attempt to compose a long poem (3 sections, totaling 23 stanzas) using the terzarima of Dante's *Divine Comedy*.[3] Perhaps he was seeking the form for the "great poem

---

[3] "For an Old Woman in a Wig" shows its debt to one aspect of Dante's structure; the later masterpiece "Notes Toward a Supreme Fiction" (1942) shows perhaps a debt to the mathematical structure of the *Divine Comedy*. A statement by Mr. Gross is interesting here: "The line and stanza patterning of *Notes Toward a Supreme Fiction* would delight a medieval poet's sense of the power and significance of number. Three, seven, ten and their related sums and multiplications figure in the poem's organization. The three largest sections are called, 'It must be abstract; It must change; It must give pleasure.' Each large section is sub-divided into

ten smaller sections; each of these smaller sections is made up of seven three-line stanzas" (p. 242). Surely in his poem Stevens came close to writing his "great poem of earth," and "For an Old Woman in a Wig" was an exercise in that direction. It follows here as it appears in the manuscripts (a great many words, phrases, and whole lines have been erased and rewritten):

I

. . There is a moment's flitter
Of silvers and of blacks across the streaking.
. . a swarming chitter

Of crows that flap away beyond the creaking
Of wooden wagons in the mountain gutters.
. .

The young dogs bark. .
. .
. .   It is the skeleton Virgil utters

The fates of men. Dogs bay their ghosts. The traces
Of morning grow large and all the cocks are crowing
And . .   the sun . .   paces

The tops of hell . . Death, . . . knowing,
Grieves . . our spirits with too poignant grieving,
. . keeps on showing

To our still envious memory, still believing,
The things we knew. For him the cocks awaken.
He spreads the thought of morning past deceiving

And yet deceives. There comes a mood that's taken
From water-deeps reflecting opening roses
And rounding, watery leaves, forever shaken,

And floating colors, which the mind supposes
In an imagination cut by sorrow.
Hell is not desolate Italy. It closes

. . above a morrow
Of common yesterdays: a wagon's rumble,
Loud cocks and barking dogs . . It does not borrow,

214

Except from dark forgetfulness, the mumble
Of sounds returning, or the phantom leaven
Of leaves so shaken in a water's tumble.

II

Is death in hell more death than death in heaven?
And is there never in that noon a turning—
One step descending one of all the seven

Implacable buttresses of sunlight, burning
In the great air? There must be spirits riven
From out contentment by too conscious yearning.

There must be spirits willing to be driven
To that immeasurable blackness, or . .
To those old landscapes, endlessly regiven,

Whence hell, and heaven itself, were both begotten.
There must be spirits wandering in the valleys,
And on the green-planed hills, that find forgotten

Beggars of earth intent
On maids with aprons lifted up to carry
Red-purples home—beggars that cry out sallies

Of half-remembered songs . .   sing, *"Tarry,
Tarry, are you gone?"* . . Such spirits are the fellows,
In heaven, of those whom hell's illusions harry.

III

When summer ends and changing autumn mellows
The nights . .   and moons glance
Over the dreamers . . and bring the yellow

Of autumn days and nights into resemblance,
The dreamers wake and watch the moonlight streaming.
They shall have much to suffer in remembrance.

They shall have much to suffer when the beaming
Of the clear moons, long afterward, returning,
Shines on them, elsewhere, in a deeper dreaming.

215

of earth." "The great poems of heaven and hell have been written," he said later in "Imagination as Value" (*N. A.*, p. 142), "and the great poem of earth remains to be written." Evidently he sent a completed version of the poem to William Carlos Williams, who commented in a June 2, 1916 letter that he liked "the last part of The old woman-in-a-wig piece because you allow yourself to become fervent for a moment." Here are the final three, almost completed stanzas from the manuscript (possibly the ones he referred to).

> *O pitiful lovers of earth, why are you keeping*
> *Such count of beauty in the ways you wander?*
> *Why are you so insistent on the sweeping*
>
> *Poetry of sky and sea? . Are you, then, fonder*
> *Of the circumference of earth's impounding*
> *Than of some sphere on which the wind might blunder,*
>
> *If you, with irrepressible will, abounding*
> *In . .   wish for revelation,*
> *Sought out the unknown new in your surrounding?*

. .   Suns, too, shall follow them with burning
Hallucinations in their turbid sleeping . .
. .

> *O pitiful lovers of earth, why are you keeping*
> *Such count of beauty in the ways you wander?*
> *Why are you so insistent on the sweeping*
>
> *Poetry of sky and sea? . Are you, then, fonder*
> *Of the circumference of earth's impounding*
> *Than of some sphere on which the mind might blunder,*
>
> *If you, with irrepressible will, abounding*
> *In . .   wish for revelation,*
> *Sought out the unknown new in your surrounding?*

216

Despite Williams' praise of fervence and despite the metrical variations in the completed lines, the accents form a monotonous rising and falling chant, falling with regularity at the end of each line. Stevens' voice seems to be constrained by his use of the tight rhyme-scheme.

Here is how he renders the "Poetry of sky and sea" in the concluding two stanzas of "Sea Surface Full of Clouds" (1924):

> The sove reign clouds came clus ter ing. The conch
> Of loy al con jur a tion trumped. The wind
> Of green blooms turn ing crisped the mot ley hue
>
> To clear ing op a les cence. Then the sea
> And hea ven rolled as one and from the two
> Came fresh trans fig ur ings of fresh est blue.

The verse moves fluently from line to line, and the variations intensify the exultation in the open-air vividness and splendor of the seascape and skyscape. In the first stanza quoted above, the combination of accents and alliteration in "clouds came clustering," with "came" in this context picking up a stress, heightens the impressiveness and drama produced by the image of the "sovereign" cloud masses "clustering"—just the right word in meaning and sound—into transitory form. The metrical regularity of the following sentence, abetted by the repetition of sound in "conch" and "conjuration," contributes to the majestic authority of the note sounded by Triton. The suspended moment of turning is caught in the hovering emphasis on "green blooms turning," even though the long spondee adds an extra accent to the line; and this prepares for the immense satisfaction of "clearing opalescence"—the jewel-like iridescence dissolving into an instant of transfiguring clarity. Such effects lead up to the triumphant finality of the concluding line, where the partial stress on "Came" and the accents on the syllables beginning with *f* heighten the finality. The series of unstressed syllables in the penultimate foot not only increases the force of "freshest" but also helps to convey the ongoing quality of the transfigurations which are not static, even at the moment when poetic insight draws heaven and sea into a unity.

THE TECHNIQUES of Symbolism, the freedom and precision in free verse and Imagism, and the fact that in his ironic and comic guises Stevens dared to take rhetorical liberties he might not have taken otherwise—all of these contributed to an extension and perfection of Stevens' prosodic powers. But also in his voice are the voices of the English tradition. His ear clung to the lyricism and stately measures of the English poets, but unlike the genteel, twilight-interval poets, he transformed the traditional into his own idiom. The echoes that pervade his work, adding the sublimity essential for a poet who considered poetry to be the supreme fiction, are elusive, seamlessly blended into his own style, so that lines here and there tantalize one with the impression that they are variations of lines he has heard before.

One critic has said that "perhaps no contemporary poet has more associations (however tenuous and qualified) with the earlier seventeenth century than Wallace Stevens";[4] possibly such an association exists between the quality of the music in "Peter Quince" and the pure, melting, rhythmical grace, the tone and details in Campion's

[4] Marius Bewley, "The Poetry of Wallace Stevens," *The Complex Fate* (London, 1952), p. 184.

"Rose-cheekt Laura": "Sing thou smoothly with thy beauty's / Silent music . . ." and

> These dull notes we sing
> Discords need for helps to grace them;
> Only beauty purely loving
> Knows no discord,
>
> But still moves delight,
> Like clear springs renew'd by flowing,
> Ever perfect, ever in themselves eternal.

Yet such "tenuous and qualified" associations are not limited to the earlier seventeenth century. The final line of "Nomad Exquisite" (1923)—"Forms, flames, and the flakes of flames"—compares with the phrase in Spenser's "Epithalamion"—"flames with many a flake." Further, Stevens knew well the grandeur of Milton's prosody. Consider the following stanza from "Palace of the Babies" (1921):

> Night nursed not him in whose dark mind
> The clambering wings of birds of black revolved,
> Making harsh torment of the solitude . . .

particularly the Miltonic syntax of the first line.

Stevens' style, however, includes more than isolated echoes of rhythms, images, and turns of phrase from previous poetry. For one thing, he responded to those currents of sensibility that run through the poetry of an age. The Romantic poets, for example, along with influencing Stevens in many other ways, no doubt inspired and deepened his absorption in the elusive but ineffable music that interpeneterates nature and the imagination. Coleridge's "Could I revive within me / Her symphony and song," Keats' "Heard melodies are sweet, but those unheard / Are sweeter," Shelley's "Music, when soft voices die, / Vibrates in the memory" and "where music and moonlight and feeling / Are one"—to cite just a few examples—express variously the refined longing, meditative sadness, or quiet exaltation so similar in effect to the nuances of tone in Stevens' poems when he explores the relationships among music, nature, and human consciousness.

But we also sense his close affinities with individual poets whose particular characteristics seem to permeate and affect his style as a whole. One of these poets is Marvell, however few parallels in specific details suggest themselves. Stevens would concur with much in Marvell's world view— the acceptance and glorification of our transient earthly existence in "To His Coy Mistress" and his concern in "Upon Appleton House" with various orders man imposes on nature. He must have been attracted to Marvell's rich, sensuous imagery of earth, especially that of gardens,[5] and to the clarity and precision of Marvell's metaphysical imagery (see Stevens' "Stars at Tallapoosa"). Also, Marvell's graceful, moving lyricism and metrical virtuosity, and his highly civilized wit that was rooted in a realization of life's paradoxes are very similar to qualities in Stevens' work. Even so, more marked affinities seem to exist between Stevens and Keats, Wordsworth, and Shakespeare.

Keats, like Marvell, rendered the sensuous beauty of the physical world, but he felt the transiency of life with even more exquisite poignancy. The beauty is intense and at the

[5] See Joseph E. Duncan, *The Revival of Metaphysical Poetry* (Minneapolis, 1959), p. 183. He says that Stevens' work suggests Donne and Marvell, and particularly Marvell's "The Garden," which "discusses problems very similar to those that haunted Stevens. Other bonds between Stevens and the metaphysicals were their use of correspondences, conceits, paradox, and wit."

same time painful because in its passing it is tenuously grasped by the imagination and barely capturable in art. Such feelings are very much a part of the tone in "Sunday Morning," "Peter Quince," and "The Idea of Order at Key West" ("The sky acutest at its vanishing"). Moreover, the impress of the physical world on Keats' volatile sensibility is reflected not only in the sensuous words and images he chose, but also in the very versification of which these are a part, a versification Stevens must have studied closely or have absorbed by a kind of poetic osmosis through his intense reading of Keats' work. Selected almost at random are these lines from "The Eve of St. Agnes": "And diamonded with panes of quaint device, / Innumerable of stains and splendid dyes." Here the diction and the interaction of repeated sounds produce a tactile quality for "the sensuous ear" and reinforce the visual particularity of the many-colored, diamonded glass. Also, Harvey Gross compares the "pulse of meditation which quickens the Keatsian sublime" in the last stanza of "Ode to Autumn" with the final seven lines of "Sunday Morning":[6]

> Deer walk upon our mountains, and the quail
> Whistle about us their spontaneous cries;
> Sweet berries ripen in the wilderness;
> And, in the isolation of the sky,
> At evening, casual flocks of pigeons make
> Ambiguous undulations as they sink
> Downward to darkness, on extended wings.

He is right, but more than intimations of Keats inspired these lines.

The central effect of the passage, with the quail and the deer, is of natural wilderness—it is a slight reminder of the

[6] Gross, *Sound and Form in Modern Poetry*, p. 239.

berries in the woods of Massachusetts in the undergraduate
story, "The Nymph," and although the details signify
earthly nature in general, the wilderness seems to be native.
Also, Stevens, despite his many differences from Wordsworth, seems to have made indigenous in the above lines
some of the qualities in this passage from "Tintern Abbey":

> Once again
> Do I behold these steep and lofty cliffs,
> That on a wild secluded scene impress
> Thoughts of more deep seclusion; and connect
> The landscape with the quiet of the sky.

J. V. Cunningham, after saying of "Sunday Morning" that
"much of the deep feeling of the poem is derived from the
exposition in sustained and traditional rhetoric of the position which is being denied" (traditional Christianity), goes
on to state that the positive argument in the poem is Wordsworthian "in detail, in feeling, and in rhetoric." He also
suggests that Stevens' stanza in "Sunday Morning" beginning

> There is not any haunt of prophecy,
> Nor any old chimera of the grave,
> Neither the golden underground, nor isle
> Melodious, where spirits gat them home . . .

was influenced by this passage in "The Recluse":

> Paradise, and groves
> Elysian, Fortunate fields,—like those of old
> Sought on the Atlantic Main—why should they be
> A history of departed things,
> Or a mere fiction of what never was?
> For the discerning intellect of Man,

222

When wedded to this goodly universe
In love and holy passion, shall find these
The simple produce of the common day.[7]

But the stanza from "Sunday Morning" is more than
Wordsworthian. In it Stevens may also, with some of the
idiom of English Renaissance poetry, have been subtly
refuting the Attendant Spirit in *Comus*—a poem in which
Milton asserts the heavenly over the earthly—when the
Spirit says,

> 'Tis not vain or fabulous
>
> . . . .
>
> What the sage poets, taught by th' heavenly Muse,
> Storied of old in high immortal verse
> Of dire Chimeras and enchanted isles,
> And rifted rocks whose entrance leads to Hell. . . .

Harvey Gross further demonstrates the complexity of the
influence of traditional English poetry on "Sunday Morning" by hearing the harmonies of Tennyson in the lines,

> Winding across wide water, without sound.
> The day is like wide water, without sound,
> Stilled for the passing of her dreaming feet. . . .

These lines are not pure Tennyson, of course, but the play
of sound and cadence, already discussed, contains a music
that Stevens surely had in his ear from youth on, a music
expressive of Tennyson's elegiac, world-weary yearnings for
a remote "dreamful ease" transcending time.[8]

[7] Cunningham, "Tradition and Modernity," *The Achievement
of Wallace Stevens*, pp. 136-137.

[8] Gross, *Sound and Form in Modern Poetry*, p. 238. Both Robert
Langbaum in *The Poetry of Experience* (New York, 1963, pp.
91-92, and Hugh Kenner in *The Invisible Poet: T. S. Eliot* (New

But there is something more: these lines in "Sunday Morning,"

> For maidens who were wont to sit and gaze
> Upon the grass relinquished to their feet,

which capture a courtly, pastoral delicacy, are invested with a Shakespearian refinement, as in these words which Hermia utters to Helena in A *Midsummer Night's Dream*:

> And in the wood, where often you and I
> Upon faint primrose-beds were wont to lie. . . .

One of Stevens' manuscript poems offers us the opportunity to observe him in the process of responding to Shakespeare and playing his own variation on a passage by the master:

> All things imagined are of earth compact,
> Strange beast and bird, strange creatures all;
> Strange minds of men, unwilling slaves to fact:
> Struggling with desperate clouds, they still proclaim

York, 1959), show how Eliot drew on Tennyson even as he reacted against Tennyson's mode. And so it was with Stevens; like Eliot, he had to guard against a "world made out of words; much of Tennyson and most of Swinburne has no more bite on the realities outside the dictionary than have the verses of *Jabberwocky*. Coherence was obtained by exploiting the sounds of the words and the implications concealed in their sounds" (Kenner, pp. 8-9). Stevens was apparently thinking of his predecessors when he said in "Credences of Summer," "Far in the woods they sang their unreal songs, / Secure. It was difficult to sing in face / Of the object." What he did was to appropriate their verbal music for his poems of earthly celebration: in "Peter Quince," it seems to me, two Tennysonian lines—"Beauty is momentary in the mind— / The fitful tracing of a portal"—lead to the non-Tennysonian point, "But in the flesh it is immortal."

224

The rushing pearl, the whirling black,
Clearly, in well-remembered word and name.

Even the dead, when they return, return
Not as these dead, concealed away;
But their old persons move again, and burn.

Notably similar, yet with a reversal, are the first line and
Theseus' statement in the opening of Act V in *A Midsummer Night's Dream*, "The lunatic, the lover, and the poet, /
Are of imagination all compact."[9] Stevens' poem, as it continues, seems partly an answer to Theseus, a defender of
fact, when he says, "More strange than true: . . . Such
shaping fantasies, that apprehend / More than cool reason ever comprehends." Theseus adds: "The poet's eye
. . . / Doth glance from heaven to earth, from earth to
heaven; . . . / . . . the poet's pen / . . . gives to airy nothing /
A local habitation and a name"; and Stevens' second stanza
indicates that this is just what men do. His final stanza then
goes on to suggest the recurrence of spirit in the flesh. Although the cadences in this manuscript poem are stiff and
heavy, far from Shakespeare's mastery of blank verse, they
show Stevens working partly in Shakespearean terms, partly
in his own, toward the nobility of tone and the command
of rhetoric and versification that he achieved on so many
later occasions.

THE ENGLISH tradition takes on a new life in Stevens'
poems, and from it Stevens gained a noble resonance; but
just as he made some of the qualities in Wordsworth's
poetry indigenous and contemporary, he also turned directly to a source of lyricism and eloquence that was al-

9 See echoes of Theseus' speech, this line in particular, in Stevens'
"A Primitive Like an Orb," especially Stanza IV.

ready indigenous. On his arrival in the new world, Crispin's mind became "free / And more than free, elate, intent, profound. . . ." He would now "Thrum with a proud douceur / His grand pronunciamento . . ." and he would now have an "aesthetic tough, diverse, untamed, / Incredible to prudes, the mint of dirt, / Green barbarism turning paradigm." Here the diction is much in the manner of Whitman, but so is the energy, the boldness, and the virility of the rhetoric. Whitman, like Stevens, was a poet for whom poetry and life had to be one, and with his great rhetorical daring he sought a poetic idiom that would carry—that would be—the very force of life itself and its delicacy too, its energy and its mystery. Here was a major inspiration for Stevens to create a freer, bolder music as well as a fresh lyricism.

Some of Whitman's lyrical feeling for the fecundity in nature and the continuity of life—especially his feeling for mothers and children ("Carrying the crescent child that carries its own full mother in its belly" in "Song of Myself")—seems to be echoed in Stevens' poem "In the Carolinas" (1917): "Already the new-born children interpret love / In the voices of mothers," and in "Sunday Morning": "Our earthly mothers waiting sleeplessly."[10] Also, as Whitman often found a lyrical beauty in seemingly ordinary or earthy physical details, so does Stevens in this stanza from "Depression Before Spring" (1918) which, except for the shortness of its lines, would not seem out of place in

[10] Joseph N. Riddel points to several important correlations between the two poets, one of them being the mother-figure in the poetry of both, in his essay "Whitman and Stevens: Functions of the 'Literatus,'" *The South Atlantic Quarterly* (Autumn 1962), pp. 506-520, reprinted in *Wallace Stevens: A Collection of Critical Essays*, ed. Marie Boroff (Englewood Cliffs, 1963), pp. 30-42.

"Song of Myself," in which a "cow crunching with depressed head surpasses any statue":

> The hair of my blonde
> Is dazzling
> As the spittle of cows
> Threading the wind.

One would not expect such lyrical delicacy from the Imagistic use of the spittle of cows.

Stevens, like Whitman, also delighted in the lyrical quality of American place names and animal names. Here is a passage from Whitman's "Starting from Paumanok":

> The red aborigines,
> Leaving natural breaths, sounds of rain and winds,
>   calls as of birds and animals in the woods,
>   syllabled to us for names,
> Okonee, Koosa, Ottawa, Monongahela, Sauk,
>   Natchez, Chattahoochee. . . .

The Indian names and the "calls as of birds . . . syllabled to us for names" bring to mind the passage in Stevens' "Primordia" (1917; *Opus*), which begins "All over Minnesota, / . . . / The syllables of the gulls and of the crows / And of the bluebird. . . ." Another example is Stevens' title "Stars at Tallapoosa" (1922).

This poem is interesting for another reason, for while it seems in part a refutation of Whitman's "Out of the Cradle Endlessly Rocking" (Stevens says, "The night is not the cradle that they cry"), it is at the same time a variation on the mood and theme of that poem and, moreover, displays an assimilation of some of Whitman's tone and manner. Like Whitman's speaker, the "secretive hunter" in Stevens' poem is alone at the sea's edge and faced with the problem

227

of "Making recoveries of young nakedness / And the lost vehemence the midnights hold." These lines certainly recall "Out of the Cradle," though Stevens' poem as a whole is less elegiac than Whitman's and less brooding. Stevens calls for an active, imaginative transcendence over the blackness: in the mind's eye of his secretive hunter the intangible lines between the stars should become "brilliant arrows" which will redeem his isolation. But if the theme is not entirely parallel, some of the manner is. Notice these lines in Stevens' poem: "Wading the sea-lines, moist and ever-mingling, / Mounting the earth-lines, long and lax, lethargic." How close they are in tone, in phrasing, and in cadence to the style of Whitman!

FOLLOWING his remarks about Eliot's music quoted at the beginning of this chapter, Stevens makes the point that the music of poetry is a form of analogy. Citing narrative poetry, he says:

In the meantime the tale is being told and the music excites us and we identify it with the story and it becomes the story and the speed with which we are following it. When it is over, we are aware that we have had an experience very much like the story just as if we had participated in what took place. It is exactly as if we had listened with complete sympathy to an emotional recital. The music was a communication of emotion. It would not have been different if it had been the music of poetry or the voice of the protagonist telling the tale or speaking out of his sense of the world. How many things we should have learned in either case! (N. A., p. 126.)

This is not a new idea, that music is a "communication of

emotion," but Stevens felt it profoundly: "Music is feeling, then, not sound." It says again that poetry and reality are one. His musical imagism is one way of achieving this, making possible the projection of a wide range of emotions, often playful, witty, or spritely. But he can also achieve in its proper place a music that is lofty and noble—not anachronistic, not "old hat" as Stevens put it, but "the voice of the protagonist . . . speaking out of his sense of the world." Stevens' prosody reflects this sense, for with freedom and variation he brought into the forms of his poetry the incipient freshness of the world as he thought about it and felt it, so that flux and fixity, life and art, become one. The fluency of his voice is indissolubly joined with a structural certainty that he heightened by his incisive use of the devices of his craft, his art. And his incorporation of the traditional within the new corresponds to his recognition of the continuity within nature's change. In "Sunday Morning" and "Peter Quince" he first proved that he could "somewhat loudly sweep the string," and that the various harmonies were his own; even the basically ironic and comic poems, such as "Le Monocle de Mon Oncle" and "The Comedian as the Letter C," have their majestic measures and their exalted tone which become part of the total effect.

IX. Phases: 1914-1923

THE great year in Stevens' development as a poet, the turning point when he overcame uncertainty and pastiche and brought his talents into focus, was 1915. Hints of the later poet occur in the *Trend* poems and in "Phases," all published in the fall of 1914; but the *Rogue* poems— "Tea," "Cy Est Pourtraicte," and "Disillusionment of Ten O'Clock"—along with "The Silver Plough-Boy," "Peter Quince" and "Sunday Morning," all in 1915, show mature command and are unmistakably marked by Stevens' own voice. One way to illustrate this remarkably sudden achievement is to compare "Phases" and "Sunday Morning," since "Phases" attempts to convey some of the very effects and attitudes which are so expertly realized in "Sunday Morning."

Fourteen years after the first inklings of "Sunday Morning" appeared in the undergraduate sequence "Street Songs," Stevens, in the fall of 1914, under the stimulus of the war in Europe, made another attempt in "Phases" to give a variation of his central theme a more sustained utterance in a longer, symbolically arranged poem or series of poems. In "Phases" Stevens sought to convert the current horror of war into a statement concerning the imagination, violence and order, war and man's spirit. The poem, both in the indirectness of its symbolism and in its inclusion of unpleasant realistic detail, was radical for its time. *The Minaret*, an obscure, conservative poetry journal—with perhaps the first post-Harvard criticism of Stevens' poetry— was thoroughly dismayed by his poem, as well as by the work in *Poetry* in general:

230

. . . if anyone could suggest to me a magazine that had worse poems through its whole existence than this individual War Poem Number had, I would like to see the magazine. Moreover, we read enough about the war in the newspaper, why should we also have ranting poems thrust into our faces, which are untruthful, and nauseating to read. Here are two excellent examples.[1]

The critic chooses for his first example the opening four lines of "Phases," lines which are weak but hardly ranting or nauseating:

> There's a little square in Paris,
> Waiting until we pass.
> They sit idly there,
> They sip the glass.

Despite the philistine reaction, however, Harriet Monroe's enthusiastic acceptance of four of the many parts of the poem for publication in the leading journal devoted to the new poetry must have had a happy effect on Stevens' confidence at a time when he was experimenting more freely and just beginning to publish.[2]

[1] Anon., "Chicago Poets and Poetry," *Minaret*, 1, 4 (February 1916), 26.

[2] See *Opus Posthumous*, p. xviii—Harriet Monroe "scrawled across the top of the manuscript: 'Jewel.' " Also, among the manuscripts is a holograph mailing card from Harriet Monroe, dated October 21, 1914, in which she says, "I was heart broken that we could not use more of your poem, especially the first section. But our war number is terribly crowded—I could give you only two pages—and II through V seemed about the best of it. Also it stands well without the rest." Despite her enthusiasm, however, none of the remaining seven sections was published until Samuel French

"Phases," like "Sunday Morning," concerns the relationship of death and beauty in the contemporary world, although it also generalizes about freedom and justice. Stevens suggests with a degree of irony that war gives the common man, ordinarily a slave to the city's ugliness and futility, a touch of heroic dignity:

> Death's nobility again
> Beautified the simplest men.
> Fallen Winkle felt the pride
> Of Agamemnon
> When he died.
>
> What could London's
> Work and waste
> Give him—
> To that salty, sacrificial taste?

In "Sunday Morning," the poet makes essentially the same point, though more positively and more serenely:

> Death is the mother of beauty; hence from her,
> Alone, shall come fulfillment to our dreams
> And our desires. . . .

Also, both poems indicate that the conception of a heaven has lost its validity: in "Phases," "There was heaven, / Full of Raphael's costumes" and in a manuscript section, "Let Heaven snuff / The tapers round her futile throne"; in "Sunday Morning," there is no "visionary south, nor cloudy palm / Remote on heaven's hill, that has endured / As April's green endures."

Both poems begin with a leisurely, hedonistic situation, which contrasts with death. The "Phases" beginning, quoted

---

Morse included two others in *Opus* "to give a sample of the rest" (p. xviii).

earlier, "They sit idly there, / They sip the glass," followed
by "There's a parrot in the window," becomes in "Sunday
Morning"

> Complacencies of the peignoir, and late
> Coffee and oranges in a sunny chair,
> And the green freedom of a cockatoo. . . .

In "Phases" the

> Arabesques of candle beams,
> Winding
> Through our heavy dreams . . .

seem to anticipate the dreaming of the woman in "Sunday
Morning":

> She dreams a little, and she feels the dark
> Encroachment of that old catastrophe, . . .

and the "procession of the dead, / Winding across wide
water . . ." enters her dream. There is a reversal though;
in the midst of the reality of war, the soldiers find beauty
in their dreams, whereas the woman, in the midst of her
"green freedom," finds the reality of death in her dreams.
Further, this manuscript section of "Phases,"

> Peace means long, delicious valleys,
> In the mode of Claude Lorraine;
> Rivers of jade,
> In serpentines,
> About the heavy grain;
> Leaning trees,
> Where the pilgrim hums
> Of the dear
> And distant door.
> Peace means these,
> And all things, as before.

seems a precursor in quality to Section VI in "Sunday Morning," beginning,

> Is there no change of death in paradise?
> Does ripe fruit never fall? Or do the boughs
> Hang always heavy in that perfect sky,
> Unchanging, yet so like our perishing earth. . . .

The serenity of setting, the sense that paradise is like a painting, forever unchanged, has been complicated in the later poem by the voiced and explicit dissatisfaction with the kind of peace or paradise that is devoid of change.[3] As a final example, the "Phases" passage,

> And earth
> A thing of shadows,
> Stiff as stone,
> Where time in fitful turns . . .

perhaps led to these lines in the final section of "Sunday Morning":

> We live in an old chaos of the sun,
> Or old dependency of day and night,
> Or island solitude. . . .

All these hints of the later poem, however, are submerged in the mixed quality of "Phases." For one thing, on the basis of the manuscript sections and those published in

---

[3] Incidentally, compare Stevens' image in this sixth section of "Sunday Morning"—"With rivers like our own that seek for seas / They never find, the same receding shores / That never touch with inarticulate pang"—with Swinburne's image in "The Garden of Proserpine": "We thank . . . / Whatever gods may be / That no life lives forever; / . . . / That even the weariest river / Winds somewhere safe to sea." The two complete poems, moreover, correspond in theme if not in tone.

Poetry, it is difficult to discover a thematic center that would unite the various statements and implications concerning war and peace, force and freedom, falseness and reality, the failure of society and religion, and, in contrast, the knowledge the soldiers have of reality and death and the necessity for an inner vision ("with the spirit's lamp, / Look deep and let the truth be known"). In the manuscripts, alternate arrangements of the sections, some tried in three different positions, seem to reflect the difficulty Stevens must have had in finding a satisfactory order for his ideas.[4] About "Sunday Morning" he was evidently much

[4] Of the final ordering, II through V appeared in *Poetry* in November 1914 as I through IV, and Miss Monroe did not return the other seven of the eleven Stevens sent her, so that his arrangement of them is unknown (see *Opus*, p. xviii). Only five of the seven unpublished sections, one of them incomplete, survive in manuscript. Following is the work as it exists in the manuscripts, omitting those sections which appear in full in *Opus* or in my text (I have included Stevens' marginal numbers, which probably suggest other orders):

I

See *Opus*, p. 5, where it is numbered VI.   12
See pp. 239-40 in text (incomplete).

II

Belgian Farm, October, 1914
See *Opus*, p. 5, where it is numbered V.   14
See p. 238 in text (incomplete).

III

Life the hangman, never came,
Near our mysteries of flame.

When we marched across his towns,
He cozened us with leafy crowns.

When we marched along his roads,
He kissed his hand to ease our loads.

235

(n. 4, cont.)

Life, the hangman, kept away,
From the field where soldiers pay.   11

IV

See p. 233 in text (complete).   15

(No manuscript sections numbered v or vi.)

Un-numbered partial section which follows IV:

The crisp, sonorous spice
Mongered after every scene.
Sluggards must be quickened: Screen,

No more, the shape of false confusion.
Bare his breast and draw the flood
Of all his Babylonian blood.

VII

Same as II, Belgian Farm, October, 1914
    (or v in *Opus*) but untitled.

VIII

What shall we say to the lovers of freedom,
Forming their states for new eras to come?
Say that the fighter is master of men.

Shall we, then, say to the lovers of freedom
That force, and not freedom, must always prevail?
Say that the fighter is master of men.

Or shall we say to the lovers of freedom
That freedom will conquer and always prevail?
Say that the fighter is master of men.

Say, too, that freedom is master of masters,
Forming their states for new eras to come.
Say that the fighter is master of men.

IX

Same as III, quoted above.

more certain: even when Harriet Monroe would publish
only five of the eight stanzas he had sent her, he wrote in
a letter to her on June 6, 1915: "Provided your selection of
the numbers of *Sunday Morning* is printed in the following
order: I, VIII, IV, V, I see no objection to cutting down.
The order is necessary to the idea."[5] Such an abridgment
must have bothered Stevens, but even in the shortened
rearrangement his central thought is clear.

Corollary to the lack of thematic certainty in "Phases"
is the discordance of styles among its different sections. The
variations in verse forms—free verse, quatrains, couplets—

X

Same as IV, quoted in text, p. 233.

XI

War has no haunt except the heart,
Which envy haunts, and hate and fear,
And malice, and ambition, near
The haunt of love. Who shall impart,

To that strange commune, strength enough
To drive the laggard phantoms out?
Who shall dispel for it the doubt
Of its own strength? Let Heaven snuff

The tapers round her futile throne.
Close tight the prophet's coffin-clamp.
Peer inward, with the spirit's lamp,
Look deep, and let the truth be known.

Peter Parasol

[5] The letter from Stevens is among the manuscript materials.
Miss Monroe included VII as the conclusion to this order in *Poetry*,
November 1915. See M. Benamou, "Wallace Stevens: Some Rela-
tions Between Poetry and Painting," *Comparative Literature*, XI, 1
(Winter 1959), 53, for a discussion of the effects of the two dif-
ferent orders of the poem.

jostle ineffectively with each other (though, of course, in "Peter Quince" Stevens did successfully unite different verse forms). Also, imperfectly assimilated styles result in pastiche, most glaringly evident in the couplets in one manuscript section which remains more Housman than Stevens:

> When we marched across his towns,
> He cozened us with leafy crowns.

Finally, the sections fluctuate awkwardly between symbolic suggestions of meaning and emotion and flat, explicit statements of theme. Section V, "Belgian Farm, October, 1914," for example, achieves a vague ominousness:

> As if some old Man of the Chimney, sick
> Of summer and that unused hearth below,
>
> Stretched out a shadowy arm to feel the night.
> The children heard him in their chilly beds,
> Mumbling and musing of the silent farm. . . .

An unpublished manuscript section, on the other hand, is abstract and declamatory:

> Say, too, that freedom is master of masters,
> Forming their states for new eras to come.
> Say that the fighter is master of men.

So is this stanza from another manuscript section:

> War has no haunt except the heart,
> Which envy haunts, and hate, and fear,
> And malice, and ambition, near
> The haunt of love. . . .

Abstract statements of theme, when they occur in "Sunday Morning," become part of the fabric of the poem; they are not to be found all together in one or two of the sections. Stevens said later in "Adagia," "Abstraction is part of idealism. It is in that sense that it is ugly."

The general subject of war obviously moved Stevens to make a major statement.[6] But frequently in "Phases" what is intended to be clear is not; what is intended to be highly charged poetry is heavy-handed, as in the case of much of the irony: "Life, the hangman, kept away, / From the field where soldiers pay," appears in one of the manuscript sections. What is meant to be impressive and shocking often becomes melodramatic: "Only an eyeball in the mud, / And Hopkins, / Flat and pale and gory!"; "fruit, / That fell / Along the walls / That bordered Hell." Much of the phrasing is simply clumsy: not only "They sip the glass," but also "the bugles, . . . / Were wings that bore / To where our comfort was." The imagery is often tritely poetic: "mysteries of flame," for example, and "Arabesques of candle beams." Such effects do not sound like the authentic Stevens, and yet some of the details already mentioned show that in this transitional poem he was on the verge of having full control of his own voice. Section VI, already referred to, comes closer to the style of Stevens:

> There was heaven,
> Full of Raphael's costumes;
> and earth,

[6] Although Stevens' statement about war in "Phases" (suggested briefly in the preceding excerpts) is not clear, the poem shows Stevens groping for a figure of heroic proportions who represents the imaginative grasp of reality. As Northrup Frye has pointed out, Stevens turned from the war hero to his "major man," personified as peace, and finally to his "central man," the poet, identical with the world. See "The Realistic Oriole: A Study of Wallace Stevens," *Hudson Review*, 10 (Fall 1957), 366.

> A thing of shadows,
> Stiff as stone . . .

And he would convert the overstatement of "Close tight the prophets' coffin-clamp," from a manuscript section, into the refinement of "There is not any haunt of prophecy" in "Sunday Morning." In "Phases," then, his wish to write a significant poem is only fitfully realized.

In "Sunday Morning" all is fused by certainty of theme and purpose, by the symbolic structure, by the tone, which balances pensiveness and celebration, and by the elevated rhetoric and subtle prosody. Even the delicate shadings of comic irony—the "insipid lutes" and "where spirits gat them home"—are subordinated to the poignance and nobility of feeling. The rather shadowy dialogue between the woman and the speaker gives the poem movement and order. The discussion of the twentieth-century human condition is not topical as it is in "Phases"; it takes on depth and a sense of the sweep of time through the references to Jesus, Jove, and the pagan worshippers of earth and sun.

At this point Stevens successfully brought into conjunction many of his resources for conveying meaning and effect. The interchange between the woman and speaker, for example, seems a highly refined variation of the woman-man relationship that has been traced from its origins in Stevens' undergraduate story "The Nymph" and the undergraduate poem "Outside the Hospital" through some of the *fêtes galantes* manuscript poems to "Peter Quince." If a Wordsworthian quality is central in the poem, it has been subtly transmuted by other voices in the English tradition and by derivations from the French Symbolists. With its incisive versification, its lofty blank verse—which extends the tradition running from the Elizabethans through Milton, the Romantics, and Tennyson—its Biblical echoes, and its symbolist ache for union with the absolute, the poem blends the pictorial freshness of the Impressionists and Matisse. But, of course, one of the triumphs of the poem is that the reader hardly thinks of influences when he reads it, so thoroughly did Stevens make the stylistic elements his own.

ALTHOUGH the comparison of "Phases" and "Sunday Morning" illustrates the sudden leap from uncertainty to mastery, it offers no satisfactory explanation for the phenomenon. About that one can only surmise: by 1914, Stevens' business career was established, avant-garde excitement had reached a high pitch, and there were stirrings in all the arts. Perhaps the war itself dramatized for him how severe the pressure of outer reality could be and helped him to purge his verse of softness. Possibly the heady stimulus of getting parts of "Phases" published in the outstanding poetry journal of the day encouraged him. But whatever the reasons, one should not forget that underlying them were the Harvard work, the manuscript poems, "Carnet de Voyage" and "Phases," as well as his "determining personality."[7] Perhaps in a rough way Stevens, in outlining a course of action for the youthful poet *"in a leaden time,"* was describing his own emergence as a mature poet: "Having elected to exercise his power to the full and at its height, and having identified his power as the power of the imagination, he may begin its exercise by studying it in exercise and proceed little by little, as he becomes his own master, to those violences which are the maturity of his desires" (*N. A.*,

[7] From a Stevens remark on Cézanne as an artist, quoted by S. F. Morse in *Opus*, p. xxvi, and again in its entirety as an introductory inscription to the book (no page number).

241

pp. 63-64). Looking back, one can see that in the poems Stevens published in 1915 he managed to combine successfully the elements which he had been studying in exercise—to unite a variety of these simultaneously in each poem. "Tea," for example, although it is basically Imagistic, has a *fêtes galantes* or rococo air, with its decorous ritual of tea-taking amidst "shining pillows," an air which is intensified by its ironic contrast with a bleak Laforguian city scene and the humorous grotesquerie of the leaves that "Ran like rats." Impressionism is apparent in the rendering of the elegant room by means of the single detail, the pillows "Of sea shades and sky shades, / Like umbrellas in Java," and the title economically defines the order and civilization which the poem itself does not explicitly treat: the experience—the feeling—of being civilized is presented symbolically in the poem.

"Peter Quince" has a *fêtes galantes* delicacy, a Verlaine-like use of the Pierrot figure subtly combined with Shakespeare's clown, as the wistful speaker plays for his love and equates her with Susanna; in doing so he wryly equates himself with the impotent elders, whose music is defined with a touch of irony that seems to derive from Laforgue and Corbière. It includes Impressionistic and Symbolic uses of color and employs both musical Imagism and Mallarméan music, and it ends on a stately note with "noble accents" reminiscent of the English tradition:

> Now, in its immortality, it plays
> On the clear viol of her memory,
> And makes a constant sacrament of praise.

All of these elements contribute to a richly symbolic statement concerning earthly beauty, the spirit and the imagination.

In "Cy Est Pourtraicte," Stevens uses several elements of his style to recreate the legend of Ursula. She is a spiritualized *femme galante,* of much tenderness and delicacy:

> "Where none can see,
> I make an offering in the grass,
> Of radishes and flowers."
> And then she wept
> For fear the Lord would not accept.

The Lord himself brings in a *fêtes galantes,* rococo element —he is a connoisseur of exquisite and subtle sense experience:

> The good Lord in His garden sought
> New leaf and shadowy tinct,
> And they were all his thought.

This is combined with what Frank Kermode detects as a "Ninetyish, even pre-Raphaelite tinge" in these lines:[8]

> She dressed in red and gold brocade
>
> .   .   .   .
>
> She said, "My dear,
> Upon your altars,
> I have placed
> The marguerite and coquelicot,
> And roses
> Frail as April snow. . . ."

Such fragile beauty is enhanced by the French names of the ordinary flowers and protected by the comic irony of the title, which, in suggesting (in the manner of a French

[8] Kermode, *Wallace Stevens* (Edinburgh & London, 1960), pp. 29-30.

museum guide describing a painting) the legend of the
eleven thousand virgins who went off in triremes to serve
the Lord, makes the reader more than ever aware of the
touch of the ribald in the Lord's reaction to Ursula, and of
the roguish, irreverent twist at the end. It includes also the
paradox that the altars on which the offering is made are
grass, and that it is the radishes, not the flowers, which inspire Ursula to dress in her red and gold brocade and make
her offering. The ordinary radishes perhaps do more than
anything else in the poem to make the tenderness and
beauty possible. Stevens later was to praise Marianne
Moore for the very same kind of achievement; avoiding the
romantic as a "relic of the imagination, . . . she hybridizes
it by association. Moon-vines are moon-vines and tedious.
But moon-vines trained on fishing twine are something
else . . ." (Opus). Further on, he quotes Miss Moore's
well-known phrase, "imaginary gardens with real toads in
them," and says, "She demands the romantic that is genuine, that is living, the enriching poetic reality." This is
what Stevens was demanding by the conjunction of radishes and flowers. The poetic reality—"not writ in any
book"—is reinforced by the color and the pictorial quality
of the poem. Finally, the theme—the union of earth and
heaven on earth—is incorporated symbolically through the
ritual of Ursula, the reaction of the very human Lord, and
the offering itself. One can say that the wit has too much
of a rococo coyness, but he must see the poem as an otherwise flawless achievement in capturing refined emotions by
joining elements of the comic and the ordinary with those
of the spiritual and the beautiful. "Cy Est Pourtraicte," like
"Peter Quince" and "Tea" and all of the best of Stevens'
work, becomes a self-sustained aesthetic entity resonant
with human feelings and meanings.

IN THESE early *Harmonium* poems, then, Stevens had brought a variety of elements under control and had avoided pastiche, a problem which he recognized in his early work. With great daring (Crispin's "violence was for aggrandizement"), he continued to extend his range in the rest of the *Harmonium* poems, as he perfected "an authentic and fluent speech" for himself.[9]

Stevens' development during the years between 1915 and the publication of *Harmonium* in 1923 does not, however, fall into a smoothly plotted curve of rising achievement. For one thing, many argue with justification that "Sunday Morning" is the major poem in the volume. For another, he took aesthetic chances and, like any other poet, had his failures. "To the one of Fictive Music" (1922) is noble in purpose, but its heavenly creature of Symbolist derivation, its Biblical phrasing, and its impassioned blank verse do not prevent a degree of sentimentality. Other more obvious and complete failures, such as "Peter Parasol" (1922), "Exposition of the Contents of a Cab" (1922) and "Mandolin and Liqueurs" (1923; all three in *Opus*), Stevens would consign to his scrap heap of thin, mannered exercises.[10] "This Vast Inelegance" (1921; *Opus*), monotonous

[9] See *Opus*, p. xx: S. F. Morse quotes from a letter written by Stevens in 1919 to Harriet Monroe, explaining that he was reluctant to publish "Peter Parasol" because of the "element of pastiche present." See also p. xxii for the quotation in the text, taken from a 1922 letter to Miss Monroe in which he mentions his general dissatisfaction with the poems soon to be published in *Harmonium*.

[10] Carl Van Vechten in "Rogue Elephant in Porcelain," *Yale University Library Gazette*, XXXVIII (1963), 49, quotes Stevens' wife as saying at a gathering at the Arensbergs' in the winter of 1914-1915—just before he read "Dolls," "Infernale" (*Opus*), and "Cy Est Pourtraicte" aloud—"I like Mr. Stevens' things when they are not affected; but he writes so much that is affected." The three

245

in its versification, fittingly received an editorial rejection.[11]

Nor do the poems in this period fall into a neat pattern of changes in style and technique. Stevens did little in such later *Harmonium* poems as "The Apostrophe to Vincentine" (1918), "Fabliau of Florida" (1919), "Infanta Marina" (1921), and "The Load of Sugar Cane" (1921) that he could not have done any time from 1915 on. But then again, he could not have written the group of poems that appeared in *The Dial* in 1922 as early as 1915 or 1916. In them he is simply too exuberantly confident of his abilities, supremely sure, as he tells the woman in "A High-Toned Old Christian Woman," that "poetry is the supreme fiction"; the speaker in "Bantams in Pine-Woods" bristles in defiance, and the wit, the words, and sounds bristle, too, in a way not evident in the earlier poems. The other poems in the group—"The Ordinary Women," "Frogs Eat Butterflies. Snakes Eat Frogs. Hogs Eat Snakes. Men Eat Hogs," "O Florida, Venereal Soil," and "The Emperor of Ice-Cream"—have, taken altogether, an extravagance of conception and an energy of language and tone that approach the violences of imagination that Stevens sought but had not found in the earlier poems. The poetry of *Harmonium* does, then, show an over-all development.

---

poems reprinted in *Opus* would attest to the validity of that sentiment.

[11] Matthew Josephson, coeditor of *The Headsman* with Gorham Munson, said in his letter of rejection (February 22, 1922): "Its first line is frankly bad. Most of the others are merely neutral—and labored. The alliterations employed are quite obvious. Here and there are glimpses of your most personal method. The whole poem, then, offers the mechanics of your art and not the fruition thereof." Josephson certainly was not carping in pointing out how little this poem reflected Stevens' real ability; he was one of the first to recognize the merits of the poet's "personal method."

As the 1922 *Dial* group indicates, he became less rococo, less exquisite and coy, and more baroque and boisterous. Though the changes in his style are of degree, the general tendency is away from Keats, Tennyson, the Pre-Raphaelites, Parnassians, and Decadents, away from Verlaine, away from the more attenuated qualities of the Symbolists and the ironic disillusionment of Laforgue, and toward Whitman and the gusto of the Elizabethans, toward the hugely fantastic situations and points of view, and the essential gaudiness of word and metaphor with which Stevens probed to the limits of the imagination's power. Also, his early Imagist techniques were absorbed into his other qualities. And he moved from Fragonard and Watteau to the Fauves and beyond, from orientalism to a more intensive use of Impressionistic technique. The differences between "Peter Quince at the Clavier" (1915) and "Le Monocle de Mon Oncle" (1918), between "Six Significant Landscapes" (1916) and "Sea Surface Full of Clouds" (1924), and between "Sunday Morning" (1915) and "The Comedian as the Letter C" (1923) suggest the general pattern of development in *Harmonium*, however many exceptions have to be made to that pattern.

Stevens composed "The Comedian" as the final flourish for the volume, as a long virtuoso piece—though it is more than that—in which, disguised as Crispin, he recorded for us his poetic development. Considering the achievement of Stevens, one must grant him the excesses of ingenuity in this poem, the intricacies of style, and the desire to disguise his autobiographical pronunciamento, all of which cause difficulties for the reader. Surely the poet who wrote "Ballade of the Pink Parasol" as an undergraduate would, as he became confident of his talent and anticipated the publication of a volume of poems, want to test his powers—

even to tax them—as he does in "The Comedian"; he uses
all the elements of his style and technique that have been
discussed in these chapters, and sometimes for the purpose
of ridiculing his earlier experiments. His delight in writing
it is apparent in a letter he sent to Harriet Monroe when he
was composing the poem in 1922: "All manner of favors
drop from it. Only it requires a skill in the varying of the
serenade that makes me feel like a Guatemalan when one
particularly wants to feel like an Italian."[12] And even the
reader who experiences great difficulty in following Crispin's
shifting perceptions of reality—though we are gradually
catching up to Stevens—must share some of this delight,
just as he must recognize the poem's essential seriousness
as a philosophical and human statement (though he might
complain that the style at times tends to overwhelm the
matter). The music of the poem is varied, although it is
chiefly in the manner of "Le Monocle de Mon Oncle."
When we call "The Comedian" to mind, we are most
likely to think first of its imaginative violence; its tropical
flamboyance, its "savage color," its Elizabethan profusion
of wit, humor, and rhetoric, its effervescent play of word and
sound and its farfetched vocabulary, its earthy details, and
its "deluging onwardness" in the manner of Whitman. But
we should not overlook some of the other qualities that
contribute to the total effect, although these qualities are
subordinated to the extravagant comic irony: the Impressionistic effects ("shifting diaphanes / Of blue and green"),
the sensuous elegance ("cream for the fig and silver for the
cream"), the delicacy and fastidiousness of phrasing and
stance ("The melon should have apposite ritual, / Per-
formed in verd apparel"), and the lyricism with roots in
the English tradition and in the Symbolists ("The spring, /

[12] This letter (October 1922) is quoted at length in *Opus*, p. xxi.

. . . contending featly in its veils, / Irised in dew and early fragrancies . . .").

Such glorious excesses marked the end of the first phase of Stevens' poetic career. And although he would say with extreme self-effacement, at the time when *Harmonium* was about to be published, that his earliest *Harmonium* poems seemed "like horrid cocoons from which later abortive insides have sprung,"[13] he must at the same time have realized that the best of the poems in *Harmonium* are major twentieth-century poems. They are major poems not simply because they brilliantly combine a variety of elements into an incomparable style but also because the style grew out of the urgency of the poet's search for meaningful relationships between imagination and reality, art and banality, order and violence, life and death—a search that first became evident in his undergraduate work and continued the rest of his life. This search gave direction to his stylistic explorations and depth to his poetry. Early in his career, he wrote in a letter to William Carlos Williams: "My idea is that in order to carry a thing to the extreme [necessary] to convey it one has to stick to it. . . . Given a fixed point of view, realistic, imagistic, or what you will, everything adjusts itself to that point of view; and the process of adjustment is a world in flux, as it should be for a poet. But to fidget with points of view leads to sterility. A single manner or mood thoroughly matured and exploited is that fresh thing, etc. . . ."[14] Stevens' own artistic point of view was hardly limited to the realistic or Imagistic. His fixed point of view was in effect his search for meaningful relationships

[13] *Ibid.*

[14] Williams quotes this letter from Stevens in Prologue to *Kora in Hell* (1918); see *Selected Essays of William Carlos Williams*, 1954, pp. 12-13.

between human longings and a world in flux, and he assimilated not only realism and Imagism but also Impressionism, Symbolism, irony, painting, the influence of his native American background, and poetry of the English tradition in order to write poems that exploit his point of view "to the extreme [necessary] to convey it." The result is a style and technique that demonstrate again and again, with "felt words," with imagery that strikes through jaded conceptions of reality, and with music that is "feeling, then, not sound," that for Stevens, poetry and reality are one.

Beyond *Harmonium*, Stevens' style continued to change and develop in a kind of exfoliation of his earlier style. A number of the later poems—"Loneliness in Jersey City" (1938), for example—would not be out of place in *Harmonium*. The later poetry is still marked by the wit, the elegance, the color, the vibrancy, the surprising perspectives, and the sharply defined visual, aural, and emotional effects that characterize the 1923 collection. But generally it is toned down, with less of the fantastic irony and the virtuoso manner; it is more reflective, more meditative, more serene, but no less intense. And yet to look back at Stevens' over-all development from the perspective of his later work is to see that even those magnificent, direct, fervent, and profound poems in *The Rock* at the end—and possibly the summit—of his career were adumbrated in *Harmonium*, in "Sunday Morning," "The Snow Man," "Another Weeping Woman," "From the Misery of Don Joost," and "The Death of a Soldier." With all the variety and intensity his style permitted, Stevens, from his earliest *Harmonium* poems on, concerned himself, as the title of one of his last poems proclaims, with presenting "Not Ideas about the Thing But the Thing Itself."

APPENDIX I

A list of Stevens' courses at Harvard, 1897-1900

1897-1898

English A (Rhetoric and English Composition)
English 28 (the history and development of English literature
      in outline)
German B
French A
History I (Medieval and Modern European History)
Government I (Constitutional Government)

1898-1899

English 22 (English Composition)
English 7 (literature from the death of Swift to the publica-
      tion of the Lyrical Ballads)
German 4 (Goethe and His Time)
French 2c (Corneille, Racine, Molière, etc.)
History 12 (European history since the middle of the 1700's)
Economics I

1899-1900

English 5 (Advanced Composition)
English 8a (literature from the publication of the Lyrical Bal-
      lads to the death of Scott)
English 8b (literature from the death of Scott to the death
      of Tennyson)
German 5 (History of German Literature to the Nineteenth
      Century)
French 6c (General View of French Literature)
History 13 (Constitutional and Political History of the United
      States)
Fine Arts 4 (Fine Arts of the Middle Ages and the Renais-
      sance)

APPENDIX II

A chronological index of the poems and stories Stevens published as an undergraduate

With one exception ("To the Morn," a poem traced by Holly Stevens to the *Harvard Monthly*, on the basis of information in Stevens' Journal and after the revision of the *Checklist*), the list below agrees with the *Wallace Stevens Checklist and Bibliography of Stevens Criticism*, Samuel French Morse, Jackson R. Bryer, and Joseph N. Riddel (Denver, 1963), pp. 50-52. The unstarred titles are poems, the starred are stories. Unless otherwise noted, the works appeared in the *Harvard Advocate*. The page numbers indicate where the poems are quoted in the text or notes and where the stories are described or discussed.

APPENDIX III

Alphabetical index of Stevens' manuscript and fugitive poems used in this study, plus some miscellaneous manuscript material. The page numbers indicate where items are quoted in the text or notes.

LETTERS, manuscript

Index

257